The Reinvention of the U.S. Academic Library

The Reinvention of the U.S. Academic Library

1990 to 2025

Donald A. Barclay

BLOOMSBURY LIBRARIES UNLIMITED
NEW YORK • LONDON • OXFORD • NEW DELHI • SYDNEY

BLOOMSBURY LIBRARIES UNLIMITED

Bloomsbury Publishing Inc, 1359 Broadway, New York, NY 10018, USA
Bloomsbury Publishing Plc, 50 Bedford Square, London, WC1B 3DP, UK
Bloomsbury Publishing Ireland, 29 Earlsfort Terrace, Dublin 2, D02 AY28, Ireland

BLOOMSBURY, BLOOMSBURY LIBRARIES UNLIMITED and the Diana logo are trademarks of Bloomsbury Publishing Plc

First published in the United States of America 2025

Copyright © Bloomsbury Publishing Inc.

For legal purposes the Acknowledgments on p. vi constitute an extension of this copyright page.

All images and textboxes in this book are sourced from Donald A. Barclay

Cover design: Kathi Ha
Cover image © iStock / Viorika

All rights reserved. No part of this publication may be: i) reproduced or transmitted in any form, electronic or mechanical, including photocopying, recording or by means of any information storage or retrieval system without prior permission in writing from the publishers; or ii) used or reproduced in any way for the training, development or operation of artificial intelligence (AI) technologies, including generative AI technologies. The rights holders expressly reserve this publication from the text and data mining exception as per Article 4(3) of the Digital Single Market Directive (EU) 2019/790.

Bloomsbury Publishing Inc does not have any control over, or responsibility for, any third-party websites referred to or in this book. All internet addresses given in this book were correct at the time of going to press. The author and publisher regret any inconvenience caused if addresses have changed or sites have ceased to exist, but can accept no responsibility for any such changes.

Library of Congress Cataloging-in-Publication Data Available

ISBN: HB: 978-1-5381-8319-9
PB: 978-1-5381-8320-5
ePDF: 979-8-7651-5481-6
eBook: 978-1-5381-8321-2

Typeset by Deanta Global Publishing Services, Chennai, India
Printed and bound in the United States of America

For product safety related questions contact productsafety@bloomsbury.com.

To find out more about our authors and books visit www.bloomsbury.com and sign up for our newsletters.

Contents

Acknowledgments vi

Introduction 1

1 Acquiring Information in Digital Containers: Old Wine in New Bottles 5

2 Electronic Journals Take the Field 37

3 The Open Access Revolution 57

4 From the Card Catalog to the Semantic Web: The Digital Odessey of Cataloging and Technical Services 89

5 Distinctive Collections Go Digital 125

6 Reference, Instruction, and Facilities: The Challenge of Meeting Changing User Expectations in the Digital Age 159

7 The Future of the U.S. Academic Library 193

Index 199
About the Author 209

Acknowledgments

If there is a truer cliché than "Nobody writes a book entirely on their own," I have yet to meet it. I will begin by thanking three constant readers who kindly read and commented on draft chapters but who bear zero responsibility for any faults or failures found in this book:

- R. Bruce Miller: Founding University Librarian, University of California, Merced. Builder of miniature houses. All-around good dude.
- Steven R. Corbett: Colonel, United States Army, Retired. Historian. Educator. Teller of amazing tales, including at least one or two that are true.
- Michael K. Buckland: Accomplished author, scholar, educator, and administrator. Member of the California Library Hall of Fame. Dispenser of wisdom and good sense.

Others who provided me with invaluable assistance and acts of kindness in writing this book include:

- Jane Anders, Jisc
- Demitra Borrero, University of California, Merced Interlibrary Loan
- Stephen J. Bosch, University of Arizona Libraries
- David W. Flaxbart, University of Texas at Austin, Libraries
- Popi Florou, Directory of Open Access Journals
- Lea DeForest, Texas Digital Library
- Ed Fox, Virginia Tech
- Nathan Garcia, University of California, Merced Interlibrary Loan
- Charles Harmon, Rowman & Littlefield
- Stevan Harnad, Cognitive Scientist
- Melanie, Heeley, Jisc
- Sara Holder, University of Illinois Urbana-Champaign Library
- Brian M. Ingrassia, West Texas A & M University Department of History
- Steven Mandeville-Gamble, University Librarian, University of California, Riverside
- Ella McDonald, University Archives, University of Illinois at Urbana-Champaign
- Helen McGettrick, Newberry Library
- Lauren Moynihan, Rowman & Littlefield

- Ann Okerson, Yale University Library
- Lindsay O'Neil, Library Consultant
- Dave Phelps, OCLC
- Daniel Pitti, University of Virginia
- Dan Russell, Independent Scholar
- Mathew Rutherford, Newberry Library
- Lisa Schiff, California Digital Library
- John Shank, Penn State University Libraries
- Peter Suber, Harvard University
- Janet Marie Swatscheno, HathiTrust Research Center
- Linda TerHaar, University of Michigan Library

If I left anyone out, I apologize.

Finally, thank you and much love to my wife, Caroline Dawson, and our three favorite young women: Tess Barclay, Emily Featherston, and Alexandra Featherston.

Introduction

There are two justifications for writing a history of U.S. academic libraries covering the years 1990 to 2025. The first reason is that those tumultuous years saw unprecedented changes in the way academic libraries operated. The second is that no history focused on that period had yet been written. Of the three most recent book-length histories of U.S. academic libraries available at the time I began work on this book, two date from 1981 while the other dates from 1991. The first, Orvin Lee Shiflett's *Origins of American Academic Librarianship* (1981), provides a good amount of historical information on academic libraries, though its focus is more on the struggle of academic librarians to achieve professional status within the academy than on academic libraries per se.[1] The second, Arthur T. Hamlin's *The University Library in the United States* (1981), provides a broader history of U.S. academic libraries than Shiflett's book, though, as is only to be expected of a book published over forty years ago, its coverage of the impact of digital technology takes readers no further than the development of computer-output microform.[2] The third, Stephen E. Atkins' *The Academic Library in the American University* (1991), was published just in time to miss the launch of the World Wide Web and all that followed, though to his credit Atkins was far from oblivious to the changes looming on the horizon. In the introduction to the 2003 reprint of *The Academic Library in the American University*, Charles B. Lowery notes that "the dilemmas of expanding access to electronic information in the academy are plainly, if imprecisely, foreshadowed in Atkin's text."[3] After I began work on this book came the publication of *The Academic Library in the United States: Historical Perspectives*, edited by Mark L. McCallon and John Mark Tucker (2022).[4] While this excellent history of U.S. academic libraries takes the reader into the twenty-first century, it includes only two brief sections focusing on the impact of digital technology on the academic library.

Choosing 1990 as a starting date for this book is both approximate and arbitrary. The Digital Age begins all the way back in the mid-twentieth century, with a number of academic library digital landmarks dating from well before 1990:

- Searchable online indexes (1964)[5]
- The MARC (MAchine Readable Cataloging) pilot project (1966)[6]
- The OCLC shared online cataloging utility (1971)[7]
- The first Online Public Access Catalog (1978).[8]

It is also true that, by 1990, personal computers running CD-ROM databases had become common fixtures in many academic library reference areas.

With that freely admitted, the year 1990 is a reasonable starting date for this history because it was in the years following 1990 that digital technology effected the greatest changes on the academic library, not the least of these being the changes brought about by the emergence of the World Wide Web in the mid-1990s. From a purely self-interested perspective, I found 1990 to be a convenient starting date because that was the year I began my career as a professional librarian. My luck was such that, in my thirty-two-year career, I was a witness to, and a participant in, the transition from a mostly analog to a mostly digital academic library. A few highlights from my career include:

- From 1990 to 1996, while working as a librarian at New Mexico State University, I went from creating printed library pathfinders to creating digital content on the Gopher and then the Web. While I cannot claim that I was looking over the shoulder of Tim Berners-Lee as he created the World Wide Web, I did get to the party early enough to create my first webpages by writing HTML directly onto a Unix server. (HTML editing software was still a few years away at the time.)
- From 1996 to 1997, my job at the University of Houston Library included managing the Electronic Publications Center, a buzzing hive of 110 networked, public-access desktop computer workstations supplemented by a dozen networked printers.
- When I started working at the Houston Academy of Medicine-Texas Medical Center (HAM-TMC) Library in November 1997, the library collection included 250 full-text electronic journals; when I left HAM-TMC Library in August 2002, the count had risen to approximately 4,000 full-text electronic journals. In the span of just under five years, I saw the electronic journal transition from a side dish thrown in as a bonus for subscribing to a print journal to becoming the pricey main course.
- In September 2002, I started work at the University of California, Merced, at that time an entirely new research university for which ground had yet to be broken. The challenge? Create a research library for the twenty-first century. The result? A library with a mostly (though not exclusively) digital collection.
- In 2020, near the end of my academic library career, I witnessed digital collections and services come to the rescue as physical library collections and services were rendered inaccessible due to the Covid-19 pandemic.

If a starting point of 1990 is merely a date of convenience, a cut-off date of 2025 is as equally so. All my plans to not write about anything that occurred after 2025 went out the window in the face of events such as the Covid-19 pandemic, the launch of ChatGPT in 2022, and the wider expansion of artificial intelligence into everyday life. Peppered throughout this text, readers will find citations to publications, as well as references to events, dating as late as 2024.

Organization and Purpose

Though the original manuscript of this book included three chapters covering the history of U.S. academic libraries from 1638 to 1990, those chapters ended up on the chopping block in the interest of keeping the price of the book more reasonable for the average reader. To compensate for this loss, various accounts of pre-1990 history are woven into the remaining chapters as needed for background. The chapters of the book break down as follows

- Chapter 1 focuses on the challenges faced by academic libraries and those they serve in adapting to new, digital forms of information, in particular the electronic book, while continuing to use, manage, and value information in non-digital formats.
- Chapter 2 reviews the origins and ongoing challenges associated with the high cost of scholarly journals. This chapter also tells the story of how the rise of electronic journals came to render the print-format journal all but redundant.
- Chapter 3 follows the history of the open access movement from early calls to liberate scholarly communications from the control of publishers to the rise of transformative agreements.
- Chapter 4 considers the history of cataloging and technical services as they transitioned from the card catalog to a digital universe of metadata, the Semantic Web, and linked data.
- Chapter 5 looks at how the mass digitization of millions of public-domain books and the flourishing of librarian-curated online archival collections enhanced the accessibility and importance of academic library archives and special collections.
- Chapter 6 explores the ways in which library services and facilities changed in response to the changing expectations of users grown accustomed to life in a digital world.
- Chapter 7 offers some very broad thoughts on the future of academic libraries as the first quarter of the twenty-first century comes to a close.

In the course of writing this book, it became obvious that each chapter could easily be expanded into a full-length book. I often imagined the voices of incensed readers calling out this book's far too many omissions of significant people, events, and trends in the history of academic libraries. My only excuse is that there is neither world enough nor time to put the full history of academic libraries into a single book. Anybody who is interested in improving or expanding any part, if not all, of this book is welcome to do so. Scholarship is a conversation, and if this book does nothing more than get a few interesting conversations started, it will have served a worthwhile purpose.

Notes

1 Orvin Lee Shiflett, *Origins of American Academic Librarianship*, Libraries and Librarianship (Norwood: Ablex Pub. Corp., 1981).
2 Arthur T. Hamlin, *The University Library in the United States: Its Origins and Development* (Philadelphia: University of Pennsylvania Press, 1981), 219–25.
3 Stephen E. Atkins, *The Academic Library in the American University* (Chicago: American Library Association, 1991), vii.

4. Mark L. McCallon and John Mark Tucker, eds., *The Academic Library in the United States: Historical Perspectives* (Jefferson: McFarland & Company, Inc., Publishers, 2022).

5. Charles J. Austin, "The Medlars System. An Application Report," *Datamation* 10, no. 12 (December 1964): 28–31.

6. Henriette D. Avram, "MARC: Its History and Implications" (Washington, DC: Library of Congress, 1975), 6–8, https://files.eric.ed.gov/fulltext/ED127954.pdf.

7. Phil Schieber, "Biographical Sketch of Frederick G. Kilgour Librarian, Educator, Entrepreneur, 1914–2006," *Journal of Library Administration* 49, no. 6 (October 19, 2009): 56e.

8. Susan L. Miller, "The Evolution of an On-Line Catalog," in *New Horizons for Academic Libraries: Papers Presented at the First National Conference of the Association of College and Research Libraries, Boston, Massachusetts, November 8–11, 1978*, ed. Robert D. Stueart and Richard David Johnson (New York: K.G. Saur Pub., 1979), 193–204.

1 Acquiring Information in Digital Containers
Old Wine in New Bottles

This chapter and the two that follow it consider the ways in which digital technology transformed not only the acquisition of academic library collections but also the economics of scholarly communications writ large. This chapter focuses (mostly) on the impact of the electronic book; the following chapter, the impact of the electronic journal; the chapter after that, the impact of open access publishing. Starting in earnest in the early 1990s, library acquisitions were caught between two very different economic models. The older, traditional economic model of library acquisitions is rooted in the technology of print and the necessity of owning physical containers of information, with the printed book being the iconic form of the old bottle. The new economic model of library acquisitions that emerged in the 1990s is rooted in digital technology and based on the provision of access to information that does not necessitate, in many cases, ownership of the new digital bottles in which familiar, old-wine forms of information—books, articles, images, and so on—began to be packaged. Because the two models exist simultaneously in a single marketplace and interact with each other in sometimes unexpected ways, separating one model from the other can never be done cleanly enough to satisfy everyone. With that said, these three chapters will set out to tell, with as much clarity and as little confusion as possible, the story of how digital technology disrupted a previously more-orderly universe of academic library collections and scholarly communication.

More Books, More Better

The true university of these days is a Collection of Books.
—Thomas Carlyle, 1840[1]

It is as if excellence were in numbers alone. How many volumes? This is always the question; never, How much and how well do you use what you have?
—Otis Robinson, 1876[2]

In times past and, in some corners, continuing into the present day, the measure of an academic library's quality has been the size of its collection as determined by the number of physical items—primarily books—in the library stacks. Besides books, physical items include such formats as journals, manuscripts, microformats, photographs, maps, video recordings, sound recordings, and more. In practice and popular parlance, the words *books*, *titles*, or *volumes* are often used generically in place of the more accurate *items*. The number of books (used generically) is a popular library metric because it is simple to calculate and provides a handy fact to recite when impressing and enlightening prospective students, candidates for faculty positions, or potential donors. The number of books in the library is as easy a metric to understand as how many NCAA championship titles the water polo team has brought home or how many beds are available in the campus dormitories. Four million books in the campus library is better than three million, right? And five million books must be better than four million. Books in the library is not a number that demands a lot of thought. Though, of course, the number should demand thought. Whether the topic is academic library collections or the number of beds on campus, raw numbers out of context cannot tell the full story. Just as a bed in an eight-bed suite is not the same as a bed in a private room, eight books nobody reads is not the same as two books a great many people want to read.

To begin making basic sense of the number of physical items counted as part of any academic library collection, it helps to understand that library items can be roughly sorted into the following categories:

- Popular items that are in demand.
- Just-in-case items that are rarely or never used.
- Rare or unique items that, for the most part, get little use but which could become inaccessible to scholars, or possibly lost forever, if not securely housed in a library or archive.

With the possible exception of student-focused community-college library collections, most of the items in academic library collections fall into the category of "just-in-case." The justification for academic libraries retaining millions of just-in-case items is that scholars never know where their research might take them. From the perspective of the scholar, this is an entirely reasonable justification for what others might condemn as biblio-hoarding. After all, items that might have been low-use for years, decades, or even centuries sometimes shift back into the high-use category due to renewed interest in a line of inquiry that has long been on the scholarly backburner. Even if an item is only used once in a hundred years, if its use is essential to a scholar that one time, having access to it becomes, in a word, essential.

A related plus of large collections of physical items is that, by virtue of being highly duplicative of each other, large physical collections help ensure the preservation of the scholarly record. Under the principle known as LOCKSS (Lots of Copies Keep Stuff Safe), the more libraries holding a copy of any given book (or other physical item), the more likely that said item will never entirely disappear.[3] Take, for example, the following book:

Homer E. Newell, Jr. High Altitude Rocket Research. New York: Academic Press, 1953.

Although Homer E. Newell, Jr. is a historically important mathematician-turned-rocket-scientist who served as a key NASA administrator in the early 1960s, the chance that anyone would wish to consult Newell's decades-old book, though never zero, remains quite low.[4] If it turned out that a copy of *High Altitude Rocket Research* were wanted, a search of OCLC WorldCat shows that, as of 2023, some 252 libraries—most of them U.S. academic libraries—hold at least one physical copy of *High Altitude Rocket Research*. Such an abundance of library copies makes it likely that physical copies of Newell's book will remain available for use into the next century and beyond. Also, because two library copies of *High Altitude Rocket Research* were digitized and made available via the HathiTrust Digital Library, it is likely that digital copies will remain accessible as far into the future as anyone can see.

On the other hand, while it is true that a large physical collection provides more complete access to the universe of information than does a small collection, no library collection that has ever been, or that ever will be, could possibly hold every item that any scholar might need at any time. Even if a large library collection could reach the impossible goal of completeness, large physical collections present serious accessibility issues. The bigger the information haystack—whether five million volumes in library stacks or billions of web pages on the internet—the harder it becomes to find any given information needle. Simply keeping an accurate inventory of large numbers of physical items is a major challenge for librarians, and a careful inventory of any large library collection will reveal that far from every item listed in the library catalog can be found where the catalog says it should be, or even found at all. An article reviewing the literature of library inventories reports that "a complete inventory is just not feasible" for collections over 100,000 volumes and that from "about 1% to well over l0%" of the items found in the typical library catalog are, in fact, missing from the stacks.[5] Misshelving is also widespread. A shelf-reading project at Princeton's Firestone Library reports a "3.5% to 10% rate of misshelving per shelf," while an inventory conducted at Washington State University reports that "misshelving ranged from a low of 1.3% to a high of 18.3% in certain areas of the collection."[6]

On campuses with very large physical collections, the items comprising those collections end up spread out among multiple campus libraries. Such scenarios present not only a challenge for users who must navigate among multiple libraries but also a challenge for collection managers who must decide which books go into which campus libraries. For example, on a campus with multiple subject libraries in addition to a main library, it is a fair question to ask which library should get the one copy of *Astrobiology and Humanism: Conversations on Science, Philosophy and Theology*?[7] The alternative to picking one campus library is buying multiple copies of books that cross disciplinary lines; however, because collection budgets are not infinite and each dollar in a collections budget can be spent only one time, every duplicate copy purchased takes the place of some other book that will not be purchased at all.

In addition to the access challenges represented by multiple campus libraries, there is the even greater access challenge presented by library storage facilities, many of which are located far from where students and faculty learn, teach, and conduct research. The first modern library storage facility, the New England Depository Library, opened its doors in March 1942.[8] As academic library collections grew at a rate that outpaced even the unprecedented construction boom higher education experienced in the 1960s, library storage facilities became increasingly common. As of 2023, there were eighty-seven library storage facilities affiliated with U.S. academic libraries plus another three facilities affiliated with nonacademic U.S. research libraries (New York Public Library, Boston Public Library, and the Library of Congress).[9]

Remote library storage facilities of the twenty-first century are nearly universal in employing automated retrieval systems for the quick retrieval and replacement of materials requested by users. Automated retrieval systems have also been employed in a few onsite library storage facilities. The first U.S. academic library to install an onsite automated retrieval system was California State University, Northridge, which deployed its system in 1991.[10] While exact numbers are not available, a rough headcount suggests approximately two dozen U.S. academic libraries were employing onsite automated retrieval systems as of 2024.

Library remote storage facilities have flourished because even though academic libraries continue to acquire significant numbers of books and other physical items, the construction of new on-campus library space for the storage of physical items ground to a halt around the turn of the millennium. (See Chapter 6.) To make room for newer, (presumably) higher-use acquisitions, low-use items must either be deaccessioned or placed in remote storage. By storing materials in densely packed formats rather than on open stacks, remote storage facilities make more efficient use of space than do libraries, lowering storage costs. The most recent estimate of the cost of keeping one book in open stacks in perpetuity adds up to $141.89 in 2009 dollars ($211.14 in 2024 dollars).[11][12] One book is, of course, one book. Storage costs really start to add up when applied to serial publications such as magazines, journals, indexes, and the like. In 2002, a time when Drexel University Library was actively transitioning from print to electronic journals, librarians there estimated the annual cost of storing the library's collection of current and bound journals at $245,000 per year ($434,629 in 2024 dollars).[13]

Shared Print

In 2009, Harvard University's Task Force on University Libraries announced in its official report that:

> the Harvard libraries can no longer harbor delusions of being a completely comprehensive collection, but instead must develop their holdings more strategically. To do so, Harvard will need to embrace a model that ensures access to—not necessarily ownership of—scholarly materials needed by faculty, students, and other library users, now and in the future.[14]

While Harvard's public admission that its libraries could not go it alone generated a mild buzz in the academic world, among academic librarians the fact that no academic library, no matter how prestigious, could meet all the information needs of its user community was not news. The impossibility of an entirely self-sufficient, stand-alone academic library was, after all, the inspiration behind every cooperative collection-building plan and interlibrary-loan agreement ever devised.

By the early 2000s, the need for academic libraries to collaborate had become more pressing than ever, not only because maintaining a comprehensive collection had been acknowledged as a "delusion" but also because of the increasingly urgent problem of too many books and no place to put them. Out of stack space, and with no realistic hope of meaningful expansion of library space, academic libraries in the U.S. and abroad turned to shared print as a partial solution to their space problems. Shared print involves libraries agreeing to share physical collections in a coordinated way that both ensures the preservation of a critical number of physical copies, typically backed up by digital copies, while also freeing up valuable stack space.

One logistical model for shared print involves libraries relying on low-use items being permanently housed in a shared library storage facility from which such items can be recalled on the rare occasions they are needed. One early example of this model of shared print is seen in the Chicago-based Center for Research Libraries (CRL), a nonprofit organization founded in 1949 as the Midwest Inter-Library Corporation and which today serves 209 member libraries with its holdings of "approximately five million newspapers, journals, books, pamphlets, dissertations, archives, government publications, and other resources."[15] In the interest of actually reducing unnecessary redundancy rather than serving as library junkyards, shared library storage facilities typically employ non-duplication policies that prevent a facility from accepting additional copies of an item once the first copy-of-record has been accepted for deposit.

A second logistical model of shared print is known as *shared print in place*. In this form of collaboration, participating libraries agree to retain copies of specific items in their local stacks with the understanding that they will be made available to other libraries on demand and will never be deaccessioned by the retaining library. Shared print in place existed well before the twenty-first century, with the Farmington Plan being the prototype for all later shared-print-in-place agreements.[16] That shared-print schemes are widespread across the entire United States is reflected in the fact that two of the largest such U.S. schemes are named, respectively, EAST: Eastern Academic Scholars' Trust and WEST: Western Regional Storage Trust. While it is common to think of shared print as involving books, other formats are included in shared-print agreements. For example, in the interest of collaboratively preserving and sharing Federal Depository Library Program (FDLP) documents, the Association of Southeastern Research Libraries (ASERL) launched its Collaborative Federal Documents Program (CFDP) in 2006. As of 2023, forty-three "centers of excellence" were participating in CFDP and "96,750 items have been added to FDLP collections in the Southeast region."[17] The extent of shared-print agreements involving serial publications is documented by the Print Archives Preservation Registry (PAPR), a directory of shared serials archiving programs. As of 2023, PAPR lists fifty-two collaborative serials archiving programs active in the United States with combined holdings of 54,751 serials titles.[18]

The Print Book as Symbol

Seen through the managerial frame, the problem of too-many-books versus not-enough-stacks boils down to a simple inventory-control problem in which the only way to make room for new books is to remove old books. Seen through the symbolic frame, however, moving books out of the library stacks appears to some as an attack on literacy, scholarship, and possibly civilization as we know it. One of the harshest criticisms over removing books from academic libraries came from a past president of the American Library Association, Michael Gorman, who in a 1994 *Library Journal* opinion piece entitled, "The Treason of the Learned: The Real Agenda of Those Who Would Destroy Libraries and Books," writes:

> *The technovandals want to use technology to break up the culture of learning and, in a weird mixture of Nineties cybervision and Sixties radicalism, to replace that world with a howling wilderness of unstructured, unrelated gobbets of "information" and random images in which the hapless individual wanders without direction or sense of value.*[19]

To be sure, Gorman got, and likely still gets, nods of approval from like-minded members of the academic community, including some academic librarians. And it is fair to acknowledge that Gorman's vision of a "howling wilderness" accurately predicts the social-media wilderness of the twenty-first century.

It certainly does not help calm the anxieties of bibliophiles that removing books from libraries—whatever the reason and wherever the final destination—resonates with the many fictional dystopian futures in which the disposal of print books serves as a prelude to an authoritarian takeover of society. In Margaret Atwood's *The Handmaid's Tale*, the conversion of books to electronic format and their subsequent shredding is a step down the path toward the imposition of a violently misogynistic theocracy.[20] In Vernor Vinge's *Rainbow's End*, one element of a global mind-control conspiracy involves the conversion of print books to digital format via a destructive digitization process carried out in the University of California, San Diego's iconic Geisel Library. In addition to fictional dystopias, history provides such real-life examples as the book burners of the Third Reich, a group with whom academic librarians are occasionally compared when talk turns to reducing the size of print collections. It is not, then, all that surprising that faculty who view books and libraries through the symbolic frame sometimes stridently object to any plans to move books out of campus libraries, as was the case at Syracuse University in 2009.[21] The feelings of many faculty are reflected by the University of Chicago faculty member who, in 2005, was quoted as saying, "The experience of most of these other libraries is that the off-site stuff doesn't get used. People go to work where books are easily available."[22] It is almost certainly true that, for example, books sitting in the open stacks of the Perry-Castañeda Library on the University of Texas at Austin campus are more likely to be used than are books that have been relocated to the Library High-Density Repository "situated on the lonely south side of the university's satellite Pickle Research Campus."[23] Not to mention those UT Austin books trucked 100 miles to the Joint Library Facility in Bryan, Texas. That said, moving books just a few feet can similarly reduce their use. Books placed on the highest shelves in a library bookstack (standard height, seven feet) get less use than books placed on middle shelves where spine titles are easier to scan and volumes easier to reach.[24]

The discouraging news for those who insist that no book leave the campus library is all the data showing that even books that remain sitting in open stacks located in "the heart of the campus" do not get much use. According to the 80/20 rule, introduced in 1969 by University of Massachusetts engineering professor and library researcher Richard Trueswell, in any academic library, 20 percent of the books account for 80 percent of the use.[25] While so tidy a ratio as 80/20 might seem more like library lore than library science, there is evidence that Trueswell's rule is not that far off the mark.[26] Along similar lines, a report published by Cornell University Library in 2010 finds that of the books in its collection published since 1990, 55 percent had never circulated.[27] The hard numbers show that, across the board, circulation in U.S. academic libraries has been steadily declining as the world marches ever further into the digital age.[28]

Even as evidence mounted that a large physical collection was no longer the most important measure of an academic library's ability to meet its users' information needs, it was not easy for many librarians and academics to acknowledge the extent to which digital technology had, to borrow Spencer Johnson's well-known analogy, moved the academic library's cheese.[29] Book-counting traditionalists stuck to their guns even though well before digital forms of information achieved critical mass, many were questioning whether the size of a library's physical collection should be considered an indicator of quality. As early as 1985, Jay K. Lucker of MIT was asking how the possibility of a library providing access without ownership might change the way libraries are assessed.[30] In 2003, Richard C. Atkinson, president of the University of California, published an opinion piece in the *Chronicle of Higher Education* in which he characterized, "The homage that we pay to the Association of Research Libraries' membership index—which ranks the association's more than 120 member libraries largely according to the number of volumes they hold on their shelves" as both "an impediment" and "self-defeating." Atkinson then goes on to call on the Association of Research Libraries (ARL) to give credit to institutions that can share collections and leverage the power of digital technology, writing, "in a networked digital age, excessive attention to the local management and ownership of physical materials impedes the responsible stewardship of the scholarly and cultural record."[31] To give ARL its due, it is not as if the association was unaware of electronic information resources. The ARL began collecting data on electronic information resources in 1992–3, and its members were spending millions of dollars annually on electronic information by the time Atkinson's piece was published. From 1993 to 2003, "the average percentage of acquisition dollars that ARL member libraries directed to electronic resources rose from 3 percent to 20 percent."[32] Of course, acknowledging that electronic information resources exist is not the same thing as giving libraries credit for providing access to those resources, and the institutional conservatism of academia plus the self-interest of academic libraries in possession of large physical collections ensured that metrics for assessing libraries did not keep pace with the digital forces disrupting the information universe.

How Academic Libraries Acquire Information

While it may seem obvious that purchasing information directly from publishers is how libraries acquire information, the fact is that purchases are just one of the many ways in which libraries add to their physical and digital collections.

Purchases

A *firm order* is a type of purchase in which librarians and, in many cases, faculty request that specific items be added to the collection. To overcome the slowness and costs incurred by direct purchases, academic libraries often employ *blanket orders* and *approval plans* to more efficiently purchase books and other items. Typically, an academic library transacts a blanket order by contracting with a publisher or jobber to purchase all or part of the output of a particular publisher or group of publishers over a fixed span of time. The terms of a contract may limit the formats and subject areas covered by a blanket order. Though similar to a blanket order, approval plans differ by allowing the receiving library to send back some agreed-upon number of unwanted items. The earliest known approval plan dates from 1884, when Albion College established "an arrangement with Phillips & Hunt, whereby we are to receive for examination monthly installments of the newest books in various departments, thus enabling us to keep up with the very best thought."[33] A *slip plan* is an approval plan for which librarians make acquisition decisions based on vendor-supplied bibliographic information rather than actual items. Historically, vendors provided bibliographic information on actual slips of paper, while in more recent times the information is provided in electronic format. Most present-day approval plans are managed via digital interfaces that allow for precise fine-tuning of such factors as subject classification, date of publication, level (e.g., undergraduate, graduate, expert, etc.), publisher, format, and price.

Academic libraries occasionally purchase information through *bulk orders*, sometimes without knowing down to the last printed page exactly what they are buying. A notable twenty-first-century example of a bulk order was the California State University, Northridge Library's purchase of the Shoah Foundation Institute's visual history archive in 2021.[34] A type of bulk purchase that emerged in the digital age involves the acquisition of large sets of digital information assembled by third-party vendors. Examples include the primary-source archival collections assembled and sold by such companies as AM (formerly Adam Matthew Digital) and Alexander Street Press.

Gifts

In the early history of U.S. academic libraries, gift books and donated money were the main ways in which libraries acquired books.[35] Harvard's library began with a collection of only 300 volumes, a gift from the college's namesake, John Harvard.[36] Especially in the case of archival and special collections, gifts of books, manuscripts, and other materials continue to play a meaningful role in building academic library collections.

Subscriptions

Subscriptions are the traditional model for acquiring periodical publications such as newspapers, journals, magazines, annuals, bibliographic indexes, and monographic series. As the output of scholarly publication increased after the Second World War, managing payments and renewals for thousands of subscriptions became so complex that academic libraries routinely outsourced this task to serials subscription agencies. In December 2002, the system took a tumble when the bankruptcy of RoweCom/Faxon, a major serials subscription agency with origins dating back to 1881, left customers holding the bag after funds libraries had transmitted to pre-pay 2003 subscriptions vanished without warning.[37] The story would be repeated again in September 2014 when serials subscription agency Swets Information

Services went bankrupt.[38] In hindsight, the unprofitability of subscription agencies should not have come as a surprise seeing that, as early as 2000, there were reports of big journal publishers cutting subscription agencies out of the picture by negotiating directly with individual libraries and library consortia.[39]

In the print-format era, paying a subscription meant receiving tangible physical items that were added to the library's permanent collection. In the digital era, when subscriptions pay for intangible digital resources, the exchange of money for information can seem more like a lease (see below) than a traditional subscription. In the case of scholarly journals and most other periodical publications, academic libraries were reluctant to accept lease or rental agreements in place of the traditional subscription agreements under which they retained permanent ownership of the information purchased. If digital information was to comprise a permanent part of the scholarly record, then academic libraries saw it as central to their mission to make that information permanently available to their users. To this end, academic libraries negotiated perpetual access rights to backfiles of subscription-based digital content.[40] One sometimes hidden cost associated with perpetual access to subscription-based digital content is the access fees (which go by a variety of other names) that some publishers charge to offset the cost of hosting and maintaining access to online information. Access fees are sometimes confused with annual update fees; however, "Access fees typically are paid for closed or static resources to which no new content is added, whereas update fees cover the costs (such as digitization and royalties paid to the original rightsholders) of adding new content to the library customer's perpetual access."[41] To prevent access fees from eating up collection budgets, libraries began negotiating access fees prior to entering into a subscription agreement, buying out access fees for existing subscriptions via lump-sum payments, or moving digital information onto in-house servers.[42] Maintaining in-house servers comes with its own costs, though these costs may be lower than paying ongoing access fees.

JSTOR began addressing concerns about perpetual access to electronic content with the 2002 launch of its Electronic-Archiving Initiative, which, in 2004, was transferred to ITHAKA where the service was renamed Portico. Portico is a nonprofit, community-supported, trusted archive of scholarly content for which access to specific content is activated only when that content is no longer accessible from its original source. An example of how the system works occurred in May 2023 when Portico initiated access to eight scholarly journals that "ceased publication and will no longer be available through the original publishers."[43] As of 2023, Portico had archived 39,396 "committed ejournal titles" as well as 2,047,195 e-books and 326 digital collections.[44] A similar trusted archival service is provided by CLOCKSS, a nonprofit digital archive founded in 2006. As of 2023, CLOCKSS had archived fifty-one million electronic journal articles, 400,000 electronic books, as well as an array of other scholarly content.[45]

Leases

For digital content, the dividing line between subscriptions and leases is so fuzzy that the terms can be used interchangeably. Broadly speaking, the difference between the two models is that subscriptions either guarantee, or offer the possibility of, perpetual access to the subscribed content, while leases do not provide such guarantees. In addition, subscriptions tend to apply to a fixed quantity of content, such as a year's worth of issues from a specific journal title, while leases often apply to a moving target of content. For example, when a library leases a collection of e-books from an aggregator, the library does not own those e-books and "the aggregator can withdraw titles from the collection without warning."[46]

Even though leased collections are most closely associated with digital information, libraries have leased physical collections for decades. The McNaughton Book Service of the Brodart Company has, for example, offered libraries a leased popular-reading print-book collection since the early 1950s.[47] Because leasing information in digital formats does not require the transfer of physical items nor incur any losses due to theft or wear and tear, digital leasing quickly became more widespread than the leasing of physical items. Examples of digital leasing include libraries paying annual fees to provide users with access to such information resources as databases, collections of e-books, online newspapers, and collections of films or sound recordings with the understanding that users will no longer have access to those information resources if the library does not continue to pay the leasing fee. While not a viable option for information resources a library wishes to permanently retain, leasing is otherwise attractive because it allows libraries to provide users with information at costs that are much lower than purchasing that same information outright.

When leasing digital content first emerged in the early twenty-first century, the idea of paying for resources that did not become the permanent property of the academic library struck those with a traditional view of collections as somewhat heretical. (In my personal experience, a history professor once told me that she would rather not have any access at all to an e-book than have leased access that could possibly go away without warning.) It is certainly true that when choices about content are left to the whims of the marketplace, there is no expectation that a publisher or aggregator will continue to provide access to content when it is no longer profitable to do so.[48] However, the notion of leasing content has come to seem less strange as the personal information marketplace has transitioned from an ownership model, in which individuals purchased physical items (books, vinyl recordings, DVDs, etc.), to downloading models like iTunes in which users purchased files to store on their personal hardware, to streaming models like Apple Music in which users pay a monthly fee to access vast amounts of content, none of which they actually own and some of which can, and does, disappear without warning, including for reasons that fly in the face of the free exchange of ideas.[49]

Demand-Driven Acquisition

A phenomenon of the digital age and, largely, of the electronic book (a.k.a. ebook, e-book, or digital book), demand-driven acquisition (DDA), which is also known as patron-driven acquisition (PDA), allows a library's user community to take some control over what is or is not added to the collection. Pilot DDA projects started up as early as 2001.[50] By 2011, DDA/PDA was so well established that a pair of co-authors affiliated with Oxford University Press confidently asserted that "it is irrelevant at this point to be 'for' or 'against' PDA. The more important issue is how to adjust our business as this model gains broader acceptance in the marketplace."[51]

Although demand-driven acquisition can take various forms, the typical scenario involves a library depositing a fixed sum of money with a book publisher or an aggregator offering e-books from multiple publishers. In exchange, the publisher or aggregator provides the library with an agreed-upon number of records that the library loads into its online public access catalog (OPAC). The library is not charged for any of the e-books represented by the catalog records until "meaningful use occurs."[52] Once meaningful use has occurred, the library is charged for the e-book which then becomes a permanent part of the library's collection. Determining when meaningful use has occurred may involve such factors as the number of clicks, the length of time viewed, the number of times downloaded, or the number of pages printed. For example, in a DDA plan implemented at Iowa State University in 2010, the purchase of an e-book was not automatically initiated until (1) ten pages were viewed in one browser session, or (2) a browser session lasted more than ten minutes, or (3) one page was printed, or (4) one page was downloaded.[53] Another model for DDA plans involves short-term loans (STL) in which the first few uses of more than five minutes incur a charge equal to a small percentage of the cost of the e-book; after a set number of STLs, the next additional use initiates an auto-purchase equal to the full cost of the e-book.[54] Once a DDA plan is in place, the economics are simple. If a library deposits $50,000 with a vendor, the library's users can trigger up to $50,000 worth of STLs or e-book purchases before the plan either terminates or is renewed through an additional deposit. Though not common, there are also DDA plans in which catalog records for print-format books are loaded into the local catalog and a print copy is purchased only if a library user accesses a record and triggers a request for that item.[55]

The advantages of DDA plans are that items are often provided at a discount from list price, there are no staff costs relating to selection and ordering, and there is a highly accurate match between items provided and user demand. The downside of DDA is the risk that users could skew purchases in unpredictable directions that may not align with the mission of the library and the campus. The question for academic librarians is, "When it comes to building a long-lasting collection, how much should any academic library rely on patrons using the immediate triggering mechanism of a DDA?"[56] William H. Waters addresses the issue more directly, arguing "that PDA is likely to diminish collection quality unless librarians implement safeguards to maintain their central role in book selection."[57] On the other hand, there is Marvin H. Scilken, creator of the U*N*A*B*A*S*H*E*D L*I*B*R*A*R*I*A*N, whose waggish comments on the profession include: "Librarians much prefer buying books nobody wants in preference to buying books they know everybody wants, or, it's better to serve a possible future reader tomorrow than an actual reader today."[58] Sardonic barbs aside, the overall distressingly low use of books in academic library collections raises a valid question: Could books selected by library users fare any worse than those selected by librarians? In a published conversation about DDA/PDA, Rick Anderson observes the disconnect between the books library selectors choose and the books that get read:

> Librarian speculation (whether expressed programmatically by means of librarian-designed approval plans or on a per-title basis by means of firm orders) leads both to the purchase of books that my particular patrons don't want and to the non-purchase of books that they do want. This

is a problem. It was a problem I could live with when my budgets were relatively flush, but drastic budget cuts make the problem much more acute, and a solution much more urgently needed. I can't keep buying books for my particular library that my particular patrons don't want.[59]

DDA provides at least the hope of a solution to the dilemma Anderson poses.

Transformative Agreements

A phenomenon of the open access movement, transformative agreements may well come drive the economics of scholarly communications for the foreseeable future. Transformative agreements are discussed in depth in Chapter 3.

The Emergence of the Electronic Book

In March 1999, Martin Eberhard, president of NuvoMedia, published an opinion piece in *Publishers Weekly*, in which he writes of the future of the e-book:

> E-books offer a sufficiently enticing value that they are very likely to succeed. Features like instant delivery of purchased books; the ability to carry a stack of 10 in a device the size of a paperback; to select a comfortable font type and size for your particular eyes, and other features, far offset the cost and other limitations. And we know one thing for certain about such products: they will only get cheaper, faster and better. Whatever limitations you might see in today's e-book will probably be gone in tomorrow's.[60]

NuvoMedia's proprietary device, the Rocket eBook, was, along with the SoftBook reader, one of the first two hand-portable e-book readers to go on the market. Although NuvoMedia, SoftBook Press, and many other start-ups in the e-book field are mostly gone and forgotten, much of what Eberhard foresaw for the e-book back in 1999 turned out to be on target. Of course, "a stack of 10" e-books is nothing for any device manufactured after, approximately, 2005. And while every flaw in the e-book and the devices for reading e-books has not been overcome in the going-on-thirty years since Eberhard's prediction, the technology of the e-book is certainly faster, better, cheaper, and more pervasive than it was at the dawn of the millennium. Developments such as the Amazon Kindle (2007), the Apple iPad (2010), and the adoption (beginning circa 2010) of responsive design techniques that render web-based content readable on almost any device—smartphones included—went a long way toward normalizing and popularizing not only e-books but more generally the practice of on-screen reading.

When it comes to answering the question of what can be considered the first electronic book, the answer depends on exactly how you define an electronic book. Long before digital technology existed, there were attempts at using analog technology to create smaller, more portable versions of full-sized books that, with some generous stretching of the imagination, can be seen as forerunners of the e-book. Even the inexpensive, portable, and somewhat disposable paperback book may count as a very distant ancestor of the e-book. Other notable ancestors include:

The Fiske Reading Machine

Patented in 1926, the Fiske Reading Machine is a device which employs a magnifying glass for reading miniaturized text.[61] Its inventor, retired U.S. Navy Rear Admiral Bradley A. Fiske (1854–1942), imagined his invention as revolutionizing publishing by reducing the costs of paper and ink while revolutionizing reading by allowing anyone to carry a small library of books in a purse or pocket.

The Readies

In 1930, inspired by the innovation of talking motion pictures (a.k.a. *the talkies*), avant-garde writer Bob Brown (1886–1959) published *The Readies*, a manifesto which calls for the creation of a "simple reading machine which I can carry . . . compact, minute, operated by electricity, the printing done microscopically by the new photographic process."[62]

The Memex

In "As We May Think," an influential article written in the late 1930s and first published in 1945, U.S. engineer and public intellectual Vannevar Bush (1890–1974) proposes the Memex, a theoretical analog device that points in the general direction of the e-book, the desktop computer, and the internet.[63]

Enciclopedia Mecánica

In 1949, Spanish educator and writer Angela Ruiz Robles (1895–1975) was granted a patent for her *Enciclopedia Mecánica*, an analog device designed to function much like a modern electronic textbook by combining reading and learning activities.[64]

Of all the above devices, only the Fiske Reading Machine was manufactured for sale, and it was not commercially successful.

Analog experiments aside, the work often cited as the first electronic book is *Index Thomisticus*, a machine-readable concordance to the works of Saint Thomas Aquinas.[65] The result of projects undertaken from the late 1940s into the 1970s by Jesuit priest Roberto Busa (1913–2011), *Index Thomisticus* is also frequently identified as the first example of a digital-humanities project. In practice, *Index Thomisticus* bears more resemblance to a database than what is generally thought of as an e-book. The 1960s would see pioneering designs that came much closer to the present-day e-book, including Project Xanadu, NLS (oN-Line System), and FRESS (File Retrieval and Editing SyStem).[66] In 1971, Alan Kay, a computer scientist working at Xerox PARC in Palo Alto, California, proposed the Dynabook, a portable, notebook-sized device that Kay predicted would exist in the millions in the 1990s. Though the technology of the time could not manifest Kay's vision for the Dynabook, in the early 1970s Kay and the team at Xerox PARC developed the ALTO, a forerunner of the desktop personal computer.[67]

From a user perspective, among the first practical e-books were those created under the auspices of Project Gutenberg. Initiated in 1971 by Michael S. Hart (1947–2011), Project Gutenberg was rooted in altruism and committed to the principle of making books readily available to the public at no cost to the end user. The texts included in Project Gutenberg were drawn from the public domain and initially hand-typed by Hart, though as the project went on, additional volunteers contributed content. To facilitate downloading over slow dial-up connections, Project Gutenberg texts were made available as plain-text files. Eventually, Project Gutenberg texts were scanned rather than typed, produced in a variety of formats in addition to plain-text, and served via the World Wide Web.[68]

The first commercial e-books came in the form of CD-ROM discs. Among the first commercially produced books available on CD-ROM was Microsoft's *Grolier Academic Encyclopedia*, which went on sale in March 1985. The Voyager Company, a pioneer in the e-book trade, released its first three books on CD-ROM—*The Complete Hitch Hiker's Guide to the Galaxy*, *The Complete Annotated Alice*, and *Jurassic Park*—in January 1992.[69] Voyager would go on to release over sixty titles on CD-ROM under their Expanded Books imprint. In 1993, Bibliobytes became the first company to sell true e-books over the internet.[70] More significant for academic libraries was the founding in 1998 of NetLibrary, the first commercial e-book aggregator to license e-books from multiple publishers and make them available to libraries.[71] NetLibrary offered libraries over 2,000 titles available either title by title, as a bundled package that worked very much along the lines of a traditional blanket order, or via patron-driven acquisition.[72] Within the next few years, academic libraries would be able to choose among a growing number of options for licensing access to significant numbers of e-books. Early examples include:

- In 2000, the University of Pennsylvania and Oxford University Press struck an agreement under which the University of Pennsylvania Library would digitize and make available to its user community from 1,500 to 2,000 Oxford University Press history titles published between 2000 and 2005.[73]
- By 2001, Princeton University Press was offering 500 backlist titles as e-books, with plans to publish ten to twelve titles per year as enhanced e-books to be made available within two months of the publication of the print version of each title.[74]
- Also in 2001, working under the umbrella of the American Council of Learned Societies, a group of seven university presses teamed up to issue front and backlist e-book titles in the field of history. The presses involved were those of Columbia University, Harvard, Johns Hopkins, the University of Michigan, Oxford University, Rutgers, and NYU.[75]
- In 2003, several large book collections became available in electronic form, including:
  - Ebsco's BookSource, a research database of over 1,660 nonfiction books and series.
  - Academic Complete, Ebrary's database of over 10,000 nonfiction titles from over 150 academic publishers.
  - The Knovel collection of reference titles aimed at scientists and engineers.
  - Oxford Reference Online, a collection of dictionaries, handbooks, and other reference works.[76]

As e-books began to be marketed to academic libraries in earnest, a bewildering number of e-book packages came and went, along with an equally bewildering array of economic models through which libraries could pay for e-books. The early period of libraries acquiring e-books was a time of uncertainty, as aggregators, publishers, and librarians all sought to find their footing in an uncertain and volatile marketplace. Questia, a Houston-based start-up founded in 1999 and launched in 2001, chose to sidestep libraries altogether by selling directly to students, offering both short- and long-term subscriptions to its database of books and periodicals.[77] For risk-averse aggregators and publishers, the main concern was whether the e-book business would prove to be profitable. For academic librarians, the main concern was how to provide the right quantity and quality of e-books to their users without blowing up collections budgets that were strained to breaking even before the e-book arrived on the scene.

Especially in the early years of the e-book, publishers were asking themselves the same simple question: "How do we make sure this newfangled electronic product does not disrupt the revenue stream produced by our bread-and-butter print product?" One common tactic used by publishers hoping to support sales of print books was delaying—in some cases for as long as eighteen months—the availability of a newly published book in e-format.[78] The thinking was that faculty pressure to acquire new books sooner rather than later would prevent librarians from skipping the print and waiting for the e-book. While delays between print and e-format availability persisted as the e-book marketplace matured, a study published in 2018 found that 47.85 percent of the e-books in the study were available within fourteen days of the release of the print version and that 75 percent of the e-books in the study had become available within 101 days of the publication of the print version.[79]

The history of the e-book is not, by any means, limited to commercial endeavors. Project Gutenberg demonstrated early on that digitizing and freely sharing works from the public domain was feasible both because such works could be shared without the need to acquire permission from a rights holder and because there was no need to take on the expense of protecting public-domain works from unauthorized use, duplication, or redistribution. But where Project Gutenberg had been a somewhat decentralized volunteer project relying, at least in its early phase, on typed, plain-text files, the public-domain e-book projects that began to take shape in the late 1990s and early 2000s were grant-funded and more systematic in their approach. Instead of relying on typing texts by hand, the new e-book projects employed scanning technology that had grown increasingly faster, better, and cheaper over the years. Most importantly, lower costs for optical character recognition (OCR) technology made it possible to not only capture page images but also to simultaneously create searchable text files that facilitate discovery of, and access to, page images. In 2005, the Internet Archive, in collaboration with a group of public and private partner institutions, launched the Open Content Alliance with the announced goal of carrying out the mass digitization of millions of public-domain books.[80] Though the Open Content Alliance would eventually give way to other projects, the Internet Archive would continue to play a significant role in the digitization of books and other content. Founded in 1996 by Brewster Kahle, a computer scientist by training and apostle of free access to information by calling, the Internet Archive digital library would, by the year 2023, offer users 20,000,000 books and texts that could be freely downloaded as well as 2.3 million copyrighted books that could be digitally borrowed by anyone who registered for a free Internet Archive account.[81] Another pioneer book digitization endeavor was the Million Book Project. Launched in 2002 by Carnegie Mellon University, the Million Book Project included international partnerships with Zhejiang University, the Indian Institute of Science, and the Library at Alexandria. By the time the Million Book Project ended in 2008, it had digitized 1.5 million books, all of which were freely available via the project's Universal Library web portal.[82]

As they set out to digitize public-domain books, the staff of the Million Book Project experimented with seeking permission to legally digitize works that were not in the public domain; however, the conclusion reached was: "Locating copyright holders is difficult, expensive, and often unsuccessful, especially for older works."[83] What the Million Book Project experienced is the "orphan works problem" that still vexes efforts to make copyrighted material freely available to the public. Orphan works are copyrighted materials, most decades old, that have no economic value but for which the rights holder cannot be readily located. A hypothetical example might be a scholarly book on ocean currents published in a single edition in the 1950s, never republished, and long out of print and out of stock. The assumption is that if the rights holder of such a work, which might well be the heirs of the original rights holder, could be contacted, permission to digitize the work would likely be granted in the interest of making the work widely available online rather than marginally available in the stacks or (more likely) the high-density storage facilities of a few hundred academic libraries. While the reality is that there would be a small risk of litigation if the typical orphan work were digitized and made freely available, doing so is nonetheless an infringement of copyright that could be contested by a rights holder. In the United States, the passage of the CASE Act of 2020 and the resultant establishment of a copyright small-claims court that makes it much faster and cheaper for legitimate copyright holders as well as unscrupulous copyright trolls to seek damages led to concern within the library and legal professions that making orphan works available had become riskier than ever.[84] Even more detrimental to early digitization projects than the passage of the CASE Act was the passage of the Sonny Bono Copyright Term Extension Act of 1998, a U.S. federal law that froze the public domain from 1999 to 2019. For example, due to the Sonny Bono Copyright Term Extension Act of 1998, F. Scott Fitzgerald's *The Great Gatsby* and Henry Clayton Metcalf's *Linking Science and Industry,* both of which were published in 1925, entered the public domain on January 1, 2021, when, without a term extension, they would have entered the public domain on January 1, 2001. At the time it finally entered the public domain, *The Great Gatsby* was world famous, had been reprinted in multiple editions, and still retained considerable economic value. *Linking Science and Industry*, on the other hand, was long forgotten, had never been reprinted, and retained no economic value. This set of circumstances made *Linking Science and Industry* far more typical of the thousands of books published in 1925 than was *The Great Gatsby*, a rare example of a work for which its economic value outlives its copyright. Thanks to the untimely extension of copyright in 1998, roughly the first two decades of serious mass-digitization projects were carried out at the same time that no additional books, films, articles, photographs, or other copyrighted works were entering the public domain. Works that could have been digitized and made freely available with no economic harm to anyone, and for which digitization might have led to such works being consulted for the first time in decades, sat in copyright limbo, serving the interests of no one.

Of all the mass-digitization projects launched in the first decades of the twenty-first century, none had a greater impact than Google Books. According to Google co-founder Larry Page, in 2002 he met with Mary Sue Coleman, then president of the University of Michigan, Page's alma mater. During their meeting, Coleman informed Page that the best estimate of the time required to scan all 7,000,000 volumes in the libraries of the University of Michigan was 1,000 years. Page replied that he believed Google could do the job in six years.[85] Page was not just talking out of his hat, as he and others at Google had been experimenting with digitization before his meeting with Coleman. Regardless of what lit the fuse, in the early 2000s Google started getting serious about creating a vast library of digitized books.

The ambitious Google mass-digitization project, which went through a series of name changes over the years, was different from digitization projects like Project Gutenberg and the Million Book Project in that it indiscriminately digitized both public-domain and in-copyright works. To carry out the hands-on work of digitization, Google set up several digitization centers where workers used Google's proprietary hardware and software to scan pages at previously unheard-of speeds. Google obtained items to scan by partnering with publishers and, most importantly, by partnering with large research libraries that agreed to supply books to be scanned by the millions. For Google's library partners, the fact that Google's scanning process did not damage the books was key to their cooperation. In the fall of 2005, with the work of digitization in full swing, Google was sued for copyright infringement by both the Authors Guild and the Association of American Publishers. Although in both cases Google would ultimately prevail in court, the lawsuits had a chilling effect. Google's digitization work started to wind down in 2007 and came to a complete halt within a few years. Even so, the amount of content digitized by Google wildly exceeded anything that had been done before. According to Google's own blog, as of 2023 Google Books contains the text of "more than 40 million books in more than 500 languages."[86]

In addition to authors and publishers concerned about copyright infringement, Google Books also had its critics among academics. There was concern among many academics that, as a for-profit business, Google might take its digital book collection in a direction that did not serve the best interests of higher education. Pragmatically, there were complaints about pages left unreadable due to scanning errors as well as problems with metadata. Shortcomings aside, libraries that loaned books to Google reaped two significant benefits. First, Google rapidly scanned millions of books at no cost to the libraries themselves, performing an amount of work that would have cost libraries millions of dollars they did not, and probably never would, have. Second, libraries that provided books for scanning received their own copies of the scanned data to use in any way they saw fit. In October 2008, under the leadership of the University of Michigan, the twelve universities in the Committee on Institutional Cooperation (later known as the Big Ten Academic Alliance) along with the ten libraries of the University of California System joined forces to found HathiTrust, a digital library created and controlled by its member libraries. Within fifteen years of its founding, the HathiTrust collection had grown to over eighteen million digitized items, while membership in the HathiTrust organization had increased to nearly 300 libraries. Though the bulk of the initial HathiTrust collection was built with data acquired through participation in the Google Books Project, HathiTrust also incorporated content provided by Internet Archive, member libraries, and Microsoft's short-lived book-scanning initiative.[87] In addition to providing access to digital books, HathiTrust served the research community through such initiatives as providing access to U.S. government documents, establishing a shared-print program, and launching the HathiTrust Research Center.[88]

Google Books and HathiTrust contain the full text of both public-domain and copyrighted works; however, for both collections, full-text access is limited to works that are in the public domain. Like Google, HathiTrust was sued by the Authors Guild only to prevail in court.[89] Unlike Google, HathiTrust did not let legal entanglements stop it from expanding its collection. In the years following the founding of HathiTrust, its member libraries have continued to contribute new content created through local digitization projects, large and small. HathiTrust also expanded full-text access through its copyright review program, which researches the copyright status of works in the HathiTrust collection with the goal of identifying and opening for full-text access any public-domain materials incorrectly assumed to be in copyright. For example, a HathiTrust project to review the copyright status of state documents determined that 101,613 of 119,918 state documents thought to be under copyright were in fact in the public domain and could be opened for full-text access.[90] HathiTrust also continued working to improve the quality of scanned documents by encouraging users to report pages containing scanning errors so they could be replaced with error-free pages. Another benefit of HathiTrust and other digital libraries is that they are permitted to allow persons with print disabilities access to the full text of copyrighted materials, though in the United States retaining that right requires governmental reapproval every three years.[91] For academic researchers, arguably the most striking example of how HathiTrust meets their needs has been the HathiTrust Research Center, a set of services that permit researchers to carry out non-consumptive text mining and data analysis of the entire HathiTrust corpus, including both copyrighted and public-domain works. Two illustrative examples of the many scholarly projects conducted via the HathiTrust Research Center include a project to "create an index of all the scientific names of the Earth's species found within the HathiTrust corpus" and another to identify "all pictorial elements in educational texts from 1800–1850."[92]

If there were any doubts among academics about the value of large collections of digital books as represented by HathiTrust, they were effectively erased by the events of the Covid pandemic that began in late 2019. With academic libraries closed and print-format books inaccessible, on March 31, 2020, HathiTrust launched its Emergency Temporary Access Service (ETAS) to provide full-text access to its digital content regardless of copyright status. HathiTrust's legal justification for ETAS was based on "fair use provisions in copyright law to provide temporary access to digitized titles in HathiTrust that correspond to physical titles held by a member library, for the duration of an emergency that prevents physical access to the library's collection."[93] In practice, ETAS worked as follows. Say, for example, a HathiTrust member library owned a single print copy of the copyrighted book *One L* by Scott Turow.[94] Under the terms of ETAS, the digital full text of *One L* could be accessed by that library's affiliated users, though by only one user at a time. If the library had two print copies of *One L*, then up to two affiliated users could access the full text simultaneously, the key being to maintain a one-to-one ratio between print copies and simultaneous uses. As a condition of participating in ETAS, HathiTrust member libraries were required to keep their print collections entirely inaccessible to users. Once the restrictions imposed by the pandemic eased up and libraries reopened to users, their participation in ETAS ended immediately. Ironically, while the long-standing fear of print-centric traditionalists had been that some hypothetical disaster could cut off access to all the electronic information libraries were so recklessly acquiring, the pandemic produced the exact opposite effect, cutting off access to print while allowing electronic access to carry on without interruption.

The process for providing access to copyrighted digital material as practiced during the period of HathiTrust's ETAS is known as *controlled digital lending*. The concept of controlled digital lending was first proposed in 2011 by Michelle M. Wu, a legal scholar and director of the Georgetown University Law Center Library. Under Wu's conception, controlled digital lending "permits circulation of the exact number of copies purchased, thereby acknowledging the rights inherent in copyright, but it liberates the form of circulation from the print format."[95] Under non-emergency conditions in which print library collections remain accessible to users, libraries practicing controlled digital lending must "limit the total number of copies in any format in circulation at any time to the number of physical copies the library lawfully owns (maintain an 'owned to loaned' ratio)."[96] For example, if a library that owns three print copies of *One L* provides access to one of those copies via controlled digital lending, then it can simultaneously lend only two of its three print copies in order to maintain the owned-to-loaned ratio. Libraries began experimenting with variations of controlled digital lending not long after Wu's article was published.[97] Perhaps the most notable implementation of controlled digital lending has been the Internet Archive's Open Library: Digital Lending Library project. Internet Archive was testing the waters of controlled digital lending as early as 2011, creating a program in which Internet Archive e-books "will only be available for download to patrons physically present at the branches that donated books [to Internet Archive] as part of the program."[98] In an effort aimed at both preserving printed books and justifying its practice of controlled digital lending, Internet Archive began acquiring and warehousing millions of physical books, storing them in shipping containers located in Richmond, California, just across the Oakland Bay Bridge from Internet Archive's San Francisco Headquarters.[99] Responding to the shutdown of libraries due to the Covid pandemic, in March 2020 the Internet Archive launched its National Emergency Library, a digital library of 1.4 million books from which anyone could borrow.[100] In 2022 industry leader Ex Libris integrated into its Alma Digital library services platform a controlled digital lending function "which will ensure the number of simultaneous digital lending transactions for a particular resource does not exceed the number of physical copies owned."[101]

On the other hand, in response to a lawsuit filed by a group of publishers against Internet Archive's National Emergency Library on June 1, 2020, the U.S. District Court in the Southern District of New York on March 24, 2023, granted a summary judgment in favor of the plaintiffs.[102] Though Internet Archive immediately appealed, the ruling cast grave doubts on the future of controlled digital lending.

The E-Book and the Reader

As e-books started to become more common, the idea that some intangible assemblage of ones and zeros might replace the print book loomed large in the imagination of more tradition-minded users. In part, this was because the printed book has for so long stood as the nearly sacred symbol of what it means for a library to be a library. For many library users, it became, and remains, reasonable to ask, "Can you even have a library without books made of paper and ink?" In the early years of e-books, fear of the unknown led to loose talk about libraries of the near future not having any books at all in their collections. One of the early rumors circulating around the halls of academia in the 1990s had it that the new California State University, Monterey Bay, would open without a library. This rumor was debunked in an article published in the *Chronicle of Higher Education* in 1996: "A suggestion that Monterey might not need a library building, since so much information is available electronically, died a week after it was made last year; most information is still available only in paper form."[103] There were similar unfounded rumors in the early 2000s that the University of California, Merced Library would not have any print books. Not only do CSU Monterey Bay and UC Merced feature libraries with physical books in the stacks, so does almost every other academic library in the nation, if not the world. The exceptions are few. Johns Hopkins University's William H. Welch Medical Library was effectively online only by 2015, though library users could still acquire print texts on request.[104] More radically, the library of the Florida Polytechnic University opened in 2014 without any physical books and has, to date, remained bookless.[105]

Thus far in the history of libraries and reading, the e-book has supplemented the print book without ever threatening to replace it. Even so, the growth in the size of academic library e-book collections since 2000 has been astounding. As Figure 1.1 illustrates, from 2000 through 2021 the number of e-books in U.S. academic library collections grew from just over 10,000 to 1,363,858,000 e-books. Yet despite the widespread adoption of the e-book by academic libraries, there remain unresolved issues around the value of e-books to the users of academic

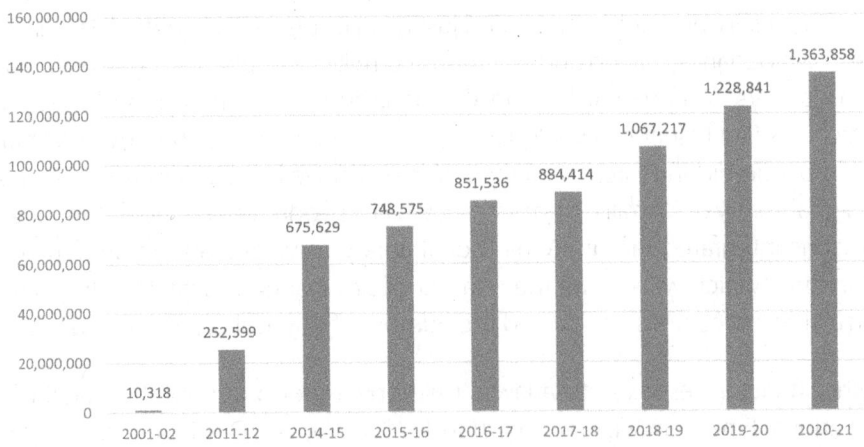

Figure 1.1 E-books in U.S. academic library collections (in thousands).
Source: National Center for Educational Statistics, "Digest of Education Statistics, 2021," IEC>NCES (National Center for Education Statistics), accessed August 6, 2023, https://nces.ed.gov/programs/digest/d21/tables/dt21_701.40.asp?current=yes..

libraries, including the problem of technological hurdles standing between users and e-books and the question of whether or not e-books meet the needs of academic library users.

Technological Hurdles

Providers who license content to academic libraries have a business interest in ensuring that their intellectual property can be accessed only by those individuals with a legitimate right to do so; in most cases, this means affiliates of a library that is paying for access. Limiting access to authorized users protects a content provider's bottom line from free riders, both individual and institutional. After all, if any random person who wants access to *The Journal of X* could obtain it simply by going to the website of subscribing Library Y, why would any other library go to the expense of subscribing to *The Journal of X*? Content providers who license digital intellectual property to libraries safeguard it from unauthorized access in two principal ways. First, by limiting access to the authorized institutional IP ranges of subscription-paying libraries, and second, through the practice of digital rights management (DRM).

Limiting access to authorized institutional IP ranges normally means that anyone using an electronic device that is physically located on the campus of a subscribing academic library is granted access to that library's licensed content. Due to the long-standing convention that anyone who walks into an academic library, whether affiliated with the campus or not, is allowed to read and make personal copies of whatever printed materials are in the stacks, one concession that academic libraries have, in most cases, been able to obtain from content providers is that the same rule applies to licensed content.[106] Unaffiliated campus visitors can typically gain access to licensed content either by using on-campus public-access terminals (if available) or by accessing a campus guest network (if one exists) via a personal electronic device.

Off-campus access to licensed content, on the other hand, is typically limited to the faculty, staff, and enrolled students of a subscribing academic library's parent institution. To obtain remote access to an academic library's licensed content, authorized users working off campus must first authenticate themselves, usually by logging into a campus proxy server or virtual private network (VPN) that then relays a user's request for access as having originated from an authorized campus IP range. As a result of the need for off-campus users to authenticate, the website of almost every academic library provides instructions, in some cases quite complex instructions, for configuring user devices to access the campus proxy server and/or VPN along with instructions for how to log on once configured. Especially for first-time users and those without sufficiently advanced computer skills, logging onto a campus network can become a barrier to accessing information that the user is, in fact, entitled to access. For some licensed content, access may be further complicated when content providers require users to establish personal provider-specific accounts in addition to authenticating through their campus VPN or proxy server.

DRM differs from IP address limitations in that it thwarts unauthorized use by employing a suite of technologies that include "data encryption, digital watermarks, and user plug-ins."[107] The use of DRM was given a boost in the United States with the passage of the Digital Millennium Copyright Act of 1998, a federal law making it a criminal offense to circumvent any technology intended to control access to a copyrighted work.[108] Content providers contend that they have good reasons to safeguard copyrighted materials from exploitation. To use an example from the realm of popular fiction, in the year 2000, Stephen King became the first bestselling author to publish a purely electronic book. Within twenty-four hours of going online, King's e-novella, *Riding the Bullet*, had been downloaded half a million times. However, within seven days of going online, the encryption protecting King's book from illegal downloading had been cracked.[109] In the academic arena, libraries and content providers must routinely deal with the problem of excessive amounts of copyrighted content being illegally downloaded via automated programs.[110]

The cumulative effect of the steps content providers take to safeguard copyrighted materials has been, in some cases, to render the use of digital content so slow and burdensome that authorized users are discouraged, if not outright prevented, from accessing library digital collections. As one organization that opposes DRM puts it, "DRM creates a damaged good; it prevents you from doing what would be possible without it."[111] Especially in the case of e-books, DRM can be a serious barrier due to the limits it places on the amount users can view, print, or download.[112] Early e-book models that limited access to a single user at a time, while intended to reassure publishers who were feeling cold feet about entering the e-book market, have been characterized as "anathema to librarians."[113] Anathema to both librarians and end users was the practice of making e-books available in proprietary formats that cannot be readily accessed on the end user's preferred device. The problem of proprietary e-book formats was lessened, though not eliminated, with the adoption of the .epub standard following its initial release in September 2007.[114] For academic librarians, the fundamental frustrations are not only that DRM is an obstacle to authorized users accessing content but also that the cost of implementing and maintaining DRM technology is passed on to the libraries as part of subscription costs.

Whether DRM measures are seen as reasonable or excessive, their existence is evidence of a fundamental difference in library acquisitions in the digital versus the print arenas. When a library purchases a print book, the First Sale Doctrine of U.S. copyright law allows that library to loan that work to another person or entity without the copyright holder being in anyway compensated.[115] In addition, copyright law further recognizes that the concept of Fair Use allows certain uses of copyrighted materials without the permission of the copyright owner.[116] Digital content, on the other hand, is controlled by both copyright law and licensing agreements, with the latter often being much more restrictive than the former. As Julie A. Murphy observes, "restrictive licensing agreements, differences between platforms, digital rights management (DRM) mechanisms, and other technological barriers make it extremely difficult to share e-books between libraries in the way that we have traditionally loaned print materials to each other."[117] In particular, e-book licensing agreements often limit or prevent the lending of whole e-books via interlibrary loan.[118] A report on three years (2013–16) of interlibrary loan in U.S. academic libraries found that interlibrary loan (ILL) of whole e-books was hindered by "license agreement restrictions, different purchasing models, unstandardized platforms, and technological barriers."[119] The restriction on ILL imposed by licensing agreements is severe enough that they have been cited as discouraging libraries from adding e-books to their collections.[120]

Do E-Books Meet the Needs of Academic Library Users?

If Netlibrary's launch of its academic e-book licensing service in 1998 can be considered the starting line, academic libraries are now twenty-plus years into the e-book era. After all that time, questions remain as to how well e-books meet the needs of individual users of academic libraries. The literature is not much help because it is so contradictory. "E-books or Textbooks: Students Prefer Textbooks" is both the title of a heavily cited article published in the journal *Computers & Education* as well as the mantra of many who work in higher education, including some librarians.[121] Finding research that reaches the opposite conclusion is, however, not hard. For one example, a study conducted at the University of Northern Iowa found that of 287 students who were asked to choose what types of books they most prefer to read in electronic format, the most popular response was textbooks.[122] Whether or not students or faculty or librarians prefer print textbooks, the fact is that textbook publishers were quick to move into the e-book market, attracted to the format in part because renting electronic textbooks to students would strike a blow against the (anathema to publishers) secondhand textbook market.[123] More altruistically, electronic textbooks have been seen as offering the potential to supplement traditional text and images with video, audio, and interactive-media components that make for more dynamic learning experiences.[124] The adoption of electronic textbooks has been furthered by the textbook industry's promotion of institutionally licensed textbook collections designed to reduce, if not eliminate, out-of-pocket textbook costs for students. As of 2022, Follett Higher Education's ACCESS textbook licensing plan had been, in one form or another, adopted by more than 1,100 North American campuses.[125] The growth of the open educational resources (OER) movement has also served to encourage the use of electronic textbooks.

The combination of site licensing of electronic textbooks, the spread of OER textbooks, and academic libraries' growing reliance on e-books as a major component of their overall collections raises an important question: "Do students use e-books because they like and learn from them, or do they use e-books because they have no other alternative?" If nothing else, the convenience of e-books has a strong appeal for students. The fact that most e-book formats have evolved to such a point of standardization that they can be read on a variety of devices, including desktops, laptops, tablets, and smartphones, has made them increasingly convenient for use by born-digital students, many of whom grew up using e-books during their years of primary and secondary education. Any student facing a looming deadline to complete a paper or project is, regardless of any personal preference for print format, far more likely to opt for an e-book that is available *now* versus waiting for a book to arrive via interlibrary loan or making a trip to the campus library to pluck a print book out of the stacks. In the case of distance learning students, for whom a trip to the campus library is not practical, the value of an e-book option is obvious. Because of their searchability, e-books lend themselves to looking up a quick supporting fact or an apt quotation to drop into a paper. Traditionalists may groan that the shortcuts provided by e-books discourage the kind of deep reading associated with print formats, but it is not unfair to ask, "How many undergraduates, before or after the coming of the e-book, have the time or inclination for much in the way of deep reading?"

Among the best explications of the contradictions of the e-book is found in Barbara Blummer and Jeffrey M. Kenton's article "A Systematic Review of E-Books in Academic Libraries: Access, Advantages, and Usage." In reviewing sixty documents relevant to the role of e-books in the academic library published from 2001 through 2017, Blummer and Kenton consider the arguments for and against the usefulness of the e-book before, in the end, concluding, "The literature illustrated the importance of E-books to all members of the academic community for research and coursework."[126] Without coming down too heavily on either side of the e-book debate, it is safe to say that the usefulness of the print book versus the usefulness of an e-book depends on both the purpose of the reading and the preference of the reader in the context of that purpose. A student who could not possibly bear to read all 677 pages of Barbara Tuckman's *A Distant Mirror: The Calamitous 14th Century* as an e-book might nonetheless turn to the e-book version of Tuckman's book to read her chapter on the Battle of Poitiers. A student who relies on e-books for all course-related reading might nonetheless prefer to dive into a print version of J. R. R. Tolkien's *Lord of the Rings* trilogy. The understanding that there is a place for both the e-book and the printed book led to the introduction of print-on-demand services. Starting in 2007, some bookstores and libraries acquired the Espresso Book Machine, a 1600-pound device capable of turning a book-length .pdf into a bound paperback in four minutes.[127] That Espresso was less than a success is reflected in the words of one of Espresso's co-founders, who in 2022 was quoted as saying that "the use of the Espresso Book Machine has stalled."[128] More successful have been online print-on-demand services such as Amazon's Kindle Direct Publishing (KDP), Lulu xPress, and IngramSpark, services through which a purchaser requests a print-on-demand copy online and receives the finished product within a few days.

In considering where the e-book may be headed, it is worth noting that the basic technology of the e-book has not changed significantly since its introduction. Though not yet widely available to consumers, technology exists that could enhance the e-book reading experience. It is easy to imagine e-books that more fully incorporate video or interactive elements. E-books and electronic reading devices may also come to better emulate the tactile characteristics that readers value in print books, including easier ways of annotating text and methods of navigating a long text that are more like turning printed pages than scrolling a flat screen. Though it is far from a certainty, there could come a day when the overall e-book reading experience is equal to, or possibly exceeds, the print reading experience.

Other Digital Formats

As much as printed books were impacted by the advent of digital surrogates, other analog technologies that underwent as much or more transformation from the 1990s through 2020 and beyond include periodicals, archival materials, non-print media, and maps. The impact of digital technology on periodicals and archival materials will be covered in detail in later chapters.

Prior to the existence of streaming technology, academic libraries routinely collected non-print media in both analog (films, filmstrips, vinyl sound recordings, photographs and slides, audio and video tapes) and digital formats (CDs and DVDs).[129] Academic libraries supporting media studies and music programs often featured full-blown media centers staffed by librarians who specialized in media acquisition and curation. The increased availability of video and audio through streaming services available via personal subscriptions, such as Netflix and iTunes, as well as through services available via institutional subscriptions, such as Kanopy and Naxos Music Library, has led some to question the need for academic libraries to continue acquiring and maintaining media collections. In considering this matter, media librarian Rachael King asks a key question: "Will streaming video databases just offer a glut of material of inferior quality that has not undergone a rigorous selection process by librarians or teaching faculty?"[130] Between subscription streaming media services and advertising-supported websites like YouTube, it is safe to assume that students and faculty will be able to access such works as *Citizen Kane*, Beethoven's Symphony No. 6, Martin Luther King's "I Have a Dream" speech, or the Beatles' "Help." As for media that falls outside of the mainstream, as well as for meeting the needs of researchers for whom the difference between the 2009 remastered version of "Help" and the 1965 mono version is crucial, such an assumption does not rise to any reasonable definition of the word *safe*.

Map collections have been strongly impacted by digital technology, yet they are much like print-book collections in that analog maps have been supplemented by digital maps without being replaced. The availability of digital Geographic Information System (GIS) programs such as ESRI GIS Mapping Software and Mapbox initiated a map-making renaissance for everyone from highly trained GIS specialists to individuals with no prior cartographic experience. In addition, the availability of GPS technology on everything from automobile entertainment systems to smartphones has all but eliminated such once-common aids to navigation as the foldable roadmap. On the other hand, there has been nothing like a rush on the part of academic libraries to divest themselves of maps in print formats. One reason for the persistence of printed maps is that their dimensions are often larger than the typical computer screen, allowing the viewer to take in an entire map without loss of detail or the need to scroll. Another reason printed maps have not gone away is that many of them will always retain their value as works of art and/or historical artifacts even when digital surrogates are available. As Mary Lynette Larsgaard stated for the benefit of her fellow map librarians at a time when GIS, GPS, and digital maps were coming into their own, "Our goal here: to have our map libraries present to our users the best of both the Paper World and the Digital World."[131]

The Best of Both Worlds

Mary Lynette Larsgaard was thinking of maps when she wrote those words back in 2006, but in the ongoing collision of analog and digital worlds, her stated goal of providing users with the best of both worlds still applies to library collections across the board and will continue to do so far into the future.

Notes

1. Thomas Carlyle, "Lecture V: The Hero as Man of Letters. Johnson. Rousseau, Burns," in *On Heroes, Hero-Worship and the Heroic in History* (London: Chapman and Hall, 1840), 192, https://catalog.hathitrust.org/Record/011627421.

2. Otis Robinson, "College Library Administration," in *Public Libraries in the United States of America; Their History, Condition, and Management. Special Report, Department of the Interior, Bureau of Education. Part I* (Washington, DC: Government Printing Office, 1876), 507, https://catalog.hathitrust.org/Record/100570955.

3. Vicky Reich and David S. Rosenthal, "LOCKSS (Lots of Copies Keep Stuff Safe)," *New Review of Academic Librarianship* 6 (2000): 155–61.

4. According to a search of Google Scholar, *High Altitude Rocket Research* was cited twelve times from 1990 to 2020.

5. Felix T. Chu, "Library Inventory: A Selected and Annotated Bibliography," *Library & Archival Security* 7, no. 3–4 (June 12, 1987): 55–65.

6. Chu, "Library Inventory," 56.

7. Julian Chela-Flores, *Astrobiology and Humanism: Conversations on Science, Philosophy and Theology* (Cambridge Scholars Publishing, 2019).

8. Francis X. Doherty, "The New England Deposit Library: History and Development," *The Library Quarterly: Information, Community, Policy* 18, no. 4 (October 1948): 249.

9. Marshall Breeding, "Library Storage Facilities," Library Technology Guides, https://librarytechnology.org/storagefacilities/ (accessed May 28, 2023).

10. David Rapp, "Robot Visions," *Library Journal*, September 15, 2011.

11. Paul N. Courant and Matthew Nielsen, "On the Cost of Keeping a Book," in *The Idea of Order: Transforming Research Collections for 21st Century Scholarship* (Washington, DC: Council on Library and Information Resources, 2010), 81–105, https://www.clir.org/wp-content/uploads/sites/6/pub147.pdf.

12. Throughout this book, all price conversions to account for inflation are based on the U.S. Bureau of Labor Statistics CPI Inflation Calculator, https://www.bls.gov/data/inflation_calculator.htm.

13. Carol Hansen Montgomery and Donald W. King, "Comparing Library and User Related Costs of Print and Electronic Journal Collections: A First Step Towards a Comprehensive Analysis," *D-Lib Magazine* 8, no. 10 (October 2002), https://doi.org/10.1045/october2002-montgomery.

14. Task Force on [Harvard] University Libraries, "Report of the Task Force on University Libraries" (Cambridge, MA: Harvard University, November 2009), https://hwpi.harvard.edu/files/provost/files/library_task_force_report.pdf.

15. "Collections | CRL," Center for Research Libraries, https://www.crl.edu/collections (accessed August 10, 2023).

16. Keyes D. Metcalf and Edwin E. Williams, "Proposal for a Division of Responsibility among American Libraries in the Acquisition and Recording of Library Materials," *College & Research Libraries* 5, no. 2 (March 1944): 105–9.

17 "ASERL Association of Southeastern Research Libraries 2020 Annual Report," Annual Report (Atlanta, Georgia: Association of Southeastern Research Libraries, 2020), 4.

18 "Dashboard," PAPR | Print Archives Preservation Registry, http://papr.crl.edu/ (accessed August 10, 2023).

19 Michael Gorman, "The Treason of the Learned," *Library Journal* 119, no. 3 (February 15, 1994): 130.

20 Margaret Atwood, *The Handmaid's Tale* (Boston and New York: Houghton Mifflin Harcourt, 1986).

21 Jennifer Howard, "In Face of Professors''Fury,' Syracuse U. Library Will Keep Books on Shelves," *The Chronicle of Higher Education*, November 12, 2009.

22 Scott Carlson, "Thoughtful Design Keeps New Libraries Relevant," *Chronicle of Higher Education*, September 30, 2005.

23 "Library Storage Facilities," *TexLibris* (blog), August 8, 2018, https://texlibris.lib.utexas.edu/category/preservation/library-storage-facilities/.

24 Matthew J. Jabaily, Rhonda Glazier, and Federico Martínez-García Jr., "Out of Reach: The Effect of Shelf Height on Book Checkouts," *Journal of Access Services* 19, no. 2/3 (June 2022): 54–66.

25 Richard L. Trueswell, "Some Behavioral Patterns of Library Users: The 80/20 Rule," *Wilson Library Bulletin* 43, no. 5 (1969): 458–61.

26 William A. Britten, "A Use Statistic for Collection Management: The 80/20 Rule Revisited," *Library Acquisitions: Practice & Theory* 14, no. 2 (January 1990): 183–9.

27 Kizer Walker et al., "Report of the Collection Development Executive Committee Task Force on Print Collection Usage Cornell University Library" (Ithaca: Cornell University Library, November 22, 2010), https://hdl.handle.net/1813/45424.

28 Charles Martell, "The Absent User: Physical Use of Academic Library Collections and Services Continues to Decline 1995–2006," *The Journal of Academic Librarianship* 34, no. 5 (September 2008): 400–7.

29 Spencer Johnson, *Who Moved My Cheese?: An Amazing Way to Deal with Change in Your Work and in Your Life* (New York: Putnam, 1998).

30 Jay K. Lucker, "Technological Advances and the Changing Research Library: From Yesterday to Tomorrow (Paper Presented at the 4th International Seminar, Kanazawa Institute of Technology, Library Center, Kanazawa, Japan, 1985)," in *Research Libraries: Yesterday, Today, and Tomorrow*, ed. William J. Welsh, Contributions in Librarianship and Information Science; No. 77 (Westport: Greenwood Press, 1993), 241–2.

31 Richard C. Atkinson, "A New World of Scholarly Communication. (Making Scholarly Publications Less Expensive and More Accessible)," *The Chronicle of Higher Education* 50, no. 11 (November 1, 2003): B16.

32 Julia C. Blixrud and Martha Kyrillidou, "E-Metrics: Next Steps for Measuring Electronic Resources," *ARL: A Bimonthly Report on Research Library Issues & Actions*, no. 230/231 (October 2003): 11.

33 John Caldwell, "Perceptions of the Academic Library Midwestern College Libraries as They Have Been Depicted in College Histories," in *The Academic Library in the United States: Historical Perspectives*, ed. Mark L. McCallon and John Mark Tucker (Jefferson: McFarland & Company, Inc., Publishers, 2022), 63.

34 "Shoah Foundation's Virtual Archive Purchased by CSUN Library to Preserve History," CSUN Today, November 3, 2021, https://csunshinetoday.csun.edu/arts-and-culture/shoah-foundations-virtual-archive-purchased-by-csun-library-to-preserve-history/.

35. Arthur T. Hamlin, *The University Library in the United States: Its Origins and Development* (Philadelphia: University of Pennsylvania Press, 1981), 35.

36. Louis Shores, *Origins of the American College Library, 1638–1800*, Contribution to Education, Published under the Direction of George Peabody College for Teachers, No. 134 (Hamden: Shoestring Press, 1934), 56, https://catalog.hathitrust.org/Record/000962175.

37. Marilyn Geller, "The Faxon Aftermath: Come Together over Me," *Serials Librarian* 47, no. 1–2 (July 2004): 89–97.

38. Stephen Bosch and Kittie Henderson, "Periodicals Price Survey 2015. Whole Lotta Shakin' Goin' On," *Library Journal* 140, no. 7 (April 15, 2015): 33–4.

39. Lee Ketcham-Van Orsdel and Kathleen Born, "Periodical Price Survey 2000. Pushing Toward More Affordable Access," *Library Journal* 125, no. 7 (April 15, 2000): 50.

40. Buddy Pennington, "Managing Perpetual Access," *Serials Review* 43, no. 3–4 (October 2, 2017): 262–4.

41. Michael Rodriguez, "Flipping Subscription and Access Fees to Perpetuity," *Serials Review* 47, no. 3–4 (October 2, 2021): 188.

42. Lizzie Cope and Elyssa M. Gould, "Access Fees: Controlling the Snowball," *Against the Grain* 33, no. 3 (June 2021): 10–11.

43. Gary Ho, "Portico Access Alert: Eight Scholarly Journals," *Portico* (blog), May 23, 2023, https://www.portico.org/news/portico-access-alert-eight-scholarly-journals/.

44. "Facts and Figures," *Portico* (blog), https://www.portico.org/coverage/facts-and-figures/ (accessed September 7, 2023).

45. "Why CLOCKSS?," *CLOCKSS* (blog), https://clockss.org/about/why-clockss/ (accessed September 7, 2023).

46. Deborah Lenares, "EBook Aggregators: A Primer," *Against the Grain* 25, no. 6 (December 1, 2013): 28, https://doi.org/10.7771/2380-176X.7405.

47. Kerri Odess-Harnish, "Making Sense of Leased Popular Literature Collections," *Collection Management* 27, no. 2 (June 2002): 56.

48. Charles Hamaker, "Ebooks on Fire: Controversies Surrounding Ebooks in Libraries," *SEARCHER Magazine*, December 2011, https://www.infotoday.com/searcher/dec11/Hamaker.shtml.

49. SCMP, "Popular Versions of 'Glory to Hong Kong' No Longer Showing on Apple Music," *Young Post*, June 14, 2023, https://www.scmp.com/yp/discover/news/hong-kong/article/3224067/popular-versions-glory-hong-kong-no-longer-showing-apple-music.

50. Michael Levine-Clark, "Developing a Model for Long-Term Management of Demand-Driven Acquisitions," *Against the Grain* 23, no. 3 (June 1, 2011): 24–6, https://doi.org/10.7771/2380-176X.5887.

51. Rebecca Seger and Lenny Allen, "A Publisher's Perspective on PDA," *Against the Grain* 23, no. 3 (June 1, 2011): 32–4, https://doi.org/10.7771/2380-176X.5889.

52. Greta Wood, "EBooks on EBSCOhost," *The Serials Librarian* 63, no. 2 (August 2012): 190.

53. Edward A. Goedeken and Karen Lawson, "The Past, Present, and Future of Demand-Driven Acquisitions in Academic Libraries," *College & Research Libraries* 76, no. 2 (March 1, 2015): 209.

54. Tina Herman Buck and Sara K. Hills, "Diminishing Short-Term Loan Returns: A Four-Year View of the Impact of Demand-Driven Acquisitions on Collection Development at a Small Academic Library," *Library Resources & Technical Services* 61, no. 1 (January 23, 2017): 52.

55. Andi Back and Sara E. Morris, "Patrons, Vendors, and Delivery: Print Demand Driven Acquisitions at the University of Kansas," *Technical Services Quarterly* 38, no. 2 (April 3, 2021): 109–22.

56. Goedeken and Lawson, "The Past, Present, and Future," 208.

57. William H. Walters, "Patron-Driven Acquisition and the Educational Mission of the Academic Library," *Library Resources & Technical Services* 56, no. 3 (July 1, 2012): 199.

58. Joseph Deitch, "A Conversation with Marvin H. Scilken," in *Getting Libraries the Credit They Deserve: A Festschrift in Honor of Marvin H. Scilken*, ed. Loriene Roy and Antony Cherian (Lanham: Scarecrow Press, 2002), 54.

59. Xan Arch, Rick Anderson, and Sanford G. Thatcher, "A Dialogue on PDA," *Against the Grain* 23, no. 3 (June 1, 2011): 28, https://doi.org/10.7771/2380-176X.5888.

60. Martin Eberhard, "E-Book Economics," *Publishers Weekly* 246, no. 10 (March 8, 1999): 22.

61. "Admiral Fiske's New Invention," *New York Times*, March 5, 1922.

62. Bob Brown, *The Readies*, edited by Craig J. Saper, Literature by Design: British and American Books 1880–1930 (Houston: Rice University Press, 2009), 28.

63. Vannevar Bush, "As We May Think," *Atlantic Monthly*, July 1945, 101–8, https://www.theatlantic.com/magazine/archive/1945/07/as-we-may-think/303881/.

64. Simon Peter Rowberry, "The Ebook Imagination," *DHQ: Digital Humanities Quarterly* 16, no. 1 (2022), http://www.digitalhumanities.org/dhq/vol/16/1/000601/000601.html.

65. Roberto Busa, "Index Thomisticus," 2005, https://www.corpusthomisticum.org/it/index.age.

66. Robert U. Ayres, "The Internet and the World Wide Web," in *The History and Future of Technology: Can Technology Save Humanity from Extinction?* (Cham, Switzerland: Springer, 2021), 519–57.

67. Susan B. Barnes, "Alan Kay: Transforming the Computer into a Communication Medium," *IEEE Annals of the History of Computing* 29, no. 2 (April 2007): 18–30, https://doi.org/10.1109/MAHC.2007.17.

68. Marie Lebert, "Project Gutenberg (1971-2008)," Project Gutenberg, 2008, https://www.gutenberg.org/ebooks/27045.

69. Andreas Kitzmann, *Hypertext Handbook: The Straight Story* (New York: Peter Lang, 2006), 21.

70. Bill Kasdorf, "The Past 25 Years of E-Books," *PublishersWeekly.com*, April 19, 2022, https://www.publishersweekly.com/pw/by-topic/digital/content-and-e-books/article/89005-the-past-25-years-of-e-books.html.

71. Lenares, "EBook Aggregators: A Primer," 28–9.

72. Laura Manley and Robert P. Holley, "History of the Ebook: The Changing Face of Books," *Technical Services Quarterly* 29, no. 4 (October 2012): 301.

73. "Penn, Oxford Make Digital History," *American Libraries* 31, no. 5 (May 2000): 30.

74. Calvin Reid, "Princeton University Press Offers 'E-Books Plus,'" *Publishers Weekly* 248, no. 19 (May 7, 2001): 22.

75. Calvin Reid, "UPs Team Up to Offer E-Books," *Publishers Weekly* 248, no. 2 (January 8, 2001): 34.

76. Gail Golderman and Bruce Connolly, "Bundles of Books," *Library Journal* 128, no. 17 (October 16, 2003): 28–35.

77. Steven M. Zeitchik, "Houston Startup Targets Undergrads," *Publishers Weekly*, April 17, 2000, 33.

78. Dracine Hodges, Cyndi Preston, and Marsha Hamilton, "Resolving the Challenge of E-Books," *Collection Management* 35, no. 3 (July 2010): 197.

79. Karen Kohn, "Worth the Wait? Using Past Patterns to Determine Wait Periods for E-Books Released After Print," *College & Research Libraries* 79, no. 1 (January 2018): 49.

80. "Consortium Forms OCA to Bring Additional Content Online," *Advanced Technology Libraries* 34, no. 11 (November 2005): 1, 9–10.

81. "Text Archive," Internet Archive, https://archive.org/details/texts?tab=collection (accessed July 27, 2023).

82. "Million Book Project Gives Access to 1.5 Million Books," *Advanced Technology Libraries* 37, no. 1 (January 2008): 7.

83. "CLIR, DLF Publish Report on Acquiring Copyright Permission," *Advanced Technology Libraries* 35, no. 1 (January 2006): 8.

84. Melody Herr, "Abusive Copyright Litigation, Proposed Solutions, and the Implications for Creative Commons Licenses," *The Journal of Academic Librarianship* 48, no. 1 (January 2022): 102475.

85. "Google Books History," Google Books, February 6, 2016, https://web.archive.org/web/20160206043510/http://books.google.com/googlebooks/about/history.html.

86. "How the Google Books Team Moved 90,000 Books across a Continent," *Google* (blog), January 27, 2023, https://blog.google/products/search/google-books-library-project/.

87. Mick O'Leary, "HathiTrust Shapes Libraries' Digital Future," *Information Today* 28, no. 10 (November 2011): 20–1.

88. Deanna Marcum and Roger C. Schonfeld, *Along Came Google: A History of Library Digitization*, 1st ed. (Princeton: Princeton University Press, 2021), 185.

89. Jonathan Band, "What Does the HathiTrust Decision Mean for Libraries?," *Research Library Issues*, no. 285 (January 2015): 7–13.

90. Kristina Hall, "HathiTrust Copyright Review of State Government Documents," *DttP: Documents to the People* 48, no. 1 (April 16, 2020): 21–3, https://doi.org/10.5860/dttp.v48i1.7337.

91. Damon Beres, "Blind People Won the Right to Break Ebook DRM. In 3 Years, They'll Have to Do It Again," *Wired*, October 27, 2021, https://www.wired.com/story/ebooks-drm-blind-accessibility-dmca/.

92. "HathiTrust Research Center Awards Five Projects," University of Indiana IT News and Events, June 17, 2019, https://news.iu.edu/live/news/29478-hathitrust-research-center-awards-five-projects.

93. Natalie Fulkerson, Sandra McIntyre, and Melissa Stewart, "HathiTrust Emergency Temporary Access Service: Reaping the Rewards of Long-Term Collaboration," *Collaborative Librarianship* 12, no. 2 (April 2020): 188.

94. Scott Turow, *One L: The Turbulent True Story of a First Year at Harvard Law School* (New York: Farrar, Straus and Giroux, 2010).

95. Michelle M. Wu, "Building a Collaborative Digital Collection: A Necessary Evolution in Libraries," *Law Library Journal* 103, no. 4 (2011): 529.

96 Lisa Bailey et al., "Position Statement," Controlled Digital Lending, March 15, 2023, https://controlleddigitallending.org/statement/.

97 David R. Hansen and Kyle K. Courtney, "A White Paper on Controlled Digital Lending of Library Books," preprint (LawArXiv, September 24, 2018): 2, https://doi.org/10.31228/osf.io/7fdyr.

98 "Internet Archive E-Lending: In-Library, License-Free," *Library Journal* 136, no. 6 (April 1, 2011): 18.

99 David Streitfeld, "In a Flood Tide of Digital Data, an Ark Full of Books," *New York Times*, March 3, 2012, sec. Technology.

100 Constance Grady, "Why Authors Are so Angry about the Internet Archive's Emergency Library," *Vox*, April 2, 2020, https://www.vox.com/culture/2020/4/2/21201193/emergency-library-internet-archive-controversy-coronavirus-pandemic.

101 Marshall Breeding, "2023 Library Systems Report: The Advance of Open Systems," *American Libraries* 54, no. 5 (May 2023): 25.

102 Matt Enis, "Judge Rules Against IA Open Library," *Library Journal* 148, no. 5 (May 2023): 12.

103 David L. Wilson, "New California State Campus Has Ambitious Plans for Technology," *Chronicle of Higher Education*, October 18, 1996.

104 Sue Woodson and Blair Anton, "Update on the Welch Medical Library," *Against the Grain* 27, no. 2 (April 1, 2015), https://doi.org/10.7771/2380-176X.7035.

105 Sharon Riley, "Academic: New Florida University Unveils Bookless Library," *Library Journal* 139, no. 15 (September 15, 2014): 13.

106 Pamela Carson and Krista Louise Alexander, "Walk-In Users and Their Access to Online Resources in Canadian Academic Libraries," *Partnership: The Canadian Journal of Library & Information Practice & Research* 15, no. 2 (July 2020): 1–25.

107 Manley and Holley, "History of the Ebook," 300.

108 "Digital Millennium Copyright Act," Public Law 105–304 (1998), https://www.govinfo.gov/content/pkg/PLAW-105publ304/pdf/PLAW-105publ304.pdf.

109 "E-Books: The Horror, the Horror," *IMI: Interactive Media International* 14, no. 4 (April 2000): 1–3.

110 Gayle Baker and Carol Tenopir, "Managing the Unmanageable: Systematic Downloading of Electronic Resources by Library Users," *Journal of Library Administration* 44, no. 3–4 (August 31, 2006): 11–24.

111 Free Software Foundation, "What Is DRM?," Defective by Design, https://www.defectivebydesign.org/what_is_drm (accessed August 4, 2023).

112 William H. Walters, "E-Books in Academic Libraries: Challenges for Sharing and Use," *Journal of Librarianship and Information Science* 46, no. 2 (June 2014): 89–895.

113 John B. Thompson, *Books in the Digital Age: The Transformation of Academic and Higher Education Publishing in Britain and The United States* (Cambridge: Polity, 2005), 338.

114 Josh Hadro, "Ebooks and .Epub at IDPF," *Library Journal* 133, no. 11 (June 15, 2008): 25–6.

115 Congress House of Representatives, "17 U.S.C. 109–Limitations on Exclusive Rights: Effect of Transfer of Particular Copy or Phonorecord," Government, govinfo.gov (U.S. Government Publishing Office, December 31, 2010), https://www.govinfo.gov/app/details/USCODE-2010-title17/USCODE-2010-title17-chap1-sec109/https%3A%2F%2Fwww.govinfo.gov%2Fapp%2Fdetails%2FUSCODE-2010-title17%2FUSCODE-2010-title17-chap1-sec109%2Fcontext.

116 Stanford University Libraries, "Copyright and Fair Use," Stanford Copyright and Fair Use Center, April 2, 2013, https://fairuse.stanford.edu/.

117 Julie A. Murphy, "Ebook Sharing Models in Academic Libraries," *Serials Review* 45, no. 3 (July 3, 2019): 176.

118 Hodges, Preston, and Hamilton, "Resolving the Challenge of E-Books," 199.

119 Xiaohua Zhu, "E-Book ILL in Academic Libraries: A Three-Year Trend Report," *The Journal of Academic Librarianship* 44, no. 3 (May 2018): 344.

120 Jolanda-Pieta (Joey) Van Arnhem and Lindsay Barnett, "Is Digital Rights Management (DRM) Impacting E-Book Adoption in Academic Libraries?," *The Charleston Advisor* 15, no. 3 (January 1, 2014): 63–5.

121 William Douglas Woody, David B. Daniel, and Crystal A. Baker, "E-Books or Textbooks: Students Prefer Textbooks," *Computers & Education* 55, no. 3 (November 2010): 945–8.

122 Leila June Rod-Welch et al., "Relative Preferences for Paper and for Electronic Books: Implications for Reference Services, Library Instruction, and Collection Management," *Internet Reference Services Quarterly* 18, no. 3–4 (July 2013): 294.

123 Josef Rill, "The Textbook Decision: Purchasing Options Affecting Students in the Classroom" (Tampa, Florida, University of South Florida, 2010), https://digitalcommons.usf.edu/etd/7910.

124 Thompson, *Books in the Digital Age,* 378.

125 Follett Higher Education, "Outcomes Made Accessible: Improving Outcomes and Retention While Lowering the Cost of College Learning Materials," Whitepaper (Follett Higher Education, 2022), https://follettaccess.follett.com/follettaccess/assets/File/Follett_ACCESS_Student_Outcomes.pdf.

126 Barbara Blummer and Jeffrey M. Kenton, "A Systematic Review of E-Books in Academic Libraries: Access, Advantages, and Usage," *New Review of Academic Librarianship* 26, no. 1 (January 2, 2020): 100.

127 Peter Brantley, "A Paperback in Four Minutes," *Library Journal*, April 16, 2007, 10–14.

128 Judith Rosen, "Is the Time Right for Espresso?," *Publishers Weekly*, March 7, 2022, 10.

129 Lori Widzinski, "'Step Away from the Machine': A Look at Our Collective Past," *Library Trends* 58, no. 3 (2010): 358–77.

130 Rachel King, "House of Cards: The Academic Library Media Center in the Era of Streaming Video," *The Serials Librarian* 67, no. 3 (October 3, 2014): 294.

131 Mary Lynette Larsgaard, "'Paper Geoscapes, or Return of the Luddites—Not!,'" *Journal of Map & Geography Libraries* 2, no. 2 (July 13, 2006): 3.

2 Electronic Journals Take the Field

Well before any book or journal first appeared in electronic form, the print-format scholarly journal had, in the estimation of most academic librarians, surpassed the print-format book as the most important component of the academic library collection. One reason for this was economic. Human beings tend to place more importance on things that cost more, and by the 1960s scholarly journals began consuming larger and larger shares of collections budget than did books. A non-budgetary reason for academic librarians ranking the importance of scholarly journals above that of books is that journals are valued above books within the STEM (Science, Technology, Engineering, Mathematics) fields that, following the end of the Second World War, rose above non-STEM fields in the academic pecking order.

Aside from a few experimental scholarly electronic journals published in the early 1980s, the first successful scholarly electronic journals surfaced in the late 1980s and early 1990s.[1] Ann Okerson identifies *New Horizons in Adult Education* (*NHAE*), which began publication in 1987, as "the oldest networked electronic journal recorded."[2] (Notably, *NHAE* was still publishing into the third decade of the twenty-first century.) Because some of the early candidates for electronic journal status started out as online academic discussion groups or newsletters, deciding if or when any such informal collaboration made the leap to a full-fledged scholarly journal is always a judgment call. The unpolished state of electronic journal publishing circa 1990 is made clear by the following facts about the pioneer electronic journals, all of which were:

- Edited and published by volunteers.
- Based at a university but not financially supported by their home institution.
- Focused on the humanities or social sciences.
  - The text-only formats of early electronic publications did not meet the needs of scholars in the STEM fields.
- Available either via FTP or email listservs.
  - The Web would not become a factor in journal distribution until after the release of the Mosaic and Netscape browsers circa 1994.[3]

For anyone studying the early history of electronic journals, a key source of information is the *Directory of Electronic Journals, Newsletters, and Academic Discussion Lists*, a seven-volume series published by the Association of Research Libraries (ARL) from 1991 to 1997. Starting in 2000, the original series was superseded by a new ARL series, the *Directory of Scholarly Electronic Journals and Academic Discussion Lists*, an annual publication that limits its coverage exclusively to peer-reviewed journals and lists. The new series was no longer updated after 2002, by which time the job of counting and listing electronic journals had become too big to manage. The inaugural 1991 edition of the *Directory of Electronic Journals, Newsletters, and Academic Discussion Lists* enumerates 110 electronic scholarly journals and newsletters plus 517 academic discussion lists. Published in 1996, the sixth edition of *Directory of Scholarly Electronic Journals and Academic Discussion Lists* enumerates 1,689 electronic journals and newsletters, of which over 90 percent indicate a web address. Only 14 percent of these publications provided distribution via email listservs, while 19 percent were available via FTP. The final seventh (1997) edition of the initial series of the *Directory of Electronic Journals, Newsletters, and Academic Discussion Lists*, which was published both in print and on the Web, lists over 3,400 scholarly electronic journals and newsletters plus over 3,800 electronic scholarly conferences.[4]

A similar compilation of statistics shows the number of electronic journals growing from a mere 27 in 1991 to 8,000 in 1999. Of the 8,000 electronic scholarly journals this compilation shows as being active in 1999, only a few were experimental niche publications. Most were electronic versions of well-established, print-format scholarly journals (Figure 2.1).[5]

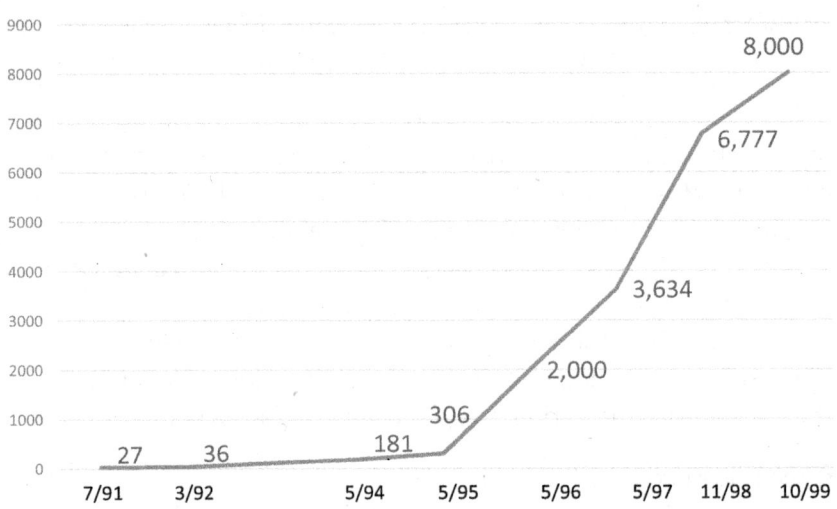

Date	E-Journals
July 1991	27
March 1992	36
May 1994	181
May 1995	306
May 1996	2,000
May 1997	3,634
November 1998	6,777
September 1999	8,000

1991-1995 Numbers: *ARL Directory*
1996-1999 Numbers: *NewJour Online Archive and List*

Figure 2.1 Number of electronic journals from 1991 to 1999.
Source: Ann Okerson, "Are We There Yet? Online E-Resources Ten Years After," *Library Trends* 48, no. 4 (Spring 2000): 676

Based on data obtained from Ulrichsweb.com, Carol Tenopir concludes, "I can say with confidence that as of the end of 2003, there are just under 50,000 scholarly journals and somewhere between one-third and just over one-half of them are in digital form."[6] Doing the quick math, that adds up to about 16,667 to 25,000 journals in digital form, though it must be noted that even as late as 2003 those numbers included a few thousand digital journals that were being distributed in CD-ROM format rather than being served online. Jumping ahead twenty years, data obtained from a 2023 search of Ulrichsweb.com show a total of 75,177 active "academic/scholarly journals" as being available online, of which 47,532 (63.23 percent) are "refereed/peer-reviewed" and 22,527 (29.97 percent) are "Electronic-only."[7]

At the dawn of the electronic journal, many believed, or at least hoped, that a transition from print to electronic would result in lower-priced, if not free, electronic journals. Such hopes were based on the reasoning that because electronic journals do not incur the costs of paper, handling, and shipping, publishers can supply them to multiple subscribers at near-zero marginal costs and therefore should, under the logic of the free market, offer their products at lower prices. Looking back from the year 2000 at these already dashed hopes, Ann Okerson writes:

> *Many believed that e-texts could be produced far more cheaply than paper ones and that numerous middlemen might be eliminated. Electronic journals would thus become very inexpensive and effective ways of competing with the behemoth print journals that were sapping universities' economic resources.*[8]

Even though journal prices did the opposite of dropping, the electronic journal caught on with users to such an extent that studies conducted at multiple institutions found that, by the early 2000s, print periodicals were sitting untouched.[9]

Academic library users readily abandoned print journals and came to rely on electronic-format journals for entirely practical reasons:

- Journal articles in electronic format can be accessed from almost anywhere at any time of the day or night.
- Electronic journals allow users to avoid the frustration of stolen or defaced articles or of discovering that an entire year's worth of print journals has been sent off to the bindery where the issues may remain inaccessible for weeks to come.
- In economic terms, a copy of a print journal is a "rivalrous good" that can be used by only one reader at a time; an electronic journal is a "non-rivalrous good" that can be used by multiple readers at the same time. Because most electronic journal subscriptions permit multiple simultaneous users, this eliminates the need for users to compete for access to an in-demand article or to report to a library reserve desk to access an article assigned to an entire class as required reading.

- Online link resolvers, which emerged in the early 2000s, reduce to a mouse click or two the transition from a citation in a bibliographic database or an online public access catalog (OPAC) to a full-text article.
- Especially as the .pdf format became standard, storing or sharing (possibly in violation of copyright) electronic articles proved easier than storing or sharing print-format articles. Even a modestly sized hard drive can store more articles than dozens of file cabinets, while a file containing a journal article can be sent by email nearly anywhere in the world without envelope, postage, or delay.
- Bibliographic software packages such as EndNote, RefWorks, Mendeley, and Zotero make it easy to organize digital articles and cite them in correct formats.
- The ability to cut and paste from electronic articles simplifies accurate quoting.
- Reading journal articles (which typically range from 3,000 to 10,000 words) in electronic format does not present an insurmountable obstacle to most readers. If for any reason a reader wants a hard copy of a journal article, printing one off is reasonably fast, cheap, and good enough for most purposes.

Despite the popularity of electronic journals and the almost complete lack of user nostalgia for print-format journals, the process of getting out from under the burden of largely unused print journals proved a slow process for many academic libraries. For example, it was not until 2020 that the University of Connecticut Library, having by that date managed to pare its once extensive collection of print-format journals to a mere 108 titles, was able to take the final step of cancelling subscriptions to all but eight of its legacy print-format journal publications.[10]

Periodical Prices and Electronic Journals

To understand how fast electronic journals sprang onto the academic library scene and how thoroughly they changed the economics and practices of academic library collections, there is no better as-it-happened primary source than the series of annual articles on periodical prices published in *Library Journal*. Before jumping into the content of the articles themselves, the story of their development and publication merits a few paragraphs.

As academic publishing flourished in the 1950s, librarians became aware of the need for reliable data as a tool for understanding the type and amount of information they were purchasing and exactly how much they were paying for it. The first effort to systematically track the overall costs of books and journals took hold in the late 1950s when the American Library Association formed national committees to investigate how to go about creating a meaningful price index.[11] An article by Helen M. Welch, "Proposed Procedure for Establishing a Cost of Periodicals Index," published in the Summer 1959 issue of *Library Resources and Technical Services*, lays out the particulars of the first protocol.[12] Under the auspices of the Library Materials Price Index Committee (LMPIC) of the American Library Association's Association of Library Collections and Technical Services (ALCTS), William H. Kurth published "U.S. Book and Periodical Prices—a Preliminary Report" in the January 1960 issue of *Library Journal*, launching what would become an annual article on the topic of periodical prices.[13] Developing a price index for periodicals and keeping it current requires a great deal of work, most of it supplied by volunteers. One challenge of creating a price index for periodicals is choosing a truly representative quantity and range of titles so that the index accurately represents the marketplace. Another challenge is the need to frequently revise the index as new periodicals are launched and existing titles fold, merge, split into multiple titles, or otherwise mutate over time. In 1983, the American National Standards Committee on Library and Information Sciences and Related Publishing Practices issued ANSI Z39.20-1983, "Criteria for Price Indexes," a formal standard for developing price indexes for library materials.[14] Among other things, ANSI Z39.20-1983 officially defines a periodical as "a publication that constitutes one issue in a continuous series under the same title, published more than once a year over an indefinite period, with individual issues in the series numbered consecutively or with each issue date. Newspapers are excluded."[15]

From 1960 through 1992, the annual periodicals price index was published in *Library Journal*. In 1993, by which time the periodicals price index had become a must-read article for many librarians, the American Library Association chose to move publication from *Library Journal* to the ALA's own publication, *American Libraries*. The periodicals price index would continue to be published in the print version of *American Libraries* through 2002. Following a two-year hiatus, *Library Journal* partnered with EBSCO Information Services to begin publishing a separate annual periodicals price survey that is still being published and remains a must-read article for librarians. The original periodicals price index employed "a hypothetical list of titles selected to represent a typical academic library collection," while the successor periodicals price survey employs a "pricing study based upon surveys of the lists of titles indexed by the Institute for Scientific Information (ISI) Arts and Humanities, Science Citation, and Social Science Citation indexes."[16] Valuable information can be found in both the *American Libraries* and *Library Journal* articles on periodical prices; however, the latter's periodicals price survey is of greater historical interest because it not only provides information on periodical prices but also conveys a narrative history of the tense intersection of scholarly publishing, academic libraries, and technology as the scholarly journal rapidly transitioned from several hundred years of print to the new world of electronic publication. Through the lens of the periodicals price surveys published in *Library Journal*, the story of the electronic journal can be seen to begin in earnest in 1995.

1995

Subtitled, "Currency Swings and Rising Costs Play Havoc with Prices," the bulk of *Library Journal's* 1995 periodicals price survey follows tradition by focusing on the cost of print subscriptions and the struggle of libraries to manage rising costs.

However, the 1995 article is notable as the first in the series to mention electronic journals, devoting a total of one paragraph to the topic. In this lone paragraph, the authors reported that there were seventy-three peer-reviewed electronic journals among the total number of publications listed in the ARL's 1994 *Directory of Electronic Journals, Newsletters and Academic Discussion Lists*. Most of these electronic journals were available for free, though for those that did require a subscription, the annual fees ranged from a high of $800 ($1,679 in 2024 dollars) for a British engineering journal to a low of $125 ($262 in 2024 dollars) for a U.S. computer-theory journal. The authors end the article with an admission and a promise: "While we have not been able to track electronic journals this year, we plan to do so in succeeding years."[17]

1996

The 1996 periodicals price survey reports that only thirteen of the journals listed in the ARL's 1995 *Directory of Electronic Journals, Newsletters and Academic Discussion Lists* charge a subscription fee. The highest of these fees—for the British journal *Current Opinions in Medicine*—came in at $4,500 a year ($9,195 in 2024 dollars). The other electronic journals that charged subscription fees were in the medical or scientific fields, with the annual average subscription coming in at $754 per year ($1,522 in 2024 dollars). The authors of the 1996 periodicals price survey reference the hope that electronic journals will prove to be much cheaper than print journals, but, in what turns out to be both an understatement and a prophetic warning, write, "It may be unrealistic to assume that the change to electronic journal formats will save libraries money in the long run."[18]

1997

The 1997 periodicals price survey article begins with a rundown of the various "powerful hopes" held by scholars, librarians, publishers, and vendors as the electronic journal "revolution" gained strength. With characteristic caution, the authors write, "It is too soon to tell whose hopes will be realized and whose dashed. But early indicators give little hope of lower prices and cheaper access." The overall library budget situation was so dire that "librarians report they are continuing to cancel print subscriptions in record numbers." In hopes of making up for revenues lost to cancellations, publishers are reported to be raising the cost of journal subscriptions, further fueling the collections death spiral of cancellations and price increases.

For the year, the EBSCO database of journals shows 850 electronic journals with active subscriptions, about half of which can be subscribed to separately from the print for prices ranging from $40 to $15,000 ($79 to $29,745 in 2024 dollars) per year. However, most libraries were still combining print and electronic subscriptions. For fields outside of STEM, most electronic journals remained available for free. The authors' scan of the three ISI citation indexes finds that access via electronic format was available for 24 percent (665/2729) of the journals indexed in *Science Citation Index*, 19 percent (546/2,866) of the journals indexed in *Social Sciences Citation Index*, and 10 percent (118/1,135) of the journals indexed in *Arts and Humanities Citation Index*.[19]

1998

The subtitle of the 1998 periodicals price survey is revealing: "E-Journals Come of Age." Though still vastly outnumbered by journals available exclusively in print format, the tide was obviously turning from print to electronic. Even so, the electronic journal remained so closely tied to print that of "the 2200 e-journal titles with active orders in EBSCO's [database of journals], more than half come free with a print subscription." The article reports that librarians were leveraging their bargaining power by joining consortia in "record numbers," while publishers were simultaneously employing a new business strategy which involved "packaging groups of e-journals into large bundles, priced like print plus a percentage above." Though the authors do not use the exact phrase to describe this new strategy, this was, in fact, the business model that would be labeled in 2001 as the *Big Deal*. (See below for more on the history of the Big Deal.)

The 1998 article also mentions electronic journal aggregators such as Blackwell's, EBSCO, Faxon, and Swets getting into the game of not only vending bundles of journals but also providing proprietary search engines to help users seamlessly access all those widely scattered electronic journals.

As if to finish off the rapidly fading hope that subscribing to electronic journals in bulk will drive down prices, the authors of "E-Journals Come of Age" report that the big takeaway from the chaotic marketplace for periodicals is that "costs to libraries are going up, not down."[20]

1999

The authors of the 1999 *Library Journal* periodicals price survey continue the previous year's theme of a chaotic marketplace for periodicals, subtitling their article "Serials Publishing in Flux" and declaring, "The web and the electronic journal are deconstructing the serials landscape." It had become clear by 1999 that digital technology was creating intriguing new opportunities for scholarly communication, including opportunities for authors to publish (in the broadest sense of the word) without the benefit of the traditional publishing infrastructure as well as opportunities for individuals to access scholarly information without the benefit of the traditional academic library infrastructure. The question in the minds of many librarians and scholars, though, was whether these opportunities would prove to be "profitable or affordable" given the risks involved when so much change was taking place so quickly. With all the change came uncertainty as publishers looked to gain marketplace advantages through mergers into ever-larger entities while libraries countered by forming coalitions big enough to leverage price concessions from publishers.

The authors of "Serials Publishing in Flux" formally announce the death of the "cyber myth" which held that subscription costs would shrink as journals went online. Subscription costs continued to rise even as the number of electronic scholarly journals grew. Though most of the "about 5000 web-based electronic journals on the market" at the time were still being offered for free with a print subscription, the truth was that print subscriptions were underwriting the real costs of nominally free electronic journals thanks to sharp increases in the costs of print subscriptions. The authors cite the example of how one of the largest U.S. journal publishers had increased the cost of print subscriptions by 19 percent in order to continue offering its electronic journals as a "free" bonus for subscribing to the print.[21]

2000

Subtitled "Pushing towards More Affordable Access," the 2000 periodicals price survey opens by discussing the difficulty library users face in trying to navigate an expanding universe of electronic scholarly journals in which the list of titles comprising that universe could no longer be squeezed onto a document of a few dozen pages. The fact that electronic journals occupied disconnected proprietary silos presented users with a discovery challenge that is difficult to understand from the perspective of a latter-day online world accustomed to sophisticated search engines and pervasive links between books, articles, data, and just about any other form of information with a digital footprint. Prior to 2000, some publishers and aggregators had offered tools for navigating electronic journals, though the proprietary-driven ineffectiveness of, and in some cases, prices charged for these aids to online navigation inspired librarians and academics to develop their own tools for linking together online scholarly content regardless of publisher. Seeing the writing on the wall, publishers took it upon themselves to knock down the silo walls, announcing in fall 1999 that twelve of the largest STEM publishers were "planning to link citations to article text across their collective boundaries."

Library consortia continued to grow in size and influence, while the number of major academic serials subscription agents had dwindled down to three, in part the result of all those library consortia cutting out subscription-service intermediaries by negotiating directly with publishers to acquire large bundles of electronic scholarly journals. While academic publishers of the year 2000 still relied on subscriptions to print journals as their principal revenue stream, a small-but-influential subset of academic publishers—Academic Press, Elsevier, Kluwer, Springer, and Wiley—offered electronic versions of every journal title they published. Medium-sized academic publishers were not far behind in getting most, if not all, of their journals online. Larger publishers had an advantage in that they were better positioned to absorb the considerable costs of taking journals online. Nonprofit journal aggregator services such as JSTOR, Highwire Press, SPARC, Project Muse, and BioOne provided appealing pathways for many smaller, nonprofit journal publishers to transition from print to electronic format. Project Muse stood out from the field due to its focus on the humanities and social sciences rather than the STEM fields. Yet another path some smaller publishers opted to follow was entering into agreements with for-profit electronic journal aggregators such as CatchWord, Ovid, Ingenta, and Bell & Howell Information and Learning (which would be renamed ProQuest Information and Learning in 2001).[22] For articles in the public domain, electronic access was being made possible by nonprofit projects like the Making of America, a joint Cornell/University of Michigan initiative to digitize older periodical articles as well as some books.[23]

2001

The 2001 periodicals price survey reports that a few leading academic libraries were already drafting plans to abandon print journals for which electronic surrogates are available; at the same time, academic journal publishers, led by the biggest academic publishers, were investing in new technologies, entering into mergers, and trying out convoluted new pricing schemes in a race to get their journals not just online, but on the Web. These moves by libraries and publishers led to a surreal situation in which libraries that asked to stop receiving print copies of journals that were available online found publishers nonetheless requiring them to continue receiving print copies. The reasons behind this insistence on the part of publishers ranged from inflexible publisher workflows to schemes for avoiding various European taxes on electronic-only publications. In scenes that would be repeated for years to come, staff at some academic libraries found themselves transporting new, unread, and unwanted print-format copies of journals straight from the mailroom to the recycling bin.

The emergence of Crossref, a nonprofit founded in 1999 to facilitate linking among content hosted at sites distributed across the internet, along with the Beta testing of SFX, the first OpenURL link resolver, are noted as important steps forward in resolving the challenges of navigating among growing numbers of siloed electronic journals and other digital objects. Another emerging concern spurred by the growth of electronic journals was the troubling question of how all those articles could be archived so that, for example, the bankruptcy of a publisher or aggregator would not cut off access to information that was not only vital to research and learning but for which libraries had already paid.

Finally, journal publishers were beginning to experiment with pay-per-view, a new way of earning income from online journals in which end users who do not otherwise have access to journal content could purchase articles on an a la carte basis.[24] This trend would continue so that by 2014 both individual users and libraries could purchase single articles through such services as Deep Dyve, ReadCube, and Get It Now.[25]

2002

Subtitling the 2002 periodicals price survey as "Doing the Digital Flip," it is with a strong sense of amazement that the authors write, "It is hard to believe the speed with which e-journals have become the standard in scholarly publishing." So thoroughly had electronic journals wrestled the crown from print that, as the authors observe, "there is evidence that many librarians are ready to give up paper for good." This evidence takes the form of library users demonstrating strong preferences for electronic journals and library consortia (including OhioLink as well as large consortia in California and Canada) insisting that pricing for electronic journals be entirely separated from pricing for print journals, demanding, in effect, that libraries be free to purchase electronic journals without also taking on the material and historical baggage of print-format subscriptions. Especially for the STEM fields, where the large publishers had, by 2002, moved all their principal journals online and readers lacked the strong attachment to print that was more common among humanists, print-format journals had become more of a burden than a benefit.

The authors of the 2002 survey paint a picture of a journal marketplace that was still somewhat chaotic as journal publishers continued experimenting with the best ways to maintain, if not increase, their revenue streams while libraries angled for better deals than they were able to negotiate when print was king. In 2000, 75 percent of journal publishers offered free (or, at least, nominally free) access to electronic journals as a bonus for having a print subscription; two years later, that figure had dropped to 61 percent, with a number of large publishers—including

Academic, Wiley, Kluwer, Dekker, Nature, Plenum, and Karger—among those charging extra for electronic access.[26]

2003

Subtitled "Big Chill on the Big Deal," the 2003 periodicals price survey focused on both the economics of scholarly publishing and the resultant librarian frustration with the whole scholarly publishing enterprise. The authors start out by bemoaning the estimated $73 million in payments gone missing with the bankruptcy of subscription agent RoweCom/Faxon. They then reference the anger of librarians working to uncouple themselves from Big Deals. Under the subheading "Serials Market Declared Dysfunctional," the authors quantify the inelastic nature of the journals market, pointing out that as STEM journal prices rose 215 percent from 1986 to 2001, the purchasing of STEM journal titles dropped by only 5.1 percent. Showing more restraint than many librarians were feeling at the time, the authors write, "Large commercial publishers profited immensely in such a favorable market."

What is most significant about the 2003 periodicals price survey is, however, not so much its expected focus on the economics of the journal marketplace as it is the first article in the series to mention open access as an alternative to traditional forms of publication. The article mentions several emerging, non-commercial alternatives to existing journals, including *Organic Letters* (an open access alternative to *Tetrahedron Letters*), BioMed Central, BioOne, and DSpace. While 2003 is hardly the end of the story for the electronic journal, the coming of open access marked the start of a new chapter in the greater story of scholarly communication.[27]

Newspapers and Magazines in the Digital Age

Scholarly journals are not, of course, the only type of serial publication to be transformed by digital technology. Physical newspapers were, at one time, an important part of academic library collections, valued as sources for both historical research as well as for keeping up on current events. As sources of historical information, physical newspapers were so challenging to store and preserve that libraries had switched to microfilm as the preferred storage medium for newspapers long before digital technology existed.[28] As sources of written information on current events, print-format newspapers were indispensable in the time before the Web and social media. Newspapers were also important sources for leisure reading. For the benefit of students and faculty studying or working far from home, U.S. academic libraries often stocked reading rooms with paper copies of newspapers from across the nation and around the world. Many former student library employees remember the ongoing chore of attaching newly arrived copies of print newspapers to wooden newspaper sticks for placement in library reading rooms.

By the 1970s, searchable newspaper citation indexes were available from such dial-up digital information services as DIALOG and BRS. In the early 1980s, the *Toronto Globe and Mail* became the first newspaper to offer full-text articles in digital format; by 1984, full-text access to a handful of major newspapers became available through such services as NEXIS,

Vu-TEXT, InfoGlobe, and Dow Jones News Retrieval.[29] In the early 1990s full-text newspapers became available on CD-ROM, with even the venerable *Times of London* being sold on disc.[30] In 1993, aggregator Newsbank was offering thirty-five U.S. newspapers on CD-ROM.[31] The drawback of CD-ROM newspapers was, of course, that the format was not much use for catching up on the very latest news. Better suited to current-events coverage were the newspaper websites launched in the mid-1990s, many of which offered at least some full-text content. The *Wall Street Journal* launched an interactive website in the summer of 1996,[32] while the *Washington Post* launched its website in February 1997.[33] The *New York Times* launched its first website on January 22, 1996.[34] It would be 2011, however, before the *New York Times* announced a digital subscription plan.[35]

For academic libraries, the most important development in digital newspapers was the ability to subscribe to online, full-text, current, and retrospective newspapers that could be made available to users via site licenses. One landmark event was the announcement in 1995 that UMI's ProQuest Direct would offer the full text of the most recent ninety days of the *New York Times* as an online product.[36] By the 2000s, libraries could subscribe to large numbers of full-text newspapers via aggregators such as Newsbank and ProQuest. By 2020, Newsbank alone offered access to 600 U.S. and 700 international newspapers. While the migration of newspapers from print to online did not eliminate newspapers from academic libraries, it marginalized the print-format newspaper's importance while simultaneously solving for academic libraries what had been a set of seemingly unsolvable newspaper access, storage, and preservation problems.

The story of the transition of magazines from print to digital is nearly identical to that of newspapers, with magazines generally following the pattern of first being indexed by online services, followed by being made available on CD-ROM, establishing websites, and ultimately being made available in full-text via packages vended by aggregators. Like the print-format newspaper, the print-format magazine moved to the margins of the academic library collection without entirely disappearing, with many academic libraries continuing to provide print-format newspapers and magazines for recreational reading.

Breaking Down, and Up, the Big Deal

In 1996, Academic Press introduced a new way of acquiring journals. Instead of subscribing to journal titles one by one, a library could instead subscribe to a large bundle of Academic Press electronic journals for a fixed term with the signing of a single contract.[37] The new business model caught on to such an extent that, not long after its introduction, most academic libraries were entering into similar contracts with multiple journal publishers.[38] However, it was not until 2001 that Kenneth Frazier, Director of Libraries at the University of Wisconsin, Madison, would coin the term *Big Deal* to describe this new business model, formally defining it as:

> *an online aggregation of journals that publishers offer as a one-price, one-size-fits-all package. In the Big Deal, libraries agree to buy electronic access to all of a commercial publisher's journals*

> *for a price based on current payments to that publisher, plus some increment. Under the terms of the contract, annual price increases are capped for a number of years.*[39]

At least in the early years, publishers based the pricing of Big Deals on the amount a library or consortia had historically spent on the publisher's print journals plus an additional 5–15 percent added on top; most contracts called for automatic annual price increases of about 6 percent for the typical three- to five-year duration of a contract.[40] The early allure of the Big Deal was that it provided an academic library or academic library consortium with a large amount of varied content available via site license to every member of the academic community served by the library or libraries signing onto the deal. In the context of the late 1990s and early 2000s, the quantity of journals provided by the Big Deal was especially attractive to academic librarians who, over the previous decades of economic struggles, had come to accept the dreaded serials-cancellation exercise as an unavoidable part of managing an academic library collection. Upon signing a Big Deal, academic librarians could, for a welcome change, announce that they were finally *adding* journal titles to the collection instead of *cutting* titles. Big deals were warmly embraced by faculty who appreciated the convenience of instant access to nearly any journal toward which their research interests or intellectual curiosity might steer them.[41] In fact, there is evidence that the increased access to journals made possible by the Big Deal enhanced the overall quality of scholarly research by introducing an "increase in references per published work and the reduction in the rate of reuse of the same references by authors."[42]

But the response to the Big Deal was not entirely positive. At the same time that Frazier was naming and defining the Big Deal, he was also warning against it:

> *Academic library directors should not sign on to the Big Deal or any comprehensive licensing agreements with commercial publishers. . . . It bundles the strongest with the weakest publisher titles, the essential with the non-essential. Once you have tumbled for the Big Deal, the library cannot continue to receive the titles it most needs unless it continues to subscribe to the full package.*[43]

Frazier was not the only academic librarian who saw the Big Deal as more like the apocryphal first free nickel bag of heroin than as a sustainable business model for acquiring scholarly journals. Or who saw the librarians buying into the Big Deal as more like desperate addicts than good stewards of scholarly information. In 2000, in advance of Frazier's warning, Robert C. Michaelson of Northwestern University cautioned against acquiring journals in large, indiscriminate bundles, expressing the view that academic librarians should take a hands-on approach to managing library collections and calling on the profession to reject the "attempt by these for-profit organizations to abrogate our role as selectors."[44] In 2010, economist Theodore C. Bergstrom published "Librarians and the Terrible Fix: Economics of the Big Deal," in which he ominously compares publishers' "exploitive . . . inelastic journal demands" to the actions of the cabal of energy suppliers (a group which included the notorious Enron Corporation) that nearly bankrupted the State of California in 2000 and 2001 by taking unprincipled advantage of the state's inelastic energy demand.[45]

Over the years, the dubious economic value of the Big Deal would undergo ever-greater scrutiny, notably from a team of economists led by Bergstrom. In undertaking their study of the economics of the Big Deal, Bergstrom and his collaborators initially found their inquiry blocked by publisher-mandated non-disclosure clauses that prevented Library A from knowing if it paid less, more, or the same as Library B for an identical bundle of electronic journals. Bergstrom's team got around this roadblock by leveraging the Freedom of Information Act to obtain data on the amounts public institutions were being charged for Big Deals. The resultant article, published in 2014, reports that Big Deal agreements produced "striking differences" in pricing among similarly sized institutions, with institutions that drove harder bargains enjoying lower prices than those that did not. The article also reports that the price-per-citation major commercial publishers charged PhD-granting universities were much higher—in some cases ten times higher—than those charged by nonprofit publishers.[46] A similar analysis of the Big Deal undertaken on behalf of the Canadian Research Knowledge Network (CRKN) that was also published in 2014 reports that the CRKN and its seventy-five Canadian university member libraries "recognize that Big Deals that grow substantially and become more expensive year after year are not cost sustainable."[47] The Big Deal, it turns out, was not the solution to the long-standing problem of journal prices increasing at rates above the consumer-price index at the same time that library collection budgets were growing at rates below the consumer-price index. As economist Bo-Christer Björk observed in 2021, "Although publisher-wide electronic licenses such as ScienceDirect or Springer Link have largely replaced subscriptions to individual titles, the same price spiral seems to be continuing."[48] Despite the problems with the economics of the Big Deal, it was in good part due to the creation of the Big Deal that the increase in journal prices leveled off at 6 percent per year in 2012 and stayed around that level for at least a decade.[49] That rate of increase was no doubt greater than librarians would have liked, but many found it preferable to the unpredictable price spikes experienced from the 1970s through the 1990s.

The authors of the 2019 version of *Library Journal*'s annual periodical survey, subtitled "Deal or No Deal," write that, while "Big Deals remain the status quo for most academic libraries, despite years of declining budgets... retooling or outright cancellations of Big Deals is becoming more common." The U.S. libraries the authors list as having recently dropped out of Big Deals include Florida State, the University of Oklahoma, and the University of California System, the latter having cut off negotiations on renewing its Big Deal with Elsevier in February 2019. Foreign universities listed as having dropped Big Deals include consortia in Hungary and Finland as well as Germany's Max Planck institute.[50] A decade and half prior to the above events, the trend of cancelling Big Deals started with Harvard's cancellation of its agreement with Elsevier in 2004. Other notable earlier cancellations of Big Deals occurred at Lafayette College in 2008 as well as at the University of Alabama at Birmingham, the University of Oregon, and Southern Illinois University—the latter three cancellations all occurring in 2009. Six years before ending its Big Deal with Elsevier, the University of California System had walked away from its consortial Big Deal with Taylor & Francis. Those academic libraries cancelling Big Deals had come to learn that, in the colorful language of journalist Richard Poynder, "the Big Deal turned out to be a cuckoo: Once in the nest, it tends to consume everything, throwing out the other fledglings in the process."[51] (SPARC's "Big Deal Cancellation" provides an updated list of cancellations.)[52]

Despite many examples of resistance from librarians, a study conducted by the ARL found that uptake of Big Deals increased from 2002 to 2012, with more than 90 percent of the academic libraries included in the study reporting that they had licensed a Big Deal with at least one of the three biggest journal publishers (Elsevier, Springer, and Wiley); however, the same study also found that academic libraries were increasingly making Big Deals for only select parts of a given publisher's output rather than for a publisher's entire journal list.[53] Instead of signing up for everything and the kitchen sink, librarians were unbundling Big Deals through the application of Evidence Based Library and Information Practice which "prioritizes the use of quantitative data as evidence for decision-making towards improving library services."[54] For what might be called the Big Deal 2.0, academic librarians sharpened their pencils to precisely calculate the value of what they were getting for their money rather than signing contracts without conducting due diligence. The Big Deal enjoyed a long run, but by 2021 the authors of the annual *Library Journal* periodicals price index survey could state with confidence that open-access-based, read-and-publish agreements were "gradually supplanting traditional Big Deal and subscription agreements."[55]

As librarians looked to unbundle Big Deals, one data point they used to calculate the value of journals was the widely accepted, though highly imperfect, *impact factor*, a quantitative measure of how frequently the average article from a given scholarly journal is cited by other scholars over time. Though the impact factor, which dates back to 1975, originated in the print era, other data points librarians turned to as they analyzed Big Deals either could not have been calculated at all in the print era or, at the very least, were less accurate and/or far more difficult to calculate before the switch to electronic formats. To extract meaningful data about the use of online information resources, standards were required. In 1998, The International Coalition of Library Consortia (ICOLC) issued its, "Guidelines for Statistical Measures of Usage of Web-Based Indexed, Abstracted, and Full Text Resources,"[56] while in February 2000 a group of ARL librarians began work on the association's E-Metrics project.[57] Another important set of standards for the extraction of meaningful data from electronic sources was unveiled in the March 2002 launch of Counting Online Usage of Networked Electronic Resources (COUNTER). COUNTER established a "Code of Practice that enabled publishers and vendors to report usage of their electronic resources in a consistent way."[58] By negotiating COUNTER-compliance into licensing agreements, librarians were finally able to obtain accurate, oranges-to-oranges data on the extent to which their community of users was accessing any given journal and, with this data, calculate cost per use. Access to such accurate data was a major improvement over the crude and inaccurate methods available to librarians in the not-so-distant ink-and-paper past. In the print era, librarians hoping to rank the value of journals in the face of a looming serial cut would conduct surveys to learn what journals the faculty thought were most important. While useful to an extent, the shortcoming of such surveys is that faculty, whether deliberately or unconsciously, tend to exaggerate their use of those journals they wish to protect from cancellation. Undertaking periodic reshelving studies of print journals was another highly inexact data-gathering technique librarians employed to calculate the usage of print-format journals.[59] While even under the best circumstances reshelving counts never produced truly reliable data, the fact that they were sometimes intentionally skewed by library users hoping to protect their favorite journals from being cut could render them useless as indicators of actual use.

The authors of "The Evolution and Revision of Big Deals: A Review from the Perspective of Libraries," provide a list of additional types of quantitative data librarians routinely use to assess the value of electronic journals, including:

- Altmetrics
- Cost-per-citation
- Cost-per-use
- Eigenfactor
- h-Index
- Interlibrary Loan Transactions
- MESUR: Metrics from Scholarly Usage of Resources data
- OpenURL statistics
- SNIP (Source-Normalized Impact per Paper)[60]

In addition to quantitative data, academic librarians unbundling Big Deals also sought out qualitative data, including old-fashioned feedback from faculty, students, and liaison librarians. Because acting upon quantitative data without putting it in context can lead to poor outcomes, "the most advanced application of evaluation in unbundling projects is combining quantitative rankings, usage statistics, and qualitative judgments into decision-making models and algorithms."[61] For one example of many journal assessment tools developed in response to the Big Deal, there is the California Digital Library (CDL) Weighted Value Algorithm, which takes into account three vectors and six data points:

- Utility
  - Usage
  - Citations
- Quality
  - Impact factor
  - SNIP
- Cost Effectiveness
  - Cost-per-use
  - Cost-per-SNIP[62]

Especially for faculty, loss of access to a journal can feel like a personal attack, and no librarian wants to be the one to break the news about a journal cut. Libraries learned that walking away from Big Deals—whether permanently or just long enough to bring a publisher back to the negotiating table—could incur faculty displeasure even when economic necessity drove such decisions. Librarians looking to cancel or renegotiate a Big Deal worked to forestall faculty resistance though such tactics as communicating with faculty right from the start, sharing data with faculty, and inviting faculty representatives to the table for both negotiation and decision-making sessions.[63]

When compelled to walk away from Big Deals, librarians found they often could meet user needs and stave off faculty revolts by selectively subscribing to the most in-demand journal titles as well as by providing articles on-demand via either standard interlibrary loan or article pay-per-view services.[64] It also became obvious that when faculty, students, and even persons unaffiliated with higher education are, in the digital age, denied access to copyrighted articles, they resort to workarounds that do not involve libraries at all. These workarounds include obtaining journal articles by emailing authors directly, hitting up friends and colleagues who happen to have access to a wanted article, obtaining preprints from repositories, accessing content providers that operate on the gray margins of copyright law (e.g., ResearchGate and Academia.com), visiting pirate sites such as the notorious SCI-Hub, and, of course, taking advantage of the ever-increasing number of articles freely available via the various forms of open access publishing.

The Electronic Journal as Mixed Blessing

For scholars and students, electronic journals proved to be easier to access, use, archive, and share than print journals. Through such innovations as the Big Deal and the various extra-library ways of accessing articles, the average information seeker enjoyed access to more journal content than did the privileged affiliates of even the most elite academic libraries in the heyday of the print-format journal. For academic libraries, the failure of the electronic journal to lower the cost of journal subscriptions was, on the one hand, a source of frustration, while on the other had become a source of inspiration as librarians and academics began the as-yet unresolved struggle to regain control of scholarly communications through the mechanism of the open access movement.

Notes

1. F. W. Lancaster, "The Evolution of Electronic Publishing," *Library Trends* 43, no. 4 (Spring 1995): 518–27.
2. Ann Okerson, "Are We There Yet? Online E-Resources Ten Years After," *Library Trends* 48, no. 4 (Spring 2000): 673.
3. Dru W. Mogge, "Seven Years of Tracking Electronic Publishing: The ARL Directory of Scholarly Electronic Journals and Academic Discussion Lists," in *Directory of Scholarly Electronic Journals and Academic Discussion Lists*, ed. Dru W. Mogge and Peter Budka, First Edition (Washington, DC: Association of Research Libraries: Office of Scholarly Communication, 2000), ix.
4. Mogge, "Seven Years of Tracking Electronic Publishing," ix–xi.
5. Okerson, "Are We There Yet?," 671–93.

6. Carol Tenopir, "Online Scholarly Journals: How Many?," *Library Journal* 129, no. 2 (February 1, 2004): 32.

7. "Search Results," ULRICHSWEB: Global Serials Directory, accessed June 15, 2023.

8. Okerson, "Are We There Yet?," 673.

9. Michael Rodriguez, "Rethinking Print Journal Subscriptions at a Large Research University," *Serials Review* 47, no. 2 (April 3, 2021): 63.

10. Rodriguez, "Rethinking Print Journal Subscriptions at a Large Research University," 66.

11. Helen W. Tuttle, "Price Indexes, Library Materials," in *Encyclopedia of Library and Information Science*, ed. Allen Kent, Harold Lancour, and Jay E. Daily (New York: Taylor & Francis, 1978).

12. Helen M. Welch, "Proposed Procedure for Establishing a Cost of Periodicals Index," *Library Resources & Technical Services* 3, no. 3 (1959): 202–8.

13. William H. Kurth, "U.S. Book and Periodical Prices–A Preliminary Report," *Library Journal* 85, no. 1 (January 1960): 54–7.

14. "American National Standard for Library and Information Sciences and Related Publishing Practices—Library Material—Criteria for Price Indexes" (New York: American National Standards Institute, 1983).

15. Adrian W. Alexander and Kathryn Hammell Carpenter, "U.S. Periodical Price Index for 1995," *American Libraries* 26, no. 5 (May 1995): 446.

16. Stephen Bosch and Kittie Henderson, "Predicting the Future in 3,000 Words and Charts: The Library Journal Serials Pricing Article," *The Serials Librarian* 74, no. 1–4 (May 31, 2018): 224.

17. Lee Ketcham and Kathleen Born, "Periodical Price Survey 1995: Serials vs. the Dollar Dilemma: Currency Swings and Rising Costs Play Havoc with Prices," *Library Journal* 120, no. 7 (April 15, 1995): 43–8.

18. Lee Ketcham and Kathleen Born, "Periodical Price Survey 1996: Projecting the Electronic Revolution While Budgeting for the Status Quo," *Library Journal* 121, no. 7 (April 15, 1996): 45–51.

19. Lee Ketcham and Kathleen Born, "Periodical Price Survey 1997: Unsettled Times, Unsettled Prices," *Library Journal* 122, no. 7 (April 15, 1997): 42–7.

20. Lee Ketcham-Van Orsdel and Kathleen Born, "Periodical Prices Survey 1998: E-Journals Come of Age," *Library Journal* 123, no. 7 (April 15, 1998): 40–5.

21. Lee Ketcham-Van Orsdel and Kathleen Born, "Periodical Price Survey: Serials Publishing in Flux," *Library Journal* 124, no. 7 (April 15, 1999): 48–53.

22. Lee Ketcham-Van Orsdel and Kathleen Born, "Periodical Price Survey 2000: Pushing Toward More Affordable Access," *Library Journal* 125, no. 7 (April 15, 2000): 47–52.

23. Mary Ellen Davis, "Making of America on the Web," *College & Research Libraries News* 58, no. 6 (June 1997): 381.

24. Kathleen Born and Lee Van Orsdel, "Periodical Price Survey 2001: Searching for Serials Utopia," *Library Journal* 126, no. 7 (April 15, 2001): 53–4.

25. Stephen Bosch and Kittie Henderson, "Periodicals Price Survey 2015: Whole Lotta Shakin' Goin' On," *Library Journal* 140, no. 7 (April 15, 2015): 31.

26. Lee Van Orsdel and Kathleen Born, "Periodical Price Survey 2002: Doing the Digital Flip," *Library Journal* 127, no. 7 (April 15, 2002): 51–6.

27. Lee Van Orsdel and Kathleen Born, "Periodicals Price Survey 2003: Big Chill on the Big Deal?," *Library Journal* 128, no. 7 (April 15, 2003): 51–6.
28. Thomas A. Bourke, "The Photostat-Microfilm War at the New York Public Library in the 1930s, the 1940s, and the 1950s," *Microform Review* 18, no. 3 (1989): 145–50.
29. Carol Tenopir, "Newspapers Online," *Library Journal* 109, no. 4 (January 1, 1984 1984): 452.
30. "Times of London/Sunday Times on CD-ROM," *Information Today* 9, no. 10 (November 1992): 25.
31. "Full-Text Newspaper Collections," *Information Today* 10, no. 5 (May 1993): 28.
32. "WSJ Site Becomes Interactive," *Online* 20, no. 4 (August 7, 1996): 67.
33. Nora Paul, "A Capital Web Site from the Capital: Washington Post Online," *Searcher* 5, no. 2 (February 1997): 31.
34. Joseph Lichterman, "20 Years Ago Today, NYTimes.Com Debuted 'on-Line' on the Web," Nieman Journalism Lab, January 22, 2016, https://web.archive.org/web/20170315124903/http://www.niemanlab.org/2016/01/20-years-ago-today-nytimes-com-debuted-on-line-on-the-web/.
35. "NY Times Launches Digital Subscription Plan," *Advanced Technology Libraries* 40, no. 4 (April 2011): 1–10.
36. "UMI's New Online Service to Include Text and Images From The New York Times," *Information Today* 12, no. 6 (June 1995): 26.
37. Richard Poynder, "The Big Deal: Not Price but Cost," *Information Today* 28, no. 8 (September 2011): 1–3, https://www.infotoday.com/it/sep11/The-Big-Deal-Not-Price-But-Cost.shtml.
38. Theodore C. Bergstrom, "Librarians and the Terrible Fix: Economics of the Big Deal," *Serials* 23, no. 2 (July 2010): 79.
39. Kenneth Frazier, "The Librarians' Dilemma: Contemplating the Costs of the 'Big Deal,'" *D-Lib Magazine* 7, no. 3 (2001), https://www.dlib.org/dlib/march01/frazier/03frazier.html.
40. Theodore C. Bergstrom et al., "Evaluating Big Deal Journal Bundles," *Proceedings of the National Academy of Sciences* 111, no. 26 (July 2014): 9425–30.
41. Kenneth Frazier, "What's the Big Deal?," *The Serials Librarian* 48, no. 1–2 (May 23, 2005): 51.
42. Blanca Rodríguez-Bravo et al., "The Evolution and Revision of Big Deals: A Review from the Perspective of Libraries," *El Profesional de La Información* 30, no. 4 (July 7, 2021): 2.
43. Frazier, "The Librarians' Dilemma."
44. Robert C. Michaelson, "The Big Deal: The Future of Electronic Publications," *Newsletter on Serials Pricing Issues*, December 19, 2000.
45. Bergstrom, "Librarians and the Terrible Fix," 77–82.
46. Bergstrom et al., "Evaluating Big Deal Journal Bundles," 9425–30.
47. Eva Jurczyka and Pamela Jacobs, "What's the Big Deal? Collection Evaluation at the National Level," *Portal: Libraries and the Academy* 14, no. 4 (2014): 619.
48. Bo-Christer Björk, "Why Is Access to the Scholarly Journal Literature So Expensive?," *Portal: Libraries & the Academy* 21, no. 2 (April 2021): 177.
49. Bosch and Henderson, "Predicting the Future," 225.
50. Stephen Bosch, Barbara Albee, and Sion Romaine, "Periodicals Price Survey 2019: Deal or No Deal," *Library Journal* 144, no. 3 (April 2019): 36–7.
51. Poynder, "The Big Deal," 1–3.

52. "Big Deal Cancellation Tracking," SPARC, https://sparcopen.org/our-work/big-deal-cancellation-tracking/ (accessed December 14, 2024).
53. Karla L. Strieb and Julia C. Blixrud, "The State of Large-Publisher Bundles in 2012," Research Library Issues (Washington, DC: Association of Research Libraries, 2013), 14, https://publications.arl.org/rli282/13.24.
54. Asen O. Ivanov, Catherine Anne Johnson, and Samuel Cassady, "Unbundling Practice: The Unbundling of Big Deal Journal Packages as an Information Practice," *Journal of Documentation* 76, no. 5 (April 4, 2020): 1056.
55. Stephen Bosch, Barbara Albee, and Sion Romaine, "Periodicals Price Survey 2021: The New Abnormal," *Library Journal* 146, no. 4 (April 2021): 21.
56. "Guidelines for Statistical Measures of Usage of Web-Based Indexed, Abstracted, and Full Text Resources | ICOLC Website," November 1, 1998, https://icolc.net/statements/guidelines-statistical-measures-usage-web-based-indexed-abstracted-and-full-text.
57. Julia C. Blixrud and Martha Kyrillidou, "E-Metrics: Next Steps for Measuring Electronic Resources," *ARL: A Bimonthly Report on Research Library Issues & Actions*, no. 230/231 (October 2003): 11–13.
58. COUNTER, "About," Project Counter, 2023, https://www.projectcounter.org/about/.
59. Pamela Tibbetts, "A Method for Estimating the In-House Use of the Periodical Collection in the University of Minnesota Bio-Medical Library," *Bulletin of the Medical Library Association* 62, no. 1 (1974): 37–48.
60. Rodríguez-Bravo et al., "The Evolution and Revision of Big Deals," 1–22.
61. Ivanov, Johnson, and Cassady, "Unbundling Practice," 1057.
62. Jacqueline Wilson and Li Chan, "Calculating Scholarly Journal Value through Objective Metrics," California Digital Library, February 13, 2012, https://cdlib.org/cdlinfo/2012/02/13/calculating-scholarly-journal-value-through-objective-metrics/.
63. Jaclyn McLean, Diane Dawson, and Charlene Sorensen, "Communicating Collections Cancellations to Campus: A Qualitative Study," *College & Research Libraries* 82, no. 1 (2021): 19, https://doi.org/10.5860/crl.82.1.19.
64. Maureen Weicher and TianXiao Zhang, "Unbundling the 'Big Deal' with Pay-Per-View of E-Journal Articles" *Serials Librarian* 63, no. 1 (July 2012): 28–37.

3 The Open Access Revolution

Open access (OA) literature is digital, online, free of charge, and free of most copyright and licensing restrictions.

—Peter Suber[1]

Over 200 years after the printing of the Gutenberg Bible came the publication of the *Journal des Sçavans* (1665), the *Philosophical Transactions of the Royal Society* (1665), and the *Mémoires de l'Académie des Sciences* (1666)—the first journals devoted to what today would be called *scholarly communication*. Articles and books printed from movable type lent themselves to scholarly communication by allowing scholars to share their discoveries and ideas on a one-to-many basis, asynchronously, across long distances. Neither the spoken word nor a handwritten text could, by itself, equal the reach of multiple printed copies of a document distributed to far-flung scholars and libraries. Printed communications further served scholars by providing a fixed, date-stamped record of who had first claim to a new discovery or groundbreaking idea. As part of the print-based system of scholarly communication, academic libraries performed the important functions of acquiring, providing access to, and permanently archiving the ever-increasing amount of scholarly information rolling off the world's presses. For a bit more than the three hundred years following the publication of the first scholarly journals, scholarly communication would be inseparably intertwined with the technologies of paper, ink, and printing.

Digital technology introduced new ways of asynchronously sharing one-to-many communications across long distances. While scholars could freely share electronic documents as early as the introduction of File Transfer Protocol (FTP) in 1971, the introduction of USENET (1979) and ListServ (1985) greatly simplified sharing and accessing electronic documents.[2] Invisible colleges of scholars were quick to organically adopt both USENET and ListServ as means of communicating among themselves at effectively zero cost and with unprecedented degrees of speed, freedom, and interactivity. For one example, within five years of its launch in May 1987, the HUMANIST listserv had grown to become a community of over 1,000 humanities scholars representing some twenty-five countries.[3] While the communications among scholars belonging to USENET and ListServ groups were more akin to the informal hallway conversations engaged in at conferences than to peer-reviewed books or journal articles, the formation of such groups constituted an early step toward the sharing of more formal types of scholarly communication via digital technology without any involvement on the part of scholarly publishers. The late 1980s and early 1990s saw the launch of such user-created, open access scholarly journals as the Syracuse-University-based *New Horizons in Adult Education*, Stevan Harnad's *Psycoloquy*, and Eyal Amiran and John Unsworth's *PostModern Culture*.[4] Another major step in the direction of openly sharing formal scholarly communication via digital technology was taken in 1991 when a collaboration begun in the late 1980s between physicists Joanne Cohn and Paul Ginsparg led to the creation of arXiv (pronounced *archive*), the world's first open access repository of scholarly preprints and postprints. Over time, the arXiv repository expanded beyond physics to include works from other fields of study. As of 2020, arXiv contained nearly two million submitted papers.[5]

If the open access revolution has a *Declaration of Independence*, it would be "Subversive Proposal," an email message posted by cognitive scientist Stevan Harnad on June 28, 1994. Distinguishing between commercial authors who write for money and scholarly authors whose "esoteric publications" are written to share ideas and findings with their scholarly peers, Harnad urges scholars to post their scholarly writing in publicly accessible FTP archives, predicting that, if this were to happen, "from this day forward, the long-heralded transition from paper publication to purely electronic publication (of esoteric research) would follow suit almost immediately."[6]

By the time Harnad posted the "Subversive Proposal," many scholars, librarians, and academic administrators were already dismayed that the price of journal subscriptions had been going up in excess of the rate of inflation for over twenty years.[7] They would grow even angrier as the transition from print to digital publication led to price increases rather than the hoped-for savings. Making matters worse, the big commercial academic publishers were perennially listed among the most profitable businesses on the planet. In the case of Elsevier's science and medical journals, the mega-publisher's profit margins for the years 1998, 1999, and 2000 were, respectively, 35.9 percent, 35.4 percent, and 36.4 percent.[8] By way of comparison, in the year 2000 Apple Computer tallied a profit margin of 27 percent.[9] One reason that journal articles have long generated such extraordinary profit is that they are written and peer-reviewed by scholars who receive no payment for their high-value labor. A study conducted in 2021 estimates that merely the reviews provided *pro bono* by the scientific community to scholarly publishers have a value of $1.1–$1.7 billion per year.[10] Even more disturbing to many is that tax monies often fund both the academic research on which scholarly articles are based as well as the subscriptions academic libraries pay to access those articles once they have been published. As a nonacademic journalist looking under the hood of scholarly publishing astutely observes, "It is as if the *New Yorker* or the *Economist* demanded that journalists write and edit each other's work for free and asked the government to foot the bill."[11]

Academic librarians showed themselves to be early and steadfast supporters of the open access revolution. The authors of the *Library Journal*'s 2003 periodicals price survey describe the growing anger over the unsustainable costs of scholarly journals and encouragingly write that "alternative approaches to disseminating scholarly information are springing up everywhere and seem to be gathering momentum.[12] The increasing affordability, ease of use, and universality of digital technology were making it obvious that industrial printing plants and physical distribution systems were no longer essential elements of scholarly communication.

On the other hand, economic reality worked against seizing the opportunity to disrupt the scholarly publishing *status quo*. Even minus the costs of printing and physical distribution, digital publications incur unavoidable costs. For example, the total expenses of running the arXiv digital repository during the year 2020 added up to $2,423,994 ($2,964,492 in 2024 dollars).[13] In 2013, the editor-in-chief of the highly selective journal *Nature* estimated that it cost his journal from $30,000 to $40,000 ($41,101 to $54,802 in 2024 dollars) to publish a single article.[14] While academics and scholarly publishers are unlikely to ever agree on how much it *really* costs to publish an article (or book), everyone agrees that publishing is not free even when no paper is consumed or ink is spilled in the process.

Open Access Gets Organized

While the concept of open access originated among a handful of visionaries, it was not until a critical mass of academics got on board and organized themselves that the revolutionary proposal transitioned to become a viable alternative. Some milestones in that transition include:

Coalition for Networked Information (CNI)

The nonprofit Coalition for Networked Information (CNI) was founded in 1990 to serve U.S. higher education and its partners as a central organization "dedicated to supporting the transformative promise of digital information technology for the advancement of scholarly communication and the enrichment of intellectual productivity."[15]

SciELO

SciELO is an open access publishing platform and database first piloted in Brazil in 1997 and officially launched in 1998 for the express purpose of meeting "the scientific communication needs of developing countries—particularly Latin America and the Caribbean countries."[16] By 2017, sixteen nations were listed on SciELO's roster of "Maintaining and Executing Organizations."[17]

Scholarly Publishing and Academic Resources Coalition (SPARC)

Founded by the Association of Research Libraries (ARL) in 1998, SPARC quickly became one of the world's leading organizations for the promotion of open access publishing.[18] SPARC's "Gaining Independence: A Manual for Planning the Launch of a Nonprofit Electronic Publishing Venture" was issued as an open access publication to "help universities, libraries, societies, and others conceive, plan, and implement alternatives to commercially published scholarly and scientific information."[19]

The Santa Fe Convention

The first scholarly conference to directly shape the future of open access was held in Santa Fe, New Mexico, in October 1999. The document resulting from this conference, *The Santa Fe Convention for the Open Access Initiative*, is noteworthy for presenting "a simple technical and organizational framework to support basic interoperability among e-print archives."[20]

Public Knowledge Project (PKP)

Founded by John Willinsky of the University of British Columbia, PKP provided would-be practitioners of open access publishing with the technological infrastructure necessary to create and maintain open access ventures capable of competing with traditional scholarly publishers. PKP open-source software packages include Open Conference Systems (2000), Open Journal Systems (2001), Open Harvester Systems (2002), and Open Monograph Press (2013).[21]

Creative Commons

In 2001, the Center for the Public Domain founded Creative Commons, an initiative chaired by legal scholar Lawrence Lessig.[22] Creative Commons provides authors who wish to share their work the option of applying one of several Creative Commons licenses as an alternative to the all-rights-reserved model enshrined in copyright law. As important as licenses have been to the development of open access publishing, in some cases differing interpretations of exactly what is or is not allowed by a given license have generated confusion and tension.[23]

Open Archives Initiative Protocol for Metadata Harvesting (OAI-PMH)

In 2002, XML-based *OAI-PMH* replaced the http-based *Santa Fe Convention* as a protocol for standardizing metadata descriptions in support of the interoperability of digital archives and search engines.[24]

Red de Revistas Científicas de América Latina y El Caribe, España y Portugal (Redalyc)

Redalyc was founded in 2002 by the Autonomous University of the State of Mexico. A digital database and library of open access journals, by 2023 the Redalyc membership consisted of 751 institutions representing 31 countries while the Redalyc collection included 1,585 online journals.[25]

Budapest, Bethesda, and Berlin

In the words of open access pioneer and thought leader Peter Suber: "OA was defined in three influential public statements: the *Budapest Open Access Initiative* (February 2002), the *Bethesda Statement on Open Access Publishing* (June 2003), and the *Berlin Declaration on Open Access to Knowledge in the Sciences and Humanities* (October 2003)."[26] The conference that produced the

Berlin Declaration had a long-lasting impact, with the to-date most-recent Berlin Conference (held in June 2023) being the sixteenth in the series.[27]

Open Access Week

In October 2008, SPARC, the Public Library of Science (PLOS), and Students for Free Culture jointly launched the first Open Access Day, a celebration of open access that was simultaneously observed in Germany as *Open-Access Tage*.[28] In 2009, Open Access Day was renamed International Open Access Week and has been observed every year since.[29]

The Growth of Open Access Content: Quantity and Prestige

All the declarations and definitions in the world mean nothing without open access publications providing a significant volume of credible scholarly content for the benefit of authors and readers. The authors of "The Development of Open Access Journal Publishing from 1993 to 2009" put the number of open access journals in 1993 at 20 and the number of open access articles they contained at 247; by 2009, those numbers had grown to 4,767 open access journals (a 23,735 percent increase) containing 191,851 open access articles (a 77,572.5 percent increase).[30] While the impressive growth in the number of both journals and articles was a key indicator of the inroads open access publishing was making, it was equally important that a critical mass of open access journals would come to rival the prestige of the established, top-tier journals produced by traditional scholarly publishers.

In 1999, Harold Varmus, then director of the U.S. National Institutes of Health, announced plans for the creation of E-biomed, an open archive of medical, biomedical, clinical, and allied health information intended to rival the prestige of traditional journals.[31] Renamed PubMed Central a year later, E-biomed, like many early open access initiatives, was met with resistance from some quarters. An article published in the *Chronicle of Higher Education* in September 1999 refers to E-biomed as "a controversial on-line archive of scholarly papers in the life sciences" and reports, "The archive has attracted the ardent opposition of some scholarly societies and for-profit journal publishers."[32] But where some saw a threat, others saw an opportunity. Partly inspired by E-biomed/PubMed Central, in the year 2000, the UK-based publisher Current Science Group announced plans for *BioMed Central*, a commercial, open access publishing juggernaut that eventually laid claim to being the first megajournal.[33]

BioMed Central and its fellow megajournals proved to be an important source of both open access quantity and quality. As outlined by economist Bo-Christer Björk, for a publication to be considered a megajournal, it must meet the following primary criteria:

- Big publishing volume or aiming for it
- Peer review of scientific soundness only
- Broad subject area
- Full open access with Article Publication Charge (APC).[34]

By 2006, *BioMed Central* had fully met the definition of a megajournal, publishing fifty-nine of its own titles while providing a publishing platform for nearly twice that number of independent journals under the control of external scientific groups or societies.[35] *BioMed Central* is also notable as the innovator of the article publication charge, which it introduced in 2002. The initial cost of a *BioMed Central* article publication charge was $500 ($891 in 2024 dollars) per accepted article manuscript. In exchange for this fee, *BioMed Central* provided "immediate, free open access to the full-text article on the Web, peer review, online re-formatting, prompt archiving in PubMed Central's permanent archives" while also allowing archiving in other open access repositories.[36] In 2008, *BioMed Central* was acquired by Springer, at that time already one of the world's largest scholarly publishers, and by 2024, the *BioMed Central* imprint included over 250 journal titles.[37]

Following closely behind *BioMed Central* came *Public Library of Science* (*PLOS*). Like many successes, *PLOS* came into existence because of a failure. In 1999, the eventual leaders of the PLOS Initiative (the aforementioned Harold Varmus in collaboration with Stanford Biochemist Patrick O. Brown and University of California computational biologist Michael Eisen) circulated a petition asking scientists to boycott, effective September 2001, journals that did not make their articles freely available within six months of publication.[38] While the petition was a success in that it garnered the signatures of some 28,000 scientists, it was a failure in that it did not result in any significant change in the scholarly communication marketplace.[39] Rather than giving up, Varmus, Brown, and Eisen shifted gears, launching the nonprofit open access journal *PLOS Biology* in October 2003. Three years later, PLOS launched

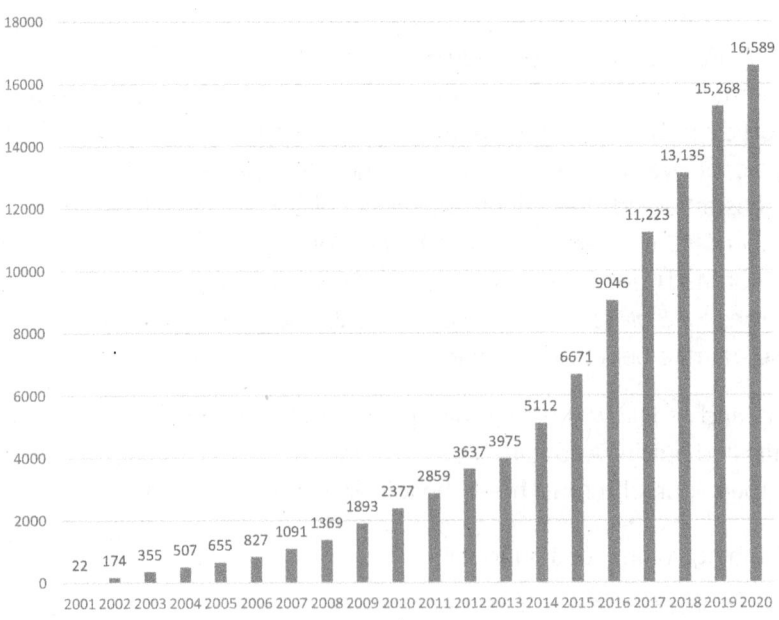

Figure 3.1 Number of open access journals indexed in the Directory of Open Access Journals 2001–2020.

its first megajournal, *PLOS One*. By 2011, *PLOS One* had become "the largest peer-reviewed journal in the world," publishing over 14,000 articles in that year.[40] Competition from established commercial journals entering the open access marketplace meant that *PLOS One* did not permanently retain its leadership, as by 2016, Springer Nature's megajournal *Scientific Reports*, which launched in 2011, had become the world's largest peer-reviewed journal.[41]

Whether for-profit or nonprofit, single subject or megajournal, traditionally or alternatively peer reviewed, funded by APCs or by other means, open access publishing grew steadily in quantity and credibility through the first two decades of the twenty-first century. By 2020, the Directory of Open Access Journals was indexing 16,589 scholarly open access journals, an 82,845 percent increase from the number of open access journals available in 1993 (Figure 3.1).[42]

The Battles over Open Access

As noted above, when the E-biomed plan that led to the creation of PubMed Central was first proposed in 1999, commercial scholarly publishers, along with a number of allies from the nonprofit sector, were quick to express their opposition on the grounds that E-biomed would weaken peer review and diminish the integrity of scientific publishing. Some opponents expressed the secondary concern that a central repository would give a single government agency too much power over the direction of biomedical research.[43] Though largely unvoiced by the opponents of open access publishing, financial considerations were also in play. Commercial publishers were concerned that open access would cut into their profits, while nonprofit scholarly societies were concerned that open access would reduce publishing income which they expended both to keep membership dues low and support their non-revenue producing activities.[44]

In the summer of 2004, both commercial and nonprofit scholarly publishers received the unwelcome news that the U.S. House of Representatives Committee on Appropriations was encouraging the National Institutes of Health (NIH), at that time the funder of one-fourth of the world's biomedical research, to change their procedures to require that "all grantees and contractors submit electronic copies of finished manuscripts for full-text release through PubMed Central," with the proviso that all manuscripts would be available within six months of their initial publication.[45] Seeing an existential threat to their business model, commercial and nonprofit scholarly publishers went on the offensive. Representatives of "more than 50 publishers visited the NIH offices in early August [2004] to voice strong opposition" to the change in policy.[46] A powerful coalition of commercial scholarly publishers, "aided mightily by a vocal core of society publishers," successfully lobbied Congress to produce a weakened proposal.[47] In the version announced in February 2005, the NIH's proposed six-month embargo period was increased, for most manuscripts, to twelve months, while the mandate that grantees must themselves deposit manuscripts in PubMed Central was eliminated. Though the outcome was a win for publishers, it was not the end of the fighting.

Less than a year later, the American Chemical Society (ACS) lobbied Congress to pull funding for the NIH's open access PubChem database on the grounds that it unfairly competed with the ACS's publications. This time, Congress sided with the NIH by voting to sustain PubChem's funding.[48] The conflict over PubChem turned out to be no more than a preliminary skirmish ahead of the protracted battle centered around the Federal Research Public Access Act (FRPAA), a bill introduced in the U.S. Senate in May 2006. If passed, FRPAA would have mandated that any journal articles resulting from research sponsored by any of the eleven U.S. agencies expending over $100 million per year on research become available via an open access repository no less than six months after publication. Like the NIH proposal of 2004, FRPAA also mandated that grantees proactively deposit their articles in an open access repository, a requirement opposed by publishers because busy scholars tend to skip this key final step in the open access lifecycle if it is left optional.

Publishers immediately went into war mode. An article published in *Nature* in January 2007 reports on how the American Association of Publishers, Professional/Scholarly Publishing Division (AAP, P/SP) was spending between $300,000 and $500,000 ($467,591 to $779,318 in 2024 dollars) on a public-relations "pit bull" whose anti-FRPAA strategies included promoting the message that "Public access equals government censorship" and involved joining forces with a conservative think tank known to have accepted oil money to discredit the science behind climate change.[49] The AAP, P/SP, and the individual publishers mentioned in the *Nature* story—the American Chemical Society, Elsevier, and Wiley—are described as having been "skewered in the scholarly and public media" for their public-relations blunder.[50] A second misstep involved the AAP, P/SP's September 2007 launch of Partnership for Research Integrity in Science and Medicine (PRISM), a public-relations campaign painting open access publishing as "junk science."[51] The response to PRISM from academics both outside and inside the scholarly publishing community was overwhelmingly negative. Thomas D. Wilson, founder of Elsevier's *International Journal of Information Management*, resigned his post as editor, writing of PRISM, "Their claim that OA threatens the peer review process is nothing less than the 'big lie'—the propaganda techniques of Dr. Goebbels."[52] Wilson was not the only scholar to resign from an editorial post over PRISM. Predictably, such pro-open-access organizations as SPARC and the ARL blasted PRISM, but more surprisingly, and more damningly, several prominent university presses publicly criticized PRISM and disassociated themselves from the whole affair.[53]

Public-relations gaffes aside, in the end the scholarly publishing community got its way. The 2006 version of FRPAA died in committee, while over the course of the years 2009 to 2012, the same fate would befall all four later iterations of FRPAA. A similar bill, the Fair Access to Science and Technology Research Act (FASTR), met the same fate as FRPAA, being introduced in 2013, 2015, and 2017 without ever being passed by the U.S. Congress. At the same time that scholarly publishers were scoring victories by successfully fighting bills that would have furthered open access, they were sustaining losses by unsuccessfully supporting bills that would have, to varying degrees, stymied open access. These bills, none of which were passed into law, include the Fair Copyright in Research Works Act (a.k.a. the Conyers Bill) introduced on February 3, 2009; the Stop Online Piracy Act (SOPA) introduced on October 26, 2011; the Preventing Real Online Threats to Economic Creativity and Theft of Intellectual Property Act

(Protect IP Act or PIPA) introduced on May 12, 2011; and the Research Works Act introduced on December 16, 2011. Both the Conyers Bill of 2009 and the Research Works Act of 2011 were explicitly drafted to eliminate the NIH open access policy.

In the end, the legislative battles over open access were rendered largely moot by a single Obama Administration Policy Memorandum entitled "Expanding Public Access to Results of Federally Funded Research." Issued by the Office of Science and Technology Policy on February 22, 2013, "Expanding Public Access" required U.S. Federal agencies with more than $100M in research and development expenditures to "develop plans to make the published results of federally funded research freely available to the public within one year of publication."[54] Remarkably, the new policy memo was described as being "praised by publishers, and open access advocates alike."[55] Scholarly publishers may have been willing to praise the White House's broadening of open access both because they were finding that open access repositories like PubMed Central were not leading to mass cancellations of journal subscriptions and, more importantly, that the gold open access model could be profitable. By 2011, Springer had become a major player in the open access marketplace through its acquisition of the open access megajournal *BioMed Central*; by this same date, Nature Publishing was offering gold open access options in 80 percent of its journals while publishing eight fully open access journals.[56]

Another reason for the softened stance taken by many scholarly publishers may have had something to do with the acts of resistance initiated by scholars and academic institutions around the world. These acts included scholar-led boycotts, editorial defections, and the implementation of institutional open access policies. Academic libraries played a part by engaging in library-led subscription cancellations and taking on the new role of academic libraries as publishers.

Library-Led Subscription Cancellations

As discussed in Chapter 2, a growing number of U.S. academic libraries began cancelling Big Deal packages in the early 2000s—a trend that continues to the present day. U.S. academic libraries were not alone in this. For one notable example, in October 2007, the Max Planck Society cancelled subscriptions to 1,200 Springer journals, defiantly holding out until February 2008 before the two parties could come to an agreement.[57] While journal cancellations were inevitably painful to the entire academic community, the availability of ever-increasing amounts of scholarship via open access sources made them less so. When the University of California (UC) System cancelled all of its Elsevier subscriptions in 2019, the UC Libraries provided explicit instructions to faculty and students on how to access tens of thousands of Elsevier articles available via open access sources.[58]

Academic library efforts to provide users with alternatives to paywalled articles were furthered by the availability of such open access discovery tools as the Open Access Button, Unpaywall, EndNote Click, Kopernio, Lean Library, and Lazy Scholar, all of which direct information seekers to open access versions of articles they might not otherwise be able to locate and access.[59] In addition, major bibliographic databases such as the freely accessible Google Scholar (starting in 2006) and the proprietary Web of Science (starting in 2018) seamlessly incorporated links to open access items into their search results. OAIster became yet another important tool for locating open access content. Funded by a Mellon grant and developed at the University of Michigan in 2002, OAIster is a union catalog that employs Open Archives Initiative Protocol for Metadata Harvesting (OAI-PMH) to locate open access content and create catalog records for each item. In 2009, OCLC was brought in as a partner on the OAIster project, and as of 2023 "OAIster includes more than 50 million records that represent digital resources from more than 2,000 contributors."[60]

Libraries as Publishers

The low infrastructure costs of digital publishing positioned academic libraries to become scholarly publishers.[61] As academic libraries entered into the world of digital publishing, they typically did so in partnership with their local faculty and, in some cases, by collaborating with university presses struggling to adapt to an increasingly digital publishing environment.[62] Academic libraries found themselves not only launching and managing largely passive open access archives of previously published work but also actively publishing new journals, monographs, dissertations and theses, gray literature, undergraduate work, data, and more. Of the eighty Association of Research Library (ARL) member libraries responding to a survey conducted in late 2007, 44 percent "were delivering publishing services," while 21 percent were planning to go into publishing; in 2007, ARL libraries were collectively publishing 265 journal titles, of which 131 were established titles, 81 new, and 53 were under development.[63] The inaugural *Library Publishing Directory 2014* reports that a combined 108 U.S. and Canadian academic libraries—plus 7 academic libraries located elsewhere—were publishing, "391 faculty-driven journals, 174 student-driven journals, 937 monographs, at least 8,746 conference papers and proceedings, and nearly 100,000 each of ETDs and technical/research reports."[64] By the appearance of *Library Publishing Directory 2023*, the worldwide number of academic library publishers had grown from 115 in 2014 to 158 (a 37.39 percent increase), and these libraries were publishing 1,282 journal titles, of which 917 were peer reviewed. Libraries also published 1,240 monographs in 2022.[65] While library publishing has not, and likely never will, completely disrupt the scholarly publishing industry, it has offered an outlet to scholars who are willing to pursue publishing alternatives that are scholar-led and wholly under the control of academic institutions.

The Colors of Open Access

By the early 2000s, it was becoming clear that there would be more than one model of open access and that these models were going to be more complex than simply posting work online. Stevan Harnad coined the terms *green open access* and *gold open access* to describe what would become the two dominant models of open access publishing.[66] In December 2004, Harnad and a team of co-authors published "The Access/Impact Problem and the Green and Gold Roads to Open Access," the first journal article to use the green/gold terminology.[67]

As more models of open access emerged, enough additional colors joined the lexicon that color coding became as much a source of confusion as clarification. The colors of open access that have stood the test of time include:

Green Open Access

Green open access operates on a self-archiving model in which an author or an author's designee deposits some version of the author's work into a verified green open access repository. Once deposited, such works may be shared at no cost to end users and, ideally, with the fewest possible restrictions on reuse attached. To ensure that the terms of use for works deposited in open access archives are clear, authors employ Creative Commons (or similar) licenses that allow for varying degrees of use and reuse without the need to obtain consent from the copyright holder. Before a previously published work can be deposited in a green open access repository, scholarly authors or their designees must license to the publisher of that work the right of publication—known in the trade as *first serial rights*—while retaining copyright for themselves and, in some cases, granting certain of their retained rights to a designee such as their home institution or research funder. Depending on the licensing terms under which an article is published, deposit in an open access repository may be delayed until an embargo period— typically six months to a year—has passed following initial publication. The version deposited may range from an unpublished, unreviewed preprint manuscript to a peer-reviewed Accepted Author Manuscript (AAM) to a peer-reviewed, edited, and formally published Version of Record (VoR). In the interest of ensuring that subscriptions are not cancelled, many publishers will agree to the deposit of the AAM of a published work while vetoing the deposit of the VoR.

Green open access repositories come in different forms, including subject repositories such as ArXiv; funder-managed repositories such as the U.S. National Institutes of Health's PubMed Central; and institutional repositories such as the University of Michigan's Deep Blue Documents, the University of Texas at Austin's Texas Scholar Works, and the Stanford Digital Repository. A study published in 2020 reports a worldwide total of 5,286 open access repositories; of this number, 898 were based in the United States.[68] The costs of developing, managing, and maintaining an open access repository are not trivial, as these costs include "budget dollars in staff time, server and storage space, subscriptions to IR [Institutional Repository] vendor platforms, programming and training expenses, marketing services, and much more."[69] Clifford A. Lynch, Executive Director of the Coalition for Networked Information, describes an institutional repository as both a "set of services" and an "organizational commitment" for the stewardship of materials created by members of its community. Lynch goes on to illustrate the complexity of the services and commitments involved in hosting an institutional repository by pointing out that "an effective institutional repository of necessity represents a collaboration among librarians, information technologists, archives and records managers, faculty, and university administrators and policy makers."[70]

Among the challenges faced by those institutional repositories managed under the sometimes-unenforceable terms of campus open access policies is the reality that faculty authors may neglect to deposit their published works in the campus's institutional repository, with the reasons for noncompliance ranging from overly complicated deposit processes to unfamiliarity with the campus open access policy to personal objections to the concept of open access.[71] Institutional repositories have responded to lackluster compliance with open access policies through such strategies as library-mediated archiving and automated content harvesting.[72]

Gold Open Access

Where traditional publishers at best tolerated green open access, they grew to actively embrace gold open access. The gold open access model flips the traditional business transaction in which the reader (or the reader's library) pays the access toll; instead, gold open access requires the author (or an entity acting on the author's behalf) to pay an article publication charge (APC) in exchange for which the article is made open access with no embargo period. In the interest of promoting brand identity, publishers typically host gold open access articles on their proprietary websites, though such articles may also be hosted in open access repositories.

For scholars, the attraction of gold open access is that it allows them to publish an article in a prestigious, brand-name journal without any paywall or embargo period restricting access. And while the idea of an APC might strike some as a form of vanity publishing, paying an APC is not entirely different from paying the page charges that scientific journals had begun levying on authors as far back as the 1930s.[73] In the eyes of some scholars, though, gold open access had the appearance of a trick designed to shift onto the ledgers of scholars' costs that had traditionally been paid out of campus library budgets. Certainly, those scholars without grant funding to pay open access fees do not find the gold open access model at all attractive, while even those with grant funding would, given the choice, rather not hand that funding over to a scholarly publisher. As much as scholars may dislike paying an APC, the act of doing so at least has the virtue of forcing scholars to become aware of the real costs of scholarly publishing. In the words of economist and librarian Jeffrey Mackie-Mason, gold open access has, for the first time, forced scholars to "have skin in the game."[74]

For scholarly publishers, the attraction of gold open access has been that, unlike green open access, it provides a revenue stream. In the case of scholarly journals, gold open access evolved to take on one of two revenue-generating forms: first, the fully open journal in which all articles are funded by APCs; second, the hybrid journal in which those articles funded by APCs are open while those that are not remain behind a paywall. The extent to which scholarly publishers embraced gold open access is reflected by the growth in the number of journals that accept APCs. A study published in 2012 reports, "As of August 2011 there were 1,825 journals listed in the Directory of Open Access Journals (DOAJ) that, at least by self-report, charge APCs. These represent just over 26% of all DOAJ journals."[75] As of November 2023, the DOAJ indexed 6,614 journals that charge APCs, a total representing a 262.41 percent increase from 2011 and accounting for 32.8 percent of all journals listed in DOAJ for 2023.[76]

As mentioned above, when BioMed Central pioneered the APC in January 2002, the cost was $500 ($891 in 2024 dollars) for each accepted article. As might be expected, over time the amount BMC charges for an APC grew far beyond the rate set in 2000. For example, the 2024 the APC charge for *BMC Biology* was $3190; *BMC Genomic Data*, $2090; and *BMC Ecology and Evolution*, $2790.[77] Looking more broadly than BMC alone, a longitudinal study of APCs found that, adjusting for inflation, from 2011 to 2021 the average APC increased by 10.78 percent while the highest APC decreased by 9.33 percent.[78]

Because the amounts charged for APCs were never in the realm of pocket change, the question of who should bear the cost of APCs immediately became an issue. A study conducted by David J. Solomon and Bo-Christer Björk that was published in 2012 identifies seven possible sources for funding APCs:

- Grant/contracts
- National OA policy funding
- Institutional OA policy funding
- Institutional discretionary funds
- Personal funds
- Fee waivers
- Other[79]

This same study found that sources of APC funding varied according to both a scholar's field of study and the GNP of the country in which a scholar works. Scholars working in either the physical sciences or the health/biological/life sciences were most likely to use grant/contract funding to pay APCs, while those in business and economics were least likely to do the same. For scholars living in countries where the average per-capita GNP was over $25,000 ($34,797 in 2024 dollars), the main sources of APC funding were grants/contracts (31 percent) and institutional discretionary funds (26 percent). For scholars living in countries where the average per-capita GNP was below $25,000 ($34,797 in 2024 dollars), the main sources of APC funding were personal funds (39 percent) and (in a tie) grants/contracts and institutional OA policy funding (both 16 percent).[80] As APCs became more common, academic libraries became directly involved in the funding of APCs either as managers of open access subvention funds or as managers of institutional memberships intended to lower the cost of APCs for campus affiliates.[81] Getting academic libraries involved in the funding of APCs was, in most ways, a reasonable strategy to pursue. The financial skills and knowledge of the scholarly publishing industry that librarians had acquired over decades of negotiating with publishers made them ideal candidates to manage institutional memberships as these are structured much like traditional journal subscriptions. However, in the case of open access subvention funds, many of which operated along lines similar to competitive grants, librarians were not necessarily in the best position to decide which campus scholars were most deserving of the limited amounts of APC subvention funding available for distribution.

For gold open access, a more important question than, "Where will the funding for APCs come from?" has been the question, "Is there enough funding to make open access economically viable?" To date, the most thorough investigation of the economic viability of a transition from a subscription model to a gold open access model is *Pay It Forward: Investigating a Sustainable Model of Open Access Article Processing Charges for Large North American Research Institutions*. Funded by the Mellon Foundation and led by the University of California, Davis Library in collaboration with U.S. and Canadian partners, the authors of *Pay It Forward* employed both qualitative and quantitative measures to gather data and input from scholarly authors and publishers. In very broad terms, the major findings reached in *Pay It Forward* are:

- The library budgets of research-intensive institutions are, by themselves, insufficient to support a complete transition to gold open access publishing.
- Grant funding could be used to bridge the gap between library budgets and the cost of transitioning to gold open access.
- If this gap is to be bridged, faculty must be incentivized to apply grant funding to publication costs, and institutions may, in some cases, need to provide additional discretionary funding to support those costs.[82]

Since the publication of *Pay It Forward* in 2016, there has been nothing like a complete transition to gold open access. The subscription model for journal acquisition remains so strong that academic libraries are in no position to unilaterally stop funding journal subscriptions and reapply those funds toward paying the costs of gold open access.

As popular as gold open access has proven to be with scholarly publishers, many of those who might be considered open access purists object to the entire concept of gold open access. The complaints leveled against gold open access include the following:

- Gold open access has been co-opted by the biggest commercial and society publishers as a means of increasing their income and solidifying their monopoly on scholarly publishing.[83]
- While gold open access has helped remove paywalls that prevent readers from accessing scholarly information, it has been detrimental to publishing scholars who lack access to the funding required to publish gold open access articles. The impacted group includes most scholars in the developing world/Global South as well as many scholars in developed nations who work in fields of study with limited or no access to grant funding.[84]
- Scholarly publishers have been criticized for the practice of "double dipping" in which the costs of subscriptions to hybrid open access journals remain high even while those journals are reaping additional income through APCs.[85]
- Gold open access fees impact research-intensive institutions, whose faculty publish frequently, far more than they impact smaller, teaching-focused institutions, whose faculty publish less frequently.[86] This has led to concerns that the libraries of smaller institutions—as well as private companies that do research but whose employees

publish infrequently—could become free riders by cancelling journal subscriptions to rely instead on the increasing number of articles available via open access. While this is advantageous to smaller institutions and private companies, mass cancellations would increase the burden on research-intensive institutions by driving up the cost of both subscriptions and APCs.

- Gold open access has led to the existence of predatory publishing.

Predatory Publishing

Predatory journals, which began to emerge alongside legitimate open access journals in the first decade of the twenty-first century, were initially brought to the widespread attention of the academic world in 2008 by Gunther Eysenbach, publisher and editor of the open access *Journal of Medical Internet Research*.[87] A phenomenon made possible by digital technology, predatory journals masquerade as legitimate open access journals by offering to publish a manuscript in exchange for the payment of an APC. While requiring the payment of an APC is not, in itself, predatory, the problem with predatory journals is that, in exchange for payment, they will publish almost any manuscript regardless of quality. Predatory journals may claim to practice rigorous peer review while, in fact, doing so at either a cursory level or not at all. Other deceptive practices for which predatory journals have been called out include aggressively soliciting manuscripts under false pretenses, falsely listing prominent scholars as members of a journal's editorial board, overstating a journal's impact factor (or other assessment metrics), hijacking legitimate journals by spoofing their identities, and holding submitted manuscripts hostage by threatening to publish them against the author's will so that they cannot be submitted elsewhere. In some cases, scholars knowingly publish with predatory journals in hopes of padding their list of publications, while other scholars innocently submit manuscripts under the mistaken impression that they are dealing with legitimate journals. The fact that predatory journals offer lower article publication charges and faster turnaround times than legitimate journals can entice unwary scholars. Beyond the problems they create for scholars, predatory journals serve to undermine confidence in science while providing a patina of scholarly legitimacy to unsound findings.

Identifying predatory journals has never been easy. For one thing, the more polished predatory journals do a credible job of passing themselves off as legitimate publications; for another, the distinction between predatory and non-predatory is not always clear-cut. The authors of a study on the effectiveness of journal whitelists and blacklists observe that it "can be a hard and tricky task" to identify which journals are predatory and which are not, reporting that "some journals and publishers appear to be in a gray area as they are included in both whitelists and blacklists at the same time."[88] Efforts to determine exactly how many publishers and/or journals qualify as predatory have led to well-qualified investigators coming up with wildly different counts.[89] The only point of agreement seems to be that the number of predatory journals is too high.

From 2008 through 2017, Jeffrey Beall, a U.S. academic librarian and coiner of the term "predatory open access publishing," maintained *Beall's List*, an often-consulted listing of journals Beall identified as predatory.[90] Beall's judgments regarding what counted as predatory could be controversial, as was seen in 2015 when Beall characterized the SciELO open access repository as a *favela*—a Brazilian Portuguese term similar in connotation to the English words *ghetto* or *slum*. The Brazilian Forum of Public Health Journals Editors and the *Associação Brasileira de Saúde Coletiva* responded by drafting the "Motion to Repudiate Mr. Jeffrey Beall's Classist Attack on SciELO," in which they characterized Beall's point of view as "neocolonial."[91] Commercial publisher Cabell developed a product similar to "Beall's List" that, in 2017, became a subscription-based service offering both whitelists and blacklists of journal titles. Rather than listing journals that fall short of the mark, the Directory of Open Access Journals (DOAJ) has, since 2003, taken the whitelist approach by providing information about open access journals that meet acceptable standards of peer review and editorial oversight.[92] Sherpa, founded in 2002, performs a similar service by providing detailed information about the policies and practices of open access publishers.[93] Taking a different approach, the multilingual "Think. Check. Submit." initiative seeks to educate scholars by providing a checklist for identifying the characteristics of predatory publications.[94]

Other Colors of Open Access

Bronze Open Access

Bronze open access articles are available to read on a publisher's website but are not licensed to allow reuse.[95]

Diamond Open Access

Diamond (also known as *platinum*) open access describes publications that are produced with no cost to authors or readers. Funding for diamond/platinum open access can come from a variety of sources, including grants, institutional support, philanthropy, and crowdfunding. The previously mentioned SciELO and Redalyc successfully operate on the diamond/platinum principle to provide scholars of the Global South with reliable alternatives to cost-prohibitive gold open access publications. Another model of diamond/platinum open access designed to keep costs low is the *overlay journal*, for which editors select promising unpublished manuscripts from existing green open access repositories, put those manuscripts through a peer-review process, and then publish the final versions as journal articles.[96]

Gray Open Access

Gray open access describes the practice of making publications accessible via scholarly social media platforms such as ResearchGate, Academia.edu, and Mendeley. It is also used to describe the informal archiving of publications on accessible personal or departmental servers.[97] Depending on one's point of view, the file sharing that is the hallmark of gray open access either pushes the boundaries of copyright law or goes beyond those boundaries to constitute a form of copyright infringement.

Black Open Access

Black open access describes the practice of making documents available in blatant violation of copyright. Black open access may be conducted through informal social media contacts or via formally organized, dark web repositories that avoid legal sanctions by employing such technologies as BitTorrent and distributed file-sharing systems. Of the many black open access operations, the best known is SCI-Hub, a website founded in 2011 by Kazakhstani computer-programmer Alexandra Elbakyan.

Funders Flex Their Power

Whether private or governmental, the funders of scholarly research were in a more powerful position than individuals and institutions to promote open access. To not put too fine a point on it, funders who favor open access have the power to dictate up front that scholars who accept funding must abide by the funder's open access policy. Funders also have leverage over scholarly publishers in that scholarly publishers must make accommodations for compliance with funder open access mandates if they wish to publish the work of the elite scholars who are most capable of getting funding for their research. The ROARMAP list of open access policies indicates that, by 2020, 142 research funders from around the world had implemented open access policies.[98]

Among high-profile funders of research, the U.S. government was not alone in its efforts to promote open access publishing. In 2004, the British Parliament's Common Science and Technology Committee published a report entitled *Scientific Publications: Free for All?*[99] While the report inspired Parliamentary interest in open access, it failed to produce immediate results.[100] This would change with the 2012 release of *Accessibility, Sustainability, Excellence: How to Expand Access to Research Publications* (commonly known as *The Finch Report*), a document recommending that "the UK should embrace the transition to open access, and accelerate the process in a measured way which promotes innovation but also what is most valuable in the research communications ecosystem."[101] *The Finch Report* was controversial, with critics objecting that it too strongly favors gold open access over green.[102] In line with the gold open access emphasis of *The Finch Report*, the Research Council of the United Kingdom "announced its intention to provide 'block grants' to UK universities which will form the basis of institutional funds to be used to pay APCs."[103] Less than a month after the appearance of *The Finch Report*, the European Commission issued a set of recommendations calling on member states to, "Define clear policies for the dissemination of and open access to scientific publications resulting from publicly funded research."[104]

Yet another notable funder-led initiative was Open Access 2020 (OA2020). Originating from the twelfth Berlin Conference held in December 2015, OA2020 produced two key documents—"Expression of Interest in the Large-Scale Implementation of Open Access to Scholarly Journals"[105] and "OA2020 Roadmap."[106] Together, these documents outline the goal of transforming "a substantial majority of today's scholarly journals from subscription to OA publishing."[107] By 2023, 174 organizations, including eighteen U.S. organizations, had signed the OA2020 *Expression of Interest*. OA2020 was followed in September 2018 by the formation of cOAlition S and its subsequent launch of Plan S. Initially, the membership of cOAlition S consisted of a number of national-level European research funders but came to include funders representing the Middle East, Africa, Australia, Canada, and the United Nations. Besides governmental entities, the membership of cOAlition S also includes such private funders as the Bill and Melinda Gates Foundation, the Wellcome Trust, Templeton World Charity Foundation, and the Howard Hughes Medical Institute. The crafters of Plan S set an ambitious goal:

> With effect from 2021, all scholarly publications on the results from research funded by public or private grants provided by national, regional and international research councils and funding bodies, must be published in Open Access Journals, on Open Access Platforms, or made immediately available through Open Access Repositories without embargo.[108]

One concession originally made by Plan S allows for "Transformative Arrangements" that provide time for hybrid journals to become compliant with the principles of Plan S, though in January 2023 cOAlition S announced that it would no longer support transformative arrangements after December 31, 2024.[109] Plan S was not universally welcomed, with some researchers going so far as to accuse it of "undermining academic freedom."[110] The Plan S rights retention strategy, under which authors are asked to negotiate directly with publishers, has also been criticized as "an administrative and legal burden, not a sustainable open access solution."[111] Tellingly, no German, Asian, or U.S. government research funders, including the NIH, have to date joined cOAlition S. In May 2019, cOAlition S and OA2020 came together to issue a joint statement confirming their shared goal of "a largescale implementation of open access to scholarly journals."[112] In October 2023, cOAlition S issued "Towards Responsible Publishing: A Proposal from cOAlition S," which it billed as a "draft proposal from cOAlition S."[113] Acknowledging that, in spite of the growth of open access publishing, "academic publishing practices are not keeping up with rapid advances in the way science is performed, openly disseminated, and used," the authors of "Towards Responsible Publishing" propose a revised "scholar-led" vision of open access that will incorporate input from scholarly authors.

Transformative Agreements

As defined by Efficiency and Standards for Article Charges (ESAC), a *transformative agreement* is a negotiated agreement between institutions and publishers in which funds that formerly went to pay subscriptions would instead be used to support open access publishing.[114]

A key document in the history of transformative agreements is *Disrupting the Subscription Journals' Business Model for the Necessary Large-Scale Transformation to Open Access*, a white paper published by the Max Planck Digital Library in April 2015. By that date, approximately two decades into the open access era, it had become clear that open access had neither solved the economic woes of academic libraries nor made the entirety of scholarly publishing freely available to all. Although the amount of open access publishing was growing, the authors of *Disrupting the Subscription Journals' Business Model* lament the fact that "the costs for open access publishing services come as an add-on to a persisting subscription system that continues to extract annual price increases above inflation from the libraries of the world."[115] Taking into account the approximately $10 billion ($13.5 billion in 2024 dollars) then being spent worldwide on scholarly publishing, the authors of the white paper contend that there is enough money in the system to end all subscription spending by instead investing in "a range of publishing services that will truly serve the scholarly endeavors of the 21st century."[116]

At the time *Disrupting the Subscription Journals' Business Model* was published, the basic idea of the transformative agreement was not entirely new. Knowledge Unlatched, which was established in September 2012, was already using a collective procurement approach to purchase the rights to monographs in order to make them freely available to all readers. In 2013 CERN launched SCOAP^3 (Sponsoring Consortium for Open Access Publishing in Particle Physics), an initiative to convert subscription-funded journals in high-energy physics to diamond open access. Throughout the 2010s, academic libraries began signing offsetting agreements under which any payment of APCs to a journal publisher from any source (grant funds, library, etc.) would go to reduce the cost of that publisher's journal subscriptions. The main benefit of offsetting agreements is that they eliminate the bane of double dipping, though full transparency on the part of publishers is required for offsetting agreements to be fully effective. By 2020, two similar, and similarly named, models of the transitional agreement had emerged. One is the *read-and-publish agreement*, a contract under which a publisher receives payment covering both publication and reading charges. The other is a *publish-and-read agreement*, a contract in which a publisher receives payment covering publication charges and reading is thrown in for free. The difference between the two types of agreements is subtle even if the end goal, at least for academic libraries, is a cost-neutral transition from the subscription model to open access.

As of December 2023, the ESAC Transformative Agreement Registry listed 872 transformative agreements involving 358,313 total publications (not all of which are unique titles); of these, U.S. institutions can lay claim to only seventy transformative agreements involving 28,997 publications (not all of which are, again, unique titles).[117] Because U.S. higher education consists primarily of a patchwork of state and private institutions, negotiating far-reaching transformative agreements has been more difficult for U.S. institutions than for institutions in those countries where higher education is under the central control of a national ministry of education.[118] For example, through Projekt DEAL the Alliance of Science Organizations in Germany, representing some 700 institutions, was able to, first, launch a nationwide boycott of Elsevier journals and, second, negotiate nationwide transformative agreements with Wiley, Springer Nature, and Elsevier.[119] The first North American transformative agreement was reached in June 2017 when the Massachusetts Institute of Technology and the Royal Society of Chemistry signed a read-and-publish agreement for scholarly articles.[120] In April 2019, the California Digital Library, negotiating on behalf of the ten-campus University of California System, reached a cost-neutral agreement involving 400 Cambridge University Press journals.[121] Though both MIT and the University of California System are large, research-intensive institutions, no U.S. institution has anything close to the power of Germany's Alliance of Science Organizations for negotiating nationwide transformative agreements.

The use of the word *transformative* is reflective of the idea that such agreements are not the ultimate solution but, rather, a step on the way to a world in which all scholarly communication is published open access. As much promise as may be seen in transformative agreements, there is nothing like a consensus that they are a step in the right direction. After making a case against transformative agreements, the librarian-authors of "Transformative Agreements: Six Myths, Busted" warn their professional colleagues, "TAs are too new to fully gauge their impact, but historical trends (Big Deals, the rise of APCs, the consolidation of publishing markets) and current data suggest that libraries should cautiously assess the 'transformative' nature of these deals."[122] In an opinion piece published in the *Scholarly Kitchen*, PLOS CEO Alison Mudditt takes the position that transformative agreements are not working, arguing that academic libraries and scholars need to find other ways to take full control over scholarly communication.[123] It will likely be at least the end of the 2020s before anyone can know for certain the extent to which transformative agreements have succeeded (or not) in achieving universal open access.

Open Access for Long-Form Scholarly Communication

When considering open access publishing, there is a tendency to focus on journal articles as the default format. This is understandable since the high cost of journals has made them the focus of the open access revolution from the outset. Even so, open access has also made its mark on long-form scholarly information.

Scholarly Monographs

In the humanities and a number of social science fields, the book has traditionally taken precedence over the journal article as the most important medium for scholarly communication. Historically, the largest market for scholarly monographs has been academic libraries, but the financial hardships brought on by decades-long increases in the cost of journals have served to redirect academic library spending away from monographs and other scholarly books. After adjusting for inflation, from 1986 to 2008, ARL-member-library's spending on serials increased by 146.2 percent while spending on monographs decreased by 3.4 percent.[124] In 2020, 75.47 percent of money spent in the scholarly publishing global marketplace went toward journals.[125] Less money spent on monographs resulted in fewer copies being printed, which in turn meant higher per-copy prices. Adjusting for inflation, from 1980 to 2010, the average cost of a history monograph had increased by 30.26 percent, a religious studies monograph by 65.12 percent, and an education monograph by 274.82 percent.[126]

Faced with the reality of unfavorable market forces, many of those who cared about the future of the scholarly book turned to open access publishing as a way of keeping the format alive. Some groundwork for the acceptance of open access book publishing was laid through Project Gutenberg, Google Books, and HathiTrust—initiatives that made millions of public domain books freely available in digital form. Although newly written works are not in the public domain and are, therefore, not usually available via repositories like HathiTrust, new scholarly monographs are potential candidates for open access publication because they tend to fit Stevan Harnad's model of "esoteric publications" that are written for reasons other than money.

Even if authors of scholarly monographs expect no payment for their work, there are unavoidable costs associated with publishing digital open access monographs. A study published in 2022 found that for fifty-seven open access scholarly monographs published by fifteen different publishers participating in the TOME open access initiative (see below), the average cost to publish a single book in an entirely digital format was $19,954 ($22,392 in 2024 dollars).[127] One way to cover the real costs of open access book publishing without charging either authors or readers has been for academic libraries and other nonprofit organizations to take on the role of publisher. Among the first open access book publishers was OAPEN, a Netherlands-based nonprofit publisher affiliated with the Royal Library of the Netherlands. Founded in 2008, OAPEN functions as a central repository for hosting and disseminating open access books, provides an open access toolkit for authors, and maintains a directory of open access books. As of 2022, the OAPEN collection consisted of 26,000 open access books that had tallied twelve million COUNTER-compliant downloads for the year.[128] Two other pioneering open access book publishers that also got their start in 2008 are Open Book Publishers and Open Humanities Press, both of which are based in the United Kingdom. In 2009, Open Humanities Press partnered with the University of Michigan Library's Scholarly Publishing Office to launch several new open access monographic series in the humanities.[129] Other notable milestones in the history of open access monograph publishing include the founding of the Radical Open Access Collective in 2015 and the aforementioned TOME (Toward an Open Monograph Ecosystem) in 2016. Declaring the business model for publishing monographs in the humanities and social sciences to be "broken," TOME's stated intention is to move "toward a new, more sustainable system in which monograph publishing costs are met by institutionally funded faculty book subsidies."[130]

TOME's institutional-subsidy funding model is one of many used to underwrite the costs of publishing open access scholarly monographs. A report from the Community-led Open Publication Infrastructures for Monographs (COPIM) published in 2020 identifies eighteen separate models for funding open access scholarly books.[131] Grants constitute one important source of funding for open access book publishing. In 2015, the National Endowment for the Humanities and the Mellon Foundation began awarding grants to "give a second life to outstanding out-of-print books in the humanities."[132] Other initiatives have been funded by organizational partners, including academic libraries, investing in the creation of digital books that are open to all, with Knowledge Unlatched's Subscribe to Open (see above), punctum books, and MIT Press's Direct to Open serving as examples of the organizational-partner approach. Unglue.it has used the crowdfunding approach to convert existing works to open access.[133] University presses have experimented with various hybrid models involving a mix of traditional sales and open access. The University of California Press's Luminos imprint, launched in 2015, underwrites the publication of new open access monographs through a combination of contributions from library partners and institutional funds raised by authors; as of 2023, the Luminos catalog listed over 170 open access titles.[134] Cambridge University Press's Flip It Open program converts scholarly books to open access once a title has earned a designated amount of revenue; as of 2023, Flip It Open had resulted in 100 high-demand titles moving to open access status.[135]

As a way of keeping down the cost of scholarly books, many publishers have moved to print-on-demand models, in which digital formats of books are offered online—freely in the case of open access books—while printed copies are produced only when ordered by a paying customer. A 2021 survey of twenty-five scholarly presses finds, "Most publishers report that more than 75% of their monograph sales are made of books that are printed on demand."[136] Regardless of whether physical copies are printed on demand or in traditional print runs, there is some evidence that readers will purchase physical copies of scholarly books in spite of access to free digital copies.[137] This phenomenon may well be due to nothing more mysterious than reader preference for printed copies of long-form works. Even so, the economic viability of hybrid models, in which digital copies are free and print copies come with a price tag, remains unproven. In summing up the hybrid print/digital model, the COPIM report states, "At present it is impossible to draw any definitive conclusions as to its future viability, with or without OA."[138]

The number of initiatives launched in support of open access monograph publishing coupled with the sheer number of titles published constitute solid evidence that publishing open access monographs has moved beyond the stage of tentative experiment. In one of the strongest endorsements to date, UK Research and Innovation (UKRI) announced in August 2021 that all monographs, book chapters, and edited collections funded by UKRI would be required to be published open access.[139] In spite of many signs of progress, open access publishing constitutes a small slice of the total monograph pie. As of 2023, the Directory of Open Access Books (DOAB) lists 76,500 academic peer-reviewed books.[140] These DOAB titles, the cumulative output of multiple years of open access publishing, amount to nearly 10,000 fewer titles than the estimated 86,000 monographs published worldwide every year.[141] The open access scholarly monograph has some catching up to do if it is to become the dominant form of long-form scholarly communication.

Other Long-Form Publications

In addition to scholarly monographs, edited collections, reference works, conference proceedings, and dissertations and theses have all been published in open access formats. Academic libraries have taken a lead role in publishing electronic dissertations and theses (ETDs) in open access formats. By 2023, Open Access Theses and Dissertations had indexed 6,810,395 open access ETDs from over 1100 colleges, universities, and research institutions worldwide.[142] The open educational resources movement has championed the replacement of commercial textbooks (and other educational materials) with open access alternatives that lower costs for students while providing more equitable access to essential course materials. Examples of major sources for open access textbooks include MERLOT,[143] the Open Textbook Library,[144] and OpenStax.[145]

Has Open Access Revolution Been a Success?

In 2012, Peter Suber wrote, "The idea [of OA] is to stop thinking of knowledge as a commodity to meter out to deserving customers, and to start thinking of it as a public good, especially when it is given away by its authors, funded with public money, or both."[146] At least within academia, those who are opposed to or dismissive of the open access revolution tend to have no problem with the idea of transforming knowledge into a public good; rather, their problem is that they see open access as having failed to achieve its goals, with some believing that open access is ultimately doomed to fail.

Whether the open access revolution is seen as succeeding or failing depends in part on the measures used to evaluate it. One obvious metric involves counting the total number of open access publications available. For the journal literature, coming up with a figure to show how much of the output is open versus how much is behind a paywall is not a simple calculation. A study published in 2018 finds that, of 300,000 articles examined, "28% of all journal articles are freely available online."[147] The authors of a different study published in 2022 find that estimates for the amount of scholarly literature that is open access range "from 27.9% to 53.7%, depending on the data source and period of investigation."[148] Taking 28 percent (the ballpark lower end of the numbers arrived at in both studies) as a conservative estimate, it remains in the eye of the beholder as to whether this represents a significant achievement or a sign of failure. In terms of sheer numbers of articles, as of 2023 Unpaywall—a database that harvests open access content from thousands of publishers and repositories—was providing access to "48,684,380 free scholarly articles."[149] Percentages of the total output aside, a number approaching fifty million is hard to brush off as a complete failure. For scholarly books, accurately estimating the percentage of the total output that is open is similarly challenging. One estimate for the monographic output of American university presses in 2022 comes up with a discouraging figure of only 5 percent to 10 percent of those titles being published open access.[150]

For users of academic libraries, rather than percentages or grand totals, the thing that matters is whether or not they are able to access the information they need for their studies and research. And in whatever way you interpret the data, there is no getting around the fact that the open access revolution has, thus far, fallen short of the goal of universal access to all knowledge. In December 2023, journalist Richard Poynder declared the open access movement a failure for having not achieved the three main goals of accessibility, affordability, and equity as well as for having allowed scholarly publishers to co-opt the movement through the dominance of gold open access and APCs. Specifically, Poynder characterizes 2023's "Towards Responsible Publishing: A Proposal from cOAlition S" as an indication that "OA is again becoming a bottom-up voluntarist movement" rather than a unified effort with the power to effect significant change in scholarly publishing.[151] Those in the trenches of the open access revolution might counter Poynder by arguing that open access already has effected significant change in scholarly publishing and is on a trajectory to do even more. The opinions of true believers and skeptics notwithstanding, whether the ongoing open access revolution goes down in history as a triumph, a failure, or something in between remains to be seen. Most likely, an unknowable number of years have yet to pass before the final chapter of the open access revolution can be written.

Notes

1. Peter Suber, *Open Access*, MIT Press Essential Knowledge Series (Cambridge, MA: MIT Press, 2012), 4, https://direct.mit.edu/books/oa-monograph/3754/Open-Access.
2. Avi Hyman, "Twenty Years of ListServ as an Academic Tool," *The Internet and Higher Education* 6, no. 1 (January 2003): 18–19.
3. Willard McCarty, "HUMANIST: Lessons from a Global Electronic Seminar," *Computers and the Humanities* 26, no. 3 (June 1992): 209.
4. Ann Okerson, "Are We There Yet? Online E-Resources Ten Years After," *Library Trends* 48, no. 4 (Spring 2000): 673.
5. Toni Feder, "Joanne Cohn and the Email List That Led to arXiv," *Physics Today*, November 8, 2021, https://doi.org/10.1063/PT.6.4.20211108a.
6. Stevan Harnad, "Subversive Proposal," Electronic Mail, June 27, 1994, https://eprints.soton.ac.uk/253351/1/subversive.pdf.
7. Lindsay Cronk, "Resourcefully: Let's End the Serials Crisis," *The Serials Librarian* 79, no. 1–2 (August 17, 2020): 78–81.
8. Glenn S. McGuigan and Robert D. Russell, "The Business of Academic Publishing: A Strategic Analysis of the Academic Journal Publishing Industry and Its Impact on the Future of Scholarly Publishing," *Electronic Journal of Academic and Special Librarianship* 9, no. 3 (Winter 2009), https://southernlibrarianship.icaap.org/content/v09n03/mcguigan_g01.html.
9. "Apple's Gross Margin Percentage (2000–2021)," Global Data, https://www.linkedin.com/company/globaldataplc/ (accessed November 8, 2023).
10. Allana G. LeBlanc et al., "Scientific Sinkhole: Estimating the Cost of Peer Review Based on Survey Data with Snowball Sampling," *Research Integrity and Peer Review* 8, no. 3 (April 24, 2023): 1–9.
11. Stephen Buranyi, "Is the Staggeringly Profitable Business of Scientific Publishing Bad for Science?," *The Guardian*, June 27, 2017, https://www.theguardian.com/science/2017/jun/27/profitable-business-scientific-publishing-bad-for-science.
12. Lee Van Orsdel and Kathleen Born, "Periodicals Price Survey 2003: Big Chill on the Big Deal?," *Library Journal* 128, no. 7 (April 15, 2003): 51–6.
13. "arXiv Annual Report 2020" (New York: Cornell University, 2020), 8, https://info.arxiv.org/about/reports/2020_arXiv_annual_report.pdf.
14. Richard Van Noorden, "The True Cost of Science Publishing," *Nature* 459 (March 28, 2013): 427.
15. "About CNI," CNI: Coalition for Networked Information, September 22, 2023, https://www.cni.org/about-cni.
16. Abel Laerte Packer, "SciELO-a Model for Cooperative Electronic Publishing in Developing Countries," *D-Lib Magazine*, 2000, https://www.dlib.org/dlib/october00/10inbrief.html#PACKER.
17. "SciELO Network," SciELO, August 28, 2023, https://scielo.org/en/about-scielo/scielo-network/.

18 John Berry et al., "ARL Venture Aims to Redefine Scholarly Publishing Model," *Library Journal* 123, no. 11 (June 15, 1998): 14.

19 Rick Johnson, "Scholarly Communication: SPARC and ACRL: Working Together to Reform Scholarly Communication," *College & Research Libraries News* 63, no. 9 (October 2002): 649, https://doi.org/10.5860/crln.63.9.648.

20 "The Santa Fe Convention for the Open Archives Initiative," Open Archives Initiative, February 15, 2000, https://www.openarchives.org/meetings/SantaFe1999/sfc_entry.htm.

21 "PKP Timeline," Public Knowledge Project, https://pkp.sfu.ca/about/timeline/ (accessed October 25, 2023).

22 Wallys W. Conhaim, "Creative Commons Nurtures the Public Domain," *Information Today* 19, no. 7 (August 2002): 52–4.

23 Ruth Mallalieu, "The Elusive Gold Mine? The Finer Details of Creative Commons Licences [Sic]– and Why They Really Matter," *Insights the UKSG Journal* 32 (January 3, 2019): 1, https://doi.org/10.1629/uksg.448.

24 Herbert Van de Sompel and Carl Lagoze, "The Open Archives Initiative Protocol for Metadata Harvesting," Open Archives Initiative, July 2, 2002, https://www.openarchives.org/OAI/1.1/openarchivesprotocol.htm.

25 "Sistema de Información Científica Redalyc, Red de Revistas Científicas," Redalyc.org, https://www.redalyc.org/home.oa (accessed October 25, 2023).

26 Suber, *Open Access*, 5.

27 "B16 Conference–OA2020," https://oa2020.org/b16-conference/ (accessed December 4, 2024).

28 "Open-Access-Tage in Berlin," *BuB: Forum Bibliothek Und Information* 60 (2008): 634, https://zs.thulb.uni-jena.de/servlets/MCRFileNodeServlet/jportal_derivate_00321837/BuB_2008_09_634.pdf.

29 Mary Curran, "Open Access Day 2008: Movement Building in a Web 2.0 World," *The Serials Librarian* 57, no. 1–2 (July 20, 2009): 34–9.

30 Mikael Laakso et al., "The Development of Open Access Journal Publishing from 1993 to 2009," ed. Marcelo Hermes-Lima, *PLoS ONE* 6, no. 6 (June 13, 2011): e20961, https://doi.org/10.1371/journal.pone.0020961.

31 Tony Delamothe, "NIH Outlines Strategy for Electronic Database," *BMJ: British Medical Journal (International Edition)* 318, no. 7192 (May 1, 1999): 1165, https://doi.org/10.1136/bmj.318.7192.1165b.

32 Vincent Kiernan, "NIH Proceeds with On-Line Archive for Papers in the Life Sciences," *Chronicle of Higher Education*, September 10, 1999.

33 Robin Peek, "Two Initiatives Support PubMed Central Model," *Information Today* 17, no. 3 (March 2000): 3.

34 Bo-Christer Björk, "Have the 'Mega-Journals' Reached the Limits to Growth?," *PeerJ* 3 (May 26, 2015): e981, https://doi.org/10.7717/peerj.981.

35 Matthew Cockerill, "The Economics of Open Access Publishing," *Information Services & Use* 26, no. 2 (April 2006): 153, https://doi.org/10.3233/ISU-2006-26221.

36 Barbara Quint, "BioMed Central Begins Charging Authors and Their Institutions for Article Publishing," *Information Today*, January 7, 2002, https://newsbreaks.infotoday.com/NewsBreaks

/BioMed-Central-Begins-Charging-Authors-and-Their-Institutions-for-Article-Publishing-17276.asp.

37. "BMC, Research in Progress," BioMed Central, https://www.biomedcentral.com/ (accessed December 5, 2024).

38. Robin Peek and Paula J. Hane, "The Future of the Public Library of Science," *Information Today* 19, no. 2 (February 2002): 28.

39. Vicki Brower, "Public Library of Science Shifts Gears: As Scientific Publishing Boycott Deadline Approached, Advocates of Free Scientific Publishing Announce That They Will Create Their Own Online, Free-access Archive," *EMBO Reports* 2, no. 11 (November 2001): 972, https://doi.org/10.1093/embo-reports/kve239.

40. Catriona J. MacCallum, "Why ONE Is More Than 5," *PLoS Biology* 9, no. 12 (December 20, 2011): e1001235, https://doi.org/10.1371/journal.pbio.1001235.

41. Stephen Pinfield, "Mega-Journals: The Future, a Stepping Stone to It or a Leap into the Abyss?," *Times Higher Education (THE)*, October 13, 2016, https://www.timeshighereducation.com/blog/mega-journals-future-stepping-stone-it-or-leap-abyss.

42. Ramesh Pandita and Shivendra Singh, "A Study of Distribution and Growth of Open Access Research Journals Across the World," *Publishing Research Quarterly* 38, no. 1 (March 2022): 134, https://doi.org/10.1007/s12109-022-09860-x.

43. Myer Kutz, "The Scholars Rebellion Against Scholarly Publishing Practices: Varmus, Vitek, and Venting," *Searcher*, January 2002, https://www.infotoday.com/searcher/jan02/kutz.htm.

44. Sally Morris, "What's so Special about Not-for-Profit Publishers?," *Learned Publishing* 14, no. 3 (July 2001): 164, https://doi.org/10.1087/095315101750240403.

45. Barbara Quint, "Future of the NIH Open Access Policy," *Information Today* 21, no. 9 (October 2004): 7.

46. Andrew Albanese, "Publishers Protest at NIH," *Library Journal* 129, no. 14 (September 1, 2004): 17.

47. Lee C. Van Orsdel and Kathleen Born, "Periodical Price Survey 2005: Choosing Sides," *Library Journal* 130, no. 7 (April 15, 2005): 47.

48. Lee C. Van Orsdel and Kathleen Born, "Periodicals Price Survey 2006: Journals in the Time of Google," *Library Journal* 131, no. 7 (April 15, 2006): 40.

49. Jim Giles, "PR's 'Pit Bull' Takes on Open Access," *Nature* 445 (January 25, 2007): 347.

50. Lee C. Van Orsdel and Kathleen Born, "Periodicals Price Survey 2007: Serial Wars," *Library Journal* 132, no. 7 (April 15, 2007): 48.

51. Mark Chillingworth, "Open Access Is Branded 'Junk Science' by US Lobby," *Information World Review*, no. 238 (September 2007): 1.

52. Mark Chillingworth, "Scientists, Publishers and Authors Rage against PRISM," *Information World Review*, no. 239 (October 2007): 3.

53. "AAP Tones down Language in Anti-Open-Access Lobbying Campaign," *Newsletter on Intellectual Freedom* 56, no. 6 (November 2007): 238, https://alair.ala.org/handle/11213/12560.

54. Michael Stebbins, "Expanding Public Access to the Results of Federally Funded Research," whitehouse.gov, February 22, 2013, https://obamawhitehouse.archives.gov/blog/2013/02/22/expanding-public-access-results-federally-funded-research.

55 "White House Issues Public Access Directive," PublishersWeekly.com, February 22, 2013, https://www.publishersweekly.com/pw/by-topic/digital/copyright/article/56076-in-historic-act-obama-administration-issues-public-access-directive.html.

56 Stephen Bosch, Kittie Henderson, and Heather Klusendorf, "Periodicals Price Survey 2011: Under Pressure, Times Are Changing," *Library Journal* 136, no. 8 (May 1, 2011): 33.

57 Lee C. Van Orsdel and Kathleen Born, "Periodicals Price Survey 2008: Embracing Openness: Global Initiatives and Startling Successes Hint at the Profound Implications of Open Access on Journal Publishing," *Library Journal* 133, no. 7 (April 15, 2008): 58.

58 University of California Office of Scholarly Communication, "UC and Elsevier: FAQs," *Office of Scholarly Communication* (blog), March 1, 2019, https://osc.universityofcalifornia.edu/2019/03/uc-and-elsevier-faqs/.

59 Yrjo Lappalainen and Nikesh Narayanan, "Harvesting Publication Data to the Institutional Repository from Scopus, Web of Science, Dimensions and Unpaywall Using a Custom R Script," *The Journal of Academic Librarianship* 49, no. 1 (January 2023): 102653.

60 "OAIster: Catalog of Open Access Resources," OCLC, https://www.oclc.org/en/oaister.html (accessed December 20, 2023).

61 Ann Okerson and Alex Holzman, "The Once and Future Publishing Library" (Washington, DC: Council on Library and Information Resources, July 2015), 4–5, https://www.clir.org/wp-content/uploads/sites/6/pub166.pdf.

62 Laura Brown, Rebecca Griffiths, and Matthew Rascoff, "University Publishing in a Digital Age," ITHAKA Report (Ithaka S+R, July 26, 2007), 21–26, https://sr.ithaka.org/wp-content/uploads/2015/08/4.13.1.pdf.

63 Karla L. Hahn, "Research Library Publishing Services: New Options for University Publishing" (Association of Research Libraries, 2008), 13–17, https://www.arl.org/wp-content/uploads/2008/03/research-library-publishing-services-mar08.pdf.

64 Sarah K. Lippincott, ed., "Library Publishing Directory 2014" (Library Publishing Coalition, 2014), x, https://librarypublishing.org/wp-content/uploads/2017/03/LPC_LPDirectory2014.pdf.

65 The Library Publishing Coalition Directory Committee, ed., "Library Publishing Directory 2023" (Library Publishing Coalition, 2023), ix, https://librarypublishing.org/wp-content/uploads/2023/06/Library-Publishing-Directory_2023_web.pdf.

66 Email from Stevan Harnad to the author sent on April 17, 2023. In that same email, Harnad expresses some regret for having coined those terms.

67 Stevan Harnad et al., "The Access/Impact Problem and the Green and Gold Roads to Open Access," *Serials Review* 30, no. 4 (December 2004): 310–14, https://search.ebscohost.com/login.aspx?direct=true&db=lxh&AN=15623239&site=ehost-live.

68 S. S. Dhanavandan, "Open Access Repositories in the World: An Overview," *Library Philosophy and Practice*, no. 2805 (2020), https://digitalcommons.unl.edu/libphilprac/3805.

69 Ellen Dubinsky, "Does Open Access Make Cents? Return on Investment in the Institutional Repository," *College & Research Libraries News* 80, no. 5 (May 3, 2019): 281, https://doi.org/10.5860/crln.80.5.281.

70 Clifford A. Lynch, "Institutional Repositories: Essential Infrastructure for Scholarship in the Digital Age," A Bimonthly Report on Research Library Issues and Actions from ARL, CNI, and SPARC

(Association of Research Libraries, February 2003), 2, https://www.cni.org/publications/cliffs-pubs/institutional-repositories-infrastructure-for-scholarship.

71. Andrea M. Quinn, "Thinking beyond *If You Build It, They Will Come*: Increasing Submissions to Campus Institutional Repositories," *New Review of Academic Librarianship* 29, no. 1 (January 2, 2023): 97–115, https://doi.org/10.1080/13614533.2022.2082990.

72. Lappalainen and Narayanan, "Harvesting Publication Data," 102653.

73. Tom Scheiding, "Paying for Knowledge One Page at a Time: The Author Fee in Physics in Twentieth-Century America," *Historical Studies in the Natural Sciences* 39, no. 2 (May 1, 2009): 223–4.

74. Jeffrey Mackie-Mason, "Authors Have the Power, Let Them Use It: Rebuttal to David Shulenburger," *madLibbing* (blog), September 25, 2016, https://madlibbing.berkeley.edu/authors-have-the-power-let-them-use-it-rebuttal-to-david-shulenburger/.

75. David J. Solomon and Bo-Christer Björk, "A Study of Open Access Journals Using Article Processing Charges," *Journal of the American Society for Information Science and Technology* 63, no. 8 (August 2012): 1486.

76. "Directory of Open Access Journals," Directory of Open Access Journals–DOAJ, November 2, 2023, https://doaj.org/.

77. APC prices as reported in the Directory of Open Access Journals.

78. Heather Morrison et al., "Change and Growth in Open Access Journal Publishing and Charging Trends 2011–2021," *Journal of the Association for Information Science and Technology* 73, no. 12 (December 2022): 1802, https://doi.org/10.1002/asi.24717.

79. David J. Solomon and Bo-Christer Björk, "Publication Fees in Open Access Publishing: Sources of Funding and Factors Influencing Choice of Journal," *Journal of the American Society for Information Science and Technology* 63, no. 1 (January 2012): 98–107.

80. Solomon and Björk, "Publication Fees," 103.

81. Ángel Borrego, "Article Processing Charges for Open Access Journal Publishing: A Review," *Learned Publishing* 36, no. 3 (July 2023): 367–8, https://doi.org/10.1002/leap.1558.

82. MacKenzie Smith et al., "Pay It Forward: Investigating a Sustainable Model of Open Access Article Processing Charges for Large North American Research Institutions [Final Report]" (Oakland: UC Office of the President: University of California Systemwide Libraries, 2016), 7, https://escholarship.org/uc/item/8326n305.

83. Sumiko Asai, "Strategies to Increase the Number of Open Access Journals: The Cases of Elsevier and Springer Nature," *Journal of Scholarly Publishing* 53, no. 2 (February 1, 2022): 75–84, https://doi.org/10.3138/jsp.53.2.02.

84. David Druelinger and Lai Ma, "Missing a Golden Opportunity? An Analysis of Publication Trends by Income Level in the Directory of Open Access Journals 1987–2020," *Learned Publishing* 36, no. 3 (July 2023): 348–58, https://doi.org/10.1002/leap.1543.

85. Daniel Cressey, "Open Access: Are Publishers 'Double Dipping,'" Nature Publishing, *Nature Newsblog* (blog), October 29, 2009, https://blogs.nature.com/news/2009/10/story_landis_resigns_from_auti.html.

86. Sara L. Rizor and Robert P. Holley, "Open Access Goals Revisited: How Green and Gold Open Access Are Meeting (or Not) Their Original Goals," *Journal of Scholarly Publishing* 45, no. 4 (July 2014): 328, https://doi.org/10.3138/jsp.45.4.01.

87 Gunther Eysenback, "Black Sheep among Open Access Journals and Publishers," *Gunther Eysenbach Random Research Rants Blog* (blog), March 8, 2008, https://webcitation.org/5YlqkyRE4.

88 Christophe Dony et al., "How Reliable and Useful Is Cabell's Blacklist ? A Data-Driven Analysis," *LIBER Quarterly* 30 (September 10, 2020): 3, https://doi.org/10.18352/lq.10339.

89 Marydee Ojala, Regina Reynolds, and Kay G. Johnson, "Predatory Journal Challenges and Responses," *The Serials Librarian* 78, no. 1–4 (June 1, 2020): 98–103.

90 Henk F. Moed et al., "Journals in Beall's List Perform as a Group Less Well than Other Open Access Journals Indexed in Scopus but Reveal Large Differences among Publishers," *Learned Publishing* 35, no. 2 (April 2022): 131.

91 Brazilian Forum of Public Health Journals Editors and Associação Brasileira de Saúde Coletiva, "Motion to Repudiate Mr. Jeffrey Beall's Classist Attack on SciELO," *SciELO in Perspective* (blog), August 2, 2015, https://blog.scielo.org/en/2015/08/02/motion-to-repudiate-mr-jeffrey-bealls-classist-attack-on-scielo/.

92 "Guide to Applying," Directory of Open Access Journals–DOAJ, https://doaj.org/apply/guide/ (accessed October 12, 2023).

93 Carolann Lee Curry, "SHERPA Services and SHERPA/RoMEO," *Journal of Electronic Resources in Medical Libraries* 14, no. 3 (July 2017): 135–8.

94 "Identify Trusted Publishers for Your Research," Think. Check. Submit., https://thinkchecksubmit.org/ (accessed October 18, 2023).

95 Eamon Costello, "Bronze, Free, or Fourrée: An Open Access Commentary," *Science Editing* 6, no. 1 (February 20, 2019): 70, https://doi.org/10.6087/kcse.157.

96 Stephanie Normand, "Is Diamond Open Access the Future of Open Access?," *The iJournal* 3, no. 2 (2018): 4, https://theijournal.ca/index.php/ijournal/article/view/29482/21973.

97 Li Zhang and Erin Watson, "The Prevalence of Green and Grey Open Access: Where Do Physical Science Researchers Archive Their Publications?," *Scientometrics* 117, no. 3 (December 2018): 2023, https://doi.org/10.1007/s11192-018-2924-2.

98 Margaret Mering, "Open Access Mandates and Policies: The Basics," *Serials Review* 46, no. 2 (April 2, 2020): 157.

99 Select Committee on Science and Technology, "Scientific Publications: Free for All?: The Government Response" (U.K. Parliament, November 8, 2004), https://publications.parliament.uk/pa/cm200304/cmselect/cmsctech/1200/120003.htm.

100 Bobby Picketing, "Government Gives Thumbs down to Open Access," *Information World Review*, no. 208 (December 2004): 15.

101 Dame Janet Finch et al., "Accessibility, Sustainability, Excellence: How to Expand Access to Research Publications" (Report of the Working Group on Expanding Access to Published Research Findings, 2012), Zenodo: 7, https://doi.org/10.5281/zenodo.8229144.

102 Martin Hall, "Green or Gold? Open Access after Finch," *Insights: The UKSG Journal* 25, no. 3 (November 1, 2012): 237–9, https://doi.org/10.1629/2048-7754.25.3.235.

103 Steven Hall, "What Does Finch Mean for Researchers, Librarians and Publishers?," *Insights: The UKSG Journal* 25, no. 3 (November 1, 2012): 242, https://doi.org/10.1629/2048-7754.25.3.241.

104 2012/417/EU: Commission Recommendation of July 17, 2012 on access to and preservation of scientific information (July 21, 2012).

105   Max Planck Digital Library, "Expression of Interest in the Large-Scale Implementation of Open Access to Scholarly Journals," Open Access 2020, March 2016, https://oa2020.org/mission/.

106   Max Planck Digital Library, "OA2020 Roadmap" (Max Planck Digital Library, August 22, 2016), https://oa2020.org/wp-content/uploads/pdfs/OA2020-Roadmap.pdf.

107   Ralf Schimmer, "The Transformation of Scientific Journal Publishing: Open Access after the Berlin 12 Conference," *Information Services & Use* 37, no. 1 (March 7, 2017): 11, https://doi.org/10.3233/ISU-160808.

108   cOAlition S, "Plan S: Making Full & Immediate Open Access A Reality," March 2021, https://www.coalition-s.org/wp-content/uploads/2021/03/Plan-S_profile_March2021.pdf.

109   "cOAlition S Confirms the End of Its Financial Support for Open Access Publishing under Transformative Arrangements after 2024," Plan S, January 26, 2023, https://www.coalition-s.org/coalition-s-confirms-the-end-of-its-financial-support-for-open-access-publishing-under-transformative-arrangements-after-2024/.

110   Tania Rabesandratana, "Open-Access Plan Draws Online Protest," *Science*, November 8, 2018, https://doi.org/10.1126/science.aav9991.

111   Shaun Yon-Seng Khoo, "The Plan S Rights Retention Strategy Is an Administrative and Legal Burden, Not a Sustainable Open Access Solution," *Insights: The UKSG Journal* 34, no. 1 (2021): 1, https://doi.org/10.1629/uksg.556.

112   cOAlition S and Max Planck Digital Library, "Joint Statement of OA2020 and cOAlition S: Research Performing and Research Funding Organizations Working Together to Accelerate the Transition to Open Access," May 2019, https://oa2020.org/wp-content/uploads/pdfs/joint-statement-oa2020-coalition-s.pdf.

113   cOAlition S, "Towards Responsible Publishing: A Proposal from cOAlition S," October 31, 2023, https://doi.org/10.5281/zenodo.8398480.

114   ESAC, "Transformative Agreements," ESAC, https://esac-initiative.org/about/transformative-agreements/ (accessed December 4, 2023).

115   Ralf Schimmer, Kai Karin Geschuhn, and Andreas Vogler, "Disrupting the Subscription Journals' Business Model for the Necessary Large-Scale Transformation to Open Access" (München, Germany: Max Planck Digital Library, April 28, 2015), 2, https://pure.mpg.de/pubman/faces/ViewItemOverviewPage.jsp?itemId=item_2148961.

116   Schimmer, Geschuhn, and Vogler, "Disrupting the Subscription Journals' Business Model," 11.

117   "ESAC Transformative Agreement Registry–ESAC Initiative," ESAC, https://esac-initiative.org/about/transformative-agreements/agreement-registry/ (accessed December 4, 2023).

118   George Machovec, "Strategies for Transformational Publish and Read Agreements in North America," *Journal of Library Administration* 59, no. 5 (July 4, 2019): 551–2.

119   Nina Leonie Weisweiler, "Im Spannungsfeld zwischen Zweckrationalität und Idealismus–Eine Analyse des Fachdiskurses zu Projekt DEAL mit Fokus auf den Begriff 'Open Access,'" *Between Pragmatism and Idealism–A Discourse Analysis on Project DEAL with Focus on the Term "Open Access,"* 45, no. 1 (April 2021): 164, https://doi.org/10.1515/bfp-2020-0116.

120   Fay Brigham, "MIT and Royal Society of Chemistry Sign First North American 'Read and Publish' Agreement for Scholarly Articles," *MIT Libraries News & Events* (blog), June 14, 2018, https://libraries.mit.edu/news/royal-society-chemistry-3/27769/.

121 "Cambridge University Press and the University of California Agree to Open Access Publishing Deal," *Office of Scholarly Communication* (blog), April 10, 2019, https://osc.universityofcalifornia.edu/2019/04/cambridge-uc/.

122 Ashley Farley et al., "Transformative Agreements: Six Myths, Busted," *College & Research Libraries News*, August 2021, https://crln.acrl.org/index.php/crlnews/article/viewFile/25032/32907.

123 Alison Mudditt, "Transitional Agreements Aren't Working: What Comes Next?," *The Scholarly Kitchen* (blog), April 4, 2024, https://scholarlykitchen.sspnet.org/2024/04/04/transitional-agreements-arent-working-what-comes-next/.

124 "ARL Statistics 2007-2008" (Washington, DC: Association of Research Libraries, 2009), 10, https://publications.arl.org/ARL-Statistics-2007-2008/1.

125 "STM Global Brief 2021–Economics & Market Size" (STM: International Association of Scientific, Technical and Medical Publishers, 2021), 6, https://www.stm-assoc.org/2022_08_24_STM_White_Report_a4_v15.pdf.

126 Albert N. Greco, "Academic Libraries and the Economics of Scholarly Publishing in the Twenty-First Century: Portfolio Theory, Product Differentiation, Economic Rent, Perfect Price Discrimination, and the Cost of Prestige," *Journal of Scholarly Publishing* 47, no. 1 (October 2015): 1–43.

127 Nancy Maron and Kimberly Schmelzinger, "The Cost to Publish TOME Monographs" (New York: Association of University Presses, 2022), 6, https://doi.org/10.18665/sr.276785.

128 "OAPEN Foundation: Stakeholder Report 2022," Annual Report (The Hague: OAPEN Foundation, 2022), https://fra1.digitaloceanspaces.com/oapen/dd478f92d96840c29ef13c409dc7a7f5.pdf.

129 "New Open Access Series from Open Humanities Press and U-Mich Library's Scholarly Publishing Office," *D-Lib Magazine* 15, no. 9/10 (October 2009), https://www.dlib.org/dlib/september09/09inbrief.html#NEWS.

130 "About," TOME: Toward an Open Monograph Ecosystem, https://www.openmonographs.org/about/ (accessed December 16, 2023).

131 Izabella Penier, Martin Paul Eve, and Tom Grady, "COPIM–Revenue Models for Open Access Monographs 2020" (Community-led Open Publication Infrastructures for Monographs, September 7, 2020), https://doi.org/10.5281/ZENODO.4011836.

132 "National Endowment for the Humanities and the Mellon Foundation Announce New Grants to Bring Back Essential Out-of-Print Books," The National Endowment for the Humanities, December 17, 2015, https://www.neh.gov/news/press-release/2015-12-17.

133 Angela Chen, "Start-Up Hopes to Create Free Digital Versions of Published Books," *The Chronicle of Higher Education*, June 19, 2019.

134 "UC Press Luminos," University of California Press: Luminos, https://www.luminosoa.org/site/ (accessed December 16, 2023).

135 Alison A. Trotta, "Cambridge University Press' OA Monograph Program Expands," *Computers in Libraries* 43, no. 1 (February 2023): 29.

136 Philip Shaw, Angus Phillips, and Maria Bajo Gutiérrez, "The Death of the Monograph?," *Publishing Research Quarterly* 38, no. 2 (June 2022): 390, https://doi.org/10.1007/s12109-022-09885-2.

137. Paul N. Courant and Elizbeth A. Jones, "Scholarly Publishing as an Economic Public Good," in *Getting the Word Out: Academic Libraries as Scholarly Publishers*, ed. Maria Bonn and Mike Furlough (Chicago: Association of College and Research Libraries, 2015), 39.

138. Penier, Eve, and Grady, "COPIM–Revenue Models," 26.

139. Judith Fathallah, "Open Access Monographs: Myths, Truths and Implications in the Wake of UKRI Open Access Policy," *LIBER Quarterly: The Journal of the Association of European Research Libraries* 32, no. 1 (February 2, 2022), https://doi.org/10.53377/lq.11068.

140. "Directory of Open Access Books," Directory of Open Access Books (DOAB), https://www.doabooks.org/ (accessed December 16, 2023).

141. Sara Grimme et al., "The State of Open Monographs," Digital Science Report (Digital Science, June 2019), 7, https://doi.org/10.6084/m9.figshare.8197625.v4.

142. "Open Access Theses and Dissertations," OATD.org, https://oatd.org/ (accessed December 20, 2023).

143. "MERLOT," MERLOT, https://www.merlot.org/merlot/ (accessed December 5, 2024).

144. "Open Textbook Library," Open Textbook Library, https://open.umn.edu/opentextbooks (accessed December 5, 2024).

145. "OpenStax | Free Textbooks Online with No Catch," OpenStax, https://openstax.org/ (accessed December 5, 2024).

146. Suber, *Open Access*, 116.

147. Heather Piwowar et al., "The State of OA: A Large-Scale Analysis of the Prevalence and Impact of Open Access Articles," *PeerJ* 6 (February 13, 2018): e4375, https://doi.org/10.7717/peerj.4375.

148. Isabel Basson et al., "The Effect of Data Sources on the Measurement of Open Access: A Comparison of Dimensions and the Web of Science," ed. Frank Havemann, *PLOS ONE* 17, no. 3 (March 31, 2022): e0265545, https://doi.org/10.1371/journal.pone.0265545.

149. "Unpaywall," Unpaywall, https://unpaywall.org/ (accessed November 15, 2023).

150. Curtis Brundy et al., "Open Access to University Press Frontlists: A Call to Action," *The Scholarly Kitchen* (blog), September 20, 2023, https://scholarlykitchen.sspnet.org/2023/09/20/guest-post-open-access-to-university-press-frontlists-a-call-to-action/.

151. Rick Anderson, "Where Did the Open Access Movement Go Wrong?: An Interview with Richard Poynder," *The Scholarly Kitchen*, December 7, 2023, https://scholarlykitchen.sspnet.org/2023/12/07/where-did-the-open-access-movement-go-wrong-an-interview-with-richard-poynder/.

4 From the Card Catalog to the Semantic Web

The Digital Odessey of Cataloging and Technical Services

In 1957, the American Library Association (ALA) launched its Resources and Technical Services Division (RTSD) with the goal of better representing the interests of everyone involved in cataloging and classification, acquisitions, and serials, all of which had previously been represented by separate, smaller subgroups within ALA's organizational structure.[1] In the winter of 1957, RTSD published the first issue of *Library Resources & Technical Services* (*LRTS*), a new journal born of two preexisting publications, *Serial Slants* and the *Journal of Cataloging and Classification*. In its first issue, *LRTS*'s founding editor promises readers that, going forward, the new journal will provide a publishing platform not just for librarians interested in cataloging and serials but also for "the newer sections joining the Division (such as acquisitions) who have not previously had an organ of their own."[2]

Obviously, the phrase *technical services* appears in both the name of the new division and the title of the new journal. Less obvious is the fact that grouping a set of once-distinct library services under the unifying banner of *technical services* was still a somewhat recent practice in 1957. Less than ten years earlier, six papers on the then-controversial topic of libraries forming technical-service departments had been presented at the June 1948 meeting of the ALA Division of Cataloging and Classification held in Atlantic City, New Jersey. In summing up these six papers, Richard H. Logsdon (1912–1997) writes, "There is a definite trend toward grouping the functions of acquisitions, cataloging, binding and related activities into technical departments or divisions."[3] In an article published in 1950, Edwin B. Colburn describes the formation of technical-services departments as "a comparatively new development, having taken place largely within the past 10 years," while also acknowledging that "considerable discussion has arisen concerning the advisability of establishing such units, the purposes they are intended to serve, and the benefits to be derived from them."[4] At the very least, it seems safe to conclude that the normalization of technical services as a department, division, or other unit within the library organizational structure post-dates the end of the Second World War. For example, a report of the University of Notre Dame Library published in 1952 includes a section describing technical services as those units that "perform a series of related operations having to do with the acquisition of books, periodicals, and other library materials, and with the cataloging and classification of these materials to make them readily available to readers."[5]

Even though the principal elements that constitute nearly all technical-services units had existed in libraries since long before the mid-point of the twentieth century, it makes sense that it was in the late 1940s and early 1950s when librarians first began to recognize the value of grouping these services together. Whereas in the decades prior to the Second World War many academic libraries—in particular, college libraries—were small enough that acquisitions might have been handled by the head librarian (with varying degrees of control ceded to faculty), and cataloging may have been the responsibility (full- or part-time) of a single librarian, the rapid expansion of U.S. academic library collections taking hold in the late 1940s required entire teams of librarians and non-librarian staff to manage the acquisitions and cataloging workload. Consolidating a library's infrastructure services into a combined technical-services department ensured those services could be well coordinated and effectively managed by a dedicated department head rather than being loosely overseen by a head librarian with too many distractions and, quite possibly, not much experience in the increasingly complex postwar arena of technical services. Besides growing in size, postwar collections were growing in variety and complexity. By the 1960s, a large academic library might employ not only multiple book catalogers and affiliated classified staff but also catalogers and classified staff specializing in rare books, visual media, music, maps, and government documents. The rapid postwar growth of journal collections meant not only more jobs for serials catalogers but also more jobs for technical-services classified staff to manage the daily grind of checking-in issues received, claiming missing issues, shelving and reshelving current periodicals, and binding old issues. Considering that it was the late 1950s when the Library of Congress first began investigating the possibility of using computers as a means of making library processes more efficient, the postwar momentum toward forming technical-services departments proved timely.[6] The first computer systems to make their way into libraries were developed as tools to support technical-services functions, and as a result, the first cohort of what would come to be known as *systems librarians* came largely from the ranks of technical-services departments. Possibly the first article to identify someone as a "systems librarian" is a 1976 profile of Harvard Libraries' Ron Diener, a former cataloger.[7] Libraries likely would have automated without the advantage provided by unified technical-services departments, but the process probably would have taken longer and cost more.

Cataloging: Tradition and Transition

From roughly the last quarter of the nineteenth century to the ascendancy of automated library systems, the primary job of catalogers was producing cards to be filed in the local card catalog. Early on, catalog cards were drafted using "library hand," a flowing script that was at one time taught to every library-school student; eventually, catalog cards would be produced on typewriters and then on computer printers, with the first computer-printed cards being produced as early as 1964.[8] Besides creating new cards, librarian catalogers and classified staff were also responsible for maintaining the physical card catalog, a quotidian chore which included keeping cards filed in the correct order, fixing errors on/updating existing cards, removing cards when items were weeded from the collection, and replacing missing or damaged cards.

Because the scope of every card catalog was, inevitably, the local collection, the focus of every library's cataloging workforce was on providing intellectual access to the finite set of physical objects held by the library in which they were employed. The stipulation found in the *Anglo-American Cataloging Rules* that calls for a catalog record's main entry to be derived from the "work in hand" reflects traditional cataloging's focus on physical objects as containers of information.[9] Each physical object in a library collection was typically represented in the card catalog by a title card, one or more author cards, and one or more subject cards. In addition, local card catalogs also contained cross-reference cards intended to help information seekers find their way among thousands, if not millions, of cards. For example, a user looking through a card catalog for books about twentieth-century art might find a "See also" card listing such alternative subject headings as "Art, Abstract," "Cubism," and "Op Art." The size of many card catalogs had grown to become nearly unmanageable by the final decades of the twentieth century. When the University of Virginia's Alderman Library closed its card catalog in 1989, its public catalog contained 4,000,000 cards.[10] When Princeton University's Firestone Library closed its public card catalog in 1981, it held an estimated 6,000,000 cards.[11] In addition to card catalogs intended for public use, libraries also routinely maintained backroom shelf-list catalogs in which cards were filed in the same order as the items in the stacks. It is not surprising to learn that, by the time the online public access catalog (OPAC) was coming to the fore, libraries were running out of space for card catalogs.[12]

Traditionally, one key responsibility of catalogers was assigning a call number to each item added to the collection, a task complicated by the fact that, while any book or other item might touch on a variety of subjects, each physical object in a collection can be assigned only one call number. When assigning call numbers, almost all U.S. academic libraries employed, and still employ, Library of Congress Classification (LCC), a system developed in 1897. A small number of academic libraries employed, and still employ, Dewey Decimal Classification, a system first published in 1876 that remains in wide use among U.S. public libraries. Somewhat astoundingly, a survey published in 2018 finds that a few U.S. academic libraries split their collections between Dewey and LC call numbers.[13] Besides Dewey and LC, two other call-number systems commonly found in U.S. academic libraries are Superintendent of Documents Classification (assigned to U.S. government documents) and National Library of Medicine Classification (employed chiefly by biomedical libraries).

Another traditional higher-level responsibility of catalogers has been the assigning of subject headings to items in a collection. For over a century, the Library of Congress Subject Headings (LCSH) have dominated subject cataloging in U.S. academic libraries. LCSH has undergone frequent revisions over the years, both to add new subjects and to revise subject headings as usage has evolved. For example, at one time the now-offensive term "spastics" was an approved Library of Congress subject heading for works about persons afflicted with cerebral palsy. The process of changing, or not changing, the subject headings included in LCSH can be controversial. In 2016, three Members of Congress from Texas objected to the Library of Congress eliminating the subject headings "illegal alien" and "alien" from LCSH.[14] One exception to the use of official LCSH has been the common practice of assigning local subject headings to highlight an item's special characteristics that cannot be expressed using only LCSH. While in theory a resource may be assigned any number of subject headings, the Library of Congress's quasi-official "20% Rule" stipulates that when subject headings for a specific, as opposed to a general, aspect of a resource are assigned, that aspect must constitute "at least 20 percent of the resource."[15] An informal cataloging rule of thumb has it that when assigning subject headings "one to six is fairly standard, but a cataloger may go up to 10 headings if necessary."[16]

Because having thousands of librarians around the country independently catalog the same book has never been efficient, the idea of sharing the work among multiple libraries has a long history. In an issue of *American Library Journal* dated September 30, 1876, Melvil Dewey addresses the topic of shared cataloging, writing of "the vast economy of labor and patience which would be brought about if the cataloging of libraries could be done on some good plan of co-operation."[17] In 1901, the Library of Congress advanced the cause of shared cataloging when it began selling pre-printed catalog cards, providing libraries with an option far less costly than paying an in-house cataloger to analyze a book and create a card from scratch. A further aid to U.S. cataloging was the Library of Congress's implementation of Cataloging in Publication (CIP) in 1971. CIP calls for the Library of Congress to work with publishers to prepare catalog information for books prior to their publication and for publishers to print that information on the verso of the title page in a format similar to that of a catalog card.[18]

The transition of cataloging away from long-standing practices rooted in the card catalog had its origins in the development of the MARC record in the mid-1960s but really took off in the early 1970s when it became possible for a library employee sitting at a terminal to perform copy cataloging via a bibliographic utility such as OCLC. As early adopters of digital technology, library catalogers were among the first professional groups to discover that the reward for adopting digital technology has been, very often, to see the services they formerly provided devalued and the status of their profession marginalized. The advent of copy cataloging meant work that had once been the exclusive domain of professional catalogers holding graduate degrees in library science could be performed at lower cost by classified staff (also known as *paraprofessionals*).

Classified staff eventually moved beyond copy cataloging to increasingly stake claims to the once-sacred ground of original cataloging. A 1995 survey of the Association of Research Libraries (ARL) reports that "64 libraries (77.1% of those responding) had paraprofessional employees who performed some original cataloging tasks, while 19 (22.9%) did not."[19] These numbers are especially telling considering that the idea of classified staff doing any cataloging whatsoever was essentially unheard of before 1970.[20] Digital technology not only de-professionalized both copy and original cataloging but also increased worker productivity to the point that libraries could get by with smaller cataloging workforces. A study published in 1998 reports that, over the previous five to ten years, only 18 percent of the libraries surveyed reported increases in the number of professional cataloging staff, while 46.4 percent reported no change and 39.3 percent reported decreases; the same study reported similar numbers for classified staff working in cataloging units.[21] A survey of professional job advertisements in *College & Research Libraries News*, the primary national outlet for advertising open positions in academic libraries, looked at a total of 4,036 professional library jobs advertised in seven sample years spanning 1975 to 2005. In 1975, of 311 jobs advertised, 18.3 percent (57 jobs) were cataloger positions; by 1990, of 823 jobs advertised, 15.6 percent (128 jobs) were cataloger positions; and by 2005, of 380 jobs advertised, 6.8 percent (26 jobs) were cataloger positions.[22] Taking a dark, but hardly unreasonable, view of the situation, in 1992 Roma Harris submitted the proposition that the de-professionalization of library cataloging was rooted not only in changing technology but also in the fact that the cataloging workforce was largely female.[23] While it is likely that the silent power of institutional sexism influenced staffing decisions, the more visible force at work was economic: libraries facing tight budgets and forced reorganizations increasingly came to see cataloging positions as expendable. For example, within eight years of a library-wide reorganization, the University of Arizona Library workforce had come to consist of "fewer classified staff in cataloging and no full-time professional catalogers."[24] In summing up the state of cataloging as a profession, Joan M. Leysen and Jeanne M. K. Boydston conclude that, as of 2005, the number of catalogers in academic libraries was at best not growing or at worst declining, and that "Recruiting for professional cataloging positions continues to be difficult."[25]

Another economic force at play in the downsizing of both cataloging and technical-services workforces was the practice of outsourcing work that had once been carried out in-house. For an extreme example, in September 1993, Wright State University shut down its entire cataloging department and began outsourcing all cataloging to OCLC's TECH-PRO service.[26] While other examples tend to be less extreme, it became increasingly common for libraries to carry out cataloging operations via mixtures of in-house and outsourced options. The abovementioned University of Arizona Library coped with the downsizing of its cataloging workforce by employing copy cataloging to process as many foreign-language books as possible while outsourcing the cataloging of the remainder.[27] By the mid-1990s, another outsourcing option was to purchase shelf-ready books that arrive at the library pre-cataloged.[28] Besides arriving fully cataloged, shelf-ready books could also come fully processed, with barcodes, labels, property stamps, and security tags already in place.

The practice of outsourcing was not without controversy. In a 1995 article provocatively entitled "The Corruption of Cataloging," Michael Gorman condemns "philistine administrators" for "the gutting and closing of catalog departments" and warns that the outsourcing of cataloging will result in the library losing control over "one of its three greatest assets: a coherent local database."[29] In a counterpoint article to "The Corruption of Cataloging," Glen Holt weighs both the advantages and limitations of outsourcing, posing in the process the two central questions underlying the entire outsourcing debate: "Will outsourced cataloging really be cheaper? Will the cataloging be customized (i.e., detailed in the way that system operation requires) to a level that justifies the cost?"[30] While the answers to each of Holt's questions have never been resolved to the satisfaction of all, the realpolitik of downsized staff left many libraries with no choice other than to outsource at least some technical-services functions, cataloging included.

Acquisitions and Collection Development: Tradition and Transition

In the academic library, there have long existed sometimes messy, sometimes nonexistent boundaries between acquisitions and collection development (also known as *collection management*). The 1996 article "Sleeping with the Enemy: The Love/Hate Relationship between Acquisitions and Collection Development" captures in a single sentence the essential difference between the traditional roles of acquisitions and collection development: "Collection development is clearly responsible for saying what will be ordered, but it is acquisitions' domain to determine from whom to order the material."[31] This statement reflects the tradition of framing collection development as an intellectual endeavor that is the domain of librarians, while acquisitions is seen as a service function largely left in the hands of classified staff. Collection development is generally conceived of as a long-term, ongoing process guided by written collection-development plans that encompass not only the addition of new materials to the collection but also such activities as assessing and weeding collections. In contrast to collection development, "Acquisitions work itself tends to be task- and process-oriented as are the acquisitions staff."[32]

The married authors of "Sleeping with the Enemy" (she, the head of an acquisitions department; he, the head of a collection development unit) write from the perspective of large academic libraries (she, the University of California, San Diego; he, San Diego State University), in which acquisitions and collection development have tended to exist as separate, if related, units within the library organizational structure. For all but larger academic libraries, it is more common for acquisitions and collection development to be organized into a combined unit that might be called either "acquisitions" or "collection development" (if not some other name entirely), while smaller academic libraries may not have any such unit and instead distribute this work among librarians and classified staff in more loosely structured ways.

In practice, even in very large academic libraries with dedicated collection-development and acquisitions units, it has long been common for nearly every librarian in the organization to have some responsibility for selecting materials as part of their portfolio. A reference-and-instruction librarian with a bachelor's degree in biology might be assigned frontline collection duties for the biosciences, while a technical-services librarian who is fluent in French may be assigned collection duties for francophone materials. Though a far from universal practice, non-librarians with special subject knowledge may also be assigned collection duties, as when a Geographic Information Systems (GIS) specialist is assigned the duty of selecting maps and other information resources relating to geography. Those persons within a library organization who have collection development responsibilities in their portfolios are often referred to as *selectors*. While the ideal circumstance is for all selectors to have formal, in-depth knowledge of their assigned subject areas, the expectation that all do has long been recognized as unrealistic.[33] In practice, selectors may find themselves assigned multiple subject areas, including areas in which they have little education, experience, or knowledge. While it is in some ways a disadvantage that a library selector's depth of knowledge in a particular subject does not equal that of someone with an advanced degree in that subject area, a conscientious selector can compensate by learning at least the basics of an unfamiliar subject area, working closely with faculty and students in that area, and bringing to the table a librarian's professional knowledge of the business of scholarly communication. Library selectors typically take great professional pride in building collections that directly contribute to research and instruction and consider their work as selectors to be a key component of their academic identity.

From colonial times into the early twentieth century, the selecting of books for campus libraries was, with some exceptions, considered too important to be left to librarians.[34] Though librarians slowly gained increased responsibility for collection development as the twentieth century wore on, they finally came to play a dominant role in collection development only during the higher-education boom of the 1950s and 1960s. One likely driver of this change was simply that the vastly increased volume of academic publishing had made the workload of collection development and acquisitions too heavy for faculty to shoulder, especially in light of the growing demand that faculty publish and secure external funding for their research. The employment of librarian subject bibliographers, whose job duties consisted largely, if not entirely, of choosing books and other materials for the collection was known in a few larger academic libraries prior to 1940, but the practice did not become widespread until the early the 1960s.[35] While the heyday of the subject bibliographer lasted somewhat longer than that of the Nehru jacket, by the late 1970s the adoption of approval plans began to turn the position of subject bibliographer into an expensive luxury for libraries running on increasingly tight collection budgets.[36]

If economics alone were not enough of a driving force to change the way academic libraries acquired materials, the 1990s saw the emergence of digital tools that streamlined the processes of evaluation and acquisition. The work of evaluating books and other materials that might be added to the collection was greatly eased once reviews could be found online with very little effort; once selected for acquisition, almost any item could be purchased online with a few clicks. Even the once specialized art of tracking down an elusive rare book was rendered obsolete by the new technology. In *Books: A Memoir*, author, bibliophile, and bookstore owner Larry McMurtry (1936–2021) writes of how, starting in 2001, book dealers stopped visiting Booked Up, McMurtry's massive secondhand bookstore in Archer City, Texas. Sizing up the issue through the eyes of book dealers, McMurtry asks, "Why spend money on overpriced gasoline when they could purchase all they could afford to buy on the Internet?"[37] Similarly, academic library administrators more than questioned the wisdom of paying people with graduate degrees to scout distant bookshops and attend book fairs in Frankfurt and Guadalajara when not only large online booksellers like Amazon and Alibris were available right on anyone's desktop, but also thousands of small bookshops and booksellers from around the world were offering up their wares online. In the case of journal titles, the onset of the big deal led to academic libraries adopting the shotgun approach of subscribing to journals in large bundles rather than picking them off title by title, further diminishing the role of the expert bibliographer. As Thomas A. Peters observes at a time when the big deal was just getting off the ground, "In the new information environment, article-level selection-for-use decisions made by end users are more important than title-level decisions made by librarians."[38]

Disagreements over the importance of developing collections based on the input of expert subject bibliographers hinge on what Ross Atkinson has identified as a "'loopy' contradiction" within the profession. On the one hand, Atkinson points to the stipulation that libraries respond reactively "to the needs and values" of the communities they serve. On the other, he points to the stipulation that "libraries must be proactive, creating or at least affecting the needs of the communities they support."[39] On one side, the avant-garde embraced digital technology for its ability to accurately respond to user needs in almost real time, while on the other side traditionalists cautioned against too readily abandoning the library's role of providing intentionally curated collections that help steer the course of scholarship.

While it is apparent that the non-traditional view has triumphed, it is also true that the role of the subject expert never vanished entirely from the academic library. Even if a twenty-first-century academic librarian with subject responsibilities is more likely to be described as a "selector," "liaison librarian," or "embedded librarian" than as a "subject bibliographer," it is still common for academic librarians to take on collection development responsibilities for specific subject areas. But rather than devoting the bulk of their subject-area activities to determining which books end up in the stacks, academic subject librarians increasingly put their time and effort into such endeavors as subject-focused reference and information-literacy activities while also liaising with the faculty and students in their assigned subject areas. A visible example of the work of liaison librarians is seen in the extensive subject-focused research guides that became a standard feature of academic library websites starting in the early years of the twenty-first century. In their role as subject liaisons, librarians function as advocates for library collections and services while also fostering communication between users and the library. As Kara M. Whatley puts it, "Building relationships is becoming the essence of what it is to be a liaison librarian—one that connects users with their information needs, whatever the format and whatever the technology."[40]

Just as the spread of digital technology and the expansion of outsourcing tended to reduce the size of cataloging units, it had much the same effect on the acquisitions workforce. As ordering and payment transactions moved from high-touch, paper-based formats to online interfaces, an army of acquisitions staff was no longer required to micro-manage the new, highly automated systems. By the turn of the twenty-first century, many librarians and classified staff working in technical services felt as if they were being treated as second-class citizens within the library community. Looking back from the perspective of 2004 at how digital technology had led to the gradual marginalization of technical services, Christine DeZelar-Tiedman describes the irony of the situation:

> Technical services has a history of being revolutionary. The MARC record, and the resulting cooperative bibliographic databases and online catalogs, are examples of using technology

to share data in a way that completely changed how catalogers, and all librarians, do their work. Since then, however, much of the innovation in the library world seems to have come from outside technical services, and catalog librarians are often seen as reactive, if not reactionary.[41]

The perception of catalogers and, to some extent, the entire technical-services workforce as "reactive, if not reactionary" may have in part arisen due to a relative handful of outspoken, traditionally minded champions of technical services who saw themselves standing fast against hordes of digital barbarians storming the gates of print-centric knowledge. Such staunch defenders of tradition aside, the evidence shows that many of those working in technical services during the rise of digital technology fully understood that the world of information was undergoing irrevocable change and that the profession had to change or be left behind. A 1991 *Library Journal* cover story, "Cataloging Must Change!," coauthored by Dorothy Gregor and Carol Mandel, provides an excellent example of how forward-thinking technical-services librarians often were. Openly acknowledging the elephant in the room, Gregor and Mandel write, "Cataloging has an image problem. It is associated with the application of a set of arcane rules."[42] They then point to a digitally generated form of empirical data—the user logs generated by OPACs—as proof that the real-world facts of how library users search catalogs did not conform to the theories long held by librarians; more disturbingly, OPAC user logs were indicating that the basic architecture of the library catalog was acting more as a hindrance than as a help to users. In the face of compelling evidence, Gregor and Mandel recommend such innovations as "simpler descriptive cataloging" and a new approach to subject cataloging which calls on catalogers to "be aware of the powerful role played by a sophisticated search system and beware of overestimating the power of subject analysis for each item."[43] They also call for library catalogs to point users to (1) externally produced data, (2) the growing amount of materials appearing in new electronic formats, and (3) the larger universe of information beyond the walls of the library, especially those items that are not part of the library's bought-and-paid-for collection but which the library can provide on demand.[44] While some traditionalists pushed back against Gregor and Mandel's timely call to rethink cataloging, "Cataloging Must Change!" exerted a strong influence on the profession. When the authors of a 1993 article entitled "Bibliographic Services of the Future" wrote, "Above all, change is necessary," they supported the truth of their blunt assertion by the simple expedient of citing Gregor and Mandel's seminal article.[45] On the international level, the authors of a different influential document, "Functional Requirements for Bibliographic Records," are in sync with the thinking of Gregor and Mandel when they write that libraries must "try to simplify the cataloguing process and to do more and more 'minimal level' cataloguing in order to keep pace with the continued growth of publishing output," and also must "adapt cataloguing codes and practices to accommodate change resulting from the emergence of new forms of electronic publishing, and the advent of networked access to information resources."[46] Such examples of visionary thinking show that the stereotype of the technical-services workforce as "reactive, if not reactionary" was, and remains, nothing more than a stereotype.

A Standards-Based History of Cataloging in the Digital Age

Efforts to standardize cataloging practice date back at least as far as the 1841 publication of Anthony Panizzi's *The Catalogue of Printed Books in the British Museum*.[47] Notable examples of cataloging standards published before 1950 include:

- Charles C. Jewett's *On the Construction of Catalogues of Libraries and Their Publication by Means of Separate Stereotyped Titles* (1853)[48]
- Charles A. Cutter's *Rules for a Printed Dictionary Catalogue* (1876)[49]
- *Catalog Rules Author and Title Entries, American Edition* (1908)[50]
- *A.L.A. Catalog Rules, Author and Title Entries* [Preliminary] (1941)[51]
- *A.L.A. Catalog Rules, Author and Title Entries* (1949).[52]
- *Rules for Descriptive Cataloging in the Library of Congress* (1949)[53]

While cataloging practice has always somewhat varied from one U.S. library to the next, standardization has meant that cataloging practices have varied less than other library functions. In 1955, to pick a year, a book cataloger who left a position at a college in Maryland for a similar position at a university in Alabama would have found the cataloging practices of both institutions to be more alike than different. The advent of digital technology and the resultant ease with which cataloging could be shared both nationally and internationally served only to strengthen the standardization of cataloging practice. What follows is a list of major milestones in the standardization of cataloging, and its resultant evolution, from the dawn of the Digital Age to the present.

1961—Paris Principles

Delegates representing sixty-five nations adopted a six-page document entitled, "Statement of Principles Adopted by the International Conference on Cataloguing Principles. Paris, October 1961."[54] Popularly known as the "Paris Principles," this multinational agreement outlined the basic function and architecture of library catalogs.

1965—MARC

Under the leadership of Henriette Avram (1919–2006), the Library of Congress began work on the MARC (MAchine Readable Cataloging) format. Finalized in 1967 as MARC II and fully released in 1968, the format "was to be both a catalyst and linchpin for the development of a broad and diverse automated library environment."[55] MARC became a national standard in 1971.[56] Two years later it became an international standard.[57]

1967—AACR

The publication of *Anglo-American Cataloging Rules* (*AACR*) established for most of the English-speaking world a standard set of rules for creating and maintaining catalogs and other bibliographic tools.[58] Edited by C. Sumner Spalding (1912–1997), *AACR* largely adhered to the higher-level cataloging principles outlined in the "Paris Principles."[59] Due to a failure to reach a complete consensus, *AACR* was initially published in two versions, the *North American Text* and the *British Text*. A revised second edition of *AACR* was published in 1970 to unify North American and British cataloging practice.[60]

1971—ISBD(M)

The International Standard Bibliographic Description for Monographic Publications (ISBD(M)) emerged as the outcome of an international meeting held in Copenhagen in 1969 at which delegates adopted "a resolution to establish international standards for the form and content of bibliographic descriptions."[61] In 1971, ISBD(M) was officially issued as the first of a series of ISBDs intended to standardize cataloging practice worldwide.[62]

1977—UNIMARC

In an increasingly networked library world, a number of national libraries recognized the need for an international standard "which would enable data created by one national agency to be incorporated into the databases of another national agency exactly as received."[63] Under the auspices of the International Federation of Library Associations and Institutions (IFLA), a new standard tailored to the needs of national libraries was published as *UNIMARC: Universal MARC Format*.[64] Having undergone regular updates since its initial publication in 1997, UNIMARC currently "covers four metadata schemas for bibliographic, classification, authorities and holdings information."[65]

1978—AARC2

The publication of the second edition of *Anglo-American Cataloging Rules (*universally known as *AACR2)* represented a major revision of *AACR*.[66] While digital technology was not the only force shaping the revision process, editors Michael Gorman and Paul W. Winkler, along with the many contributors involved in the creation of *AACR2*, certainly had "in mind developments in machine processing of catalog records that might affect cataloging."[67] The changes called for by *AACR2* were at first controversial. An article from 1980 quotes a distraught librarian as saying, "People were just hysterical at a workshop on *AACR2*."[68] Another article published in the same year proposed a six-step "Plan of Action" for remedying what the author sees as flaws in *AACR2*; the author then ends her article with the admonition that librarians "should not tolerate future upheavals which are costly in resources and potentially destructive to the credibility of libraries."[69] Early criticisms notwithstanding, *AACR2* quickly attained the status of a cataloging Bible, undergoing a series of revisions and updates until all further changes ceased in 2005.

1995—Dublin Core

A March 1995 meeting held at OCLC headquarters in Dublin, Ohio, resulted in the creation of the Dublin Core Metadata Element Set (DCMES), more familiarly known as "Dublin Core."

Developed with a close eye on the growing importance of the World Wide Web as a conduit for information, Dublin Core has been defined as "a general-purpose scheme for resource description originally intended to facilitate discovery of information objects on the Web."[70] The original Dublin Core consisted of a set of thirteen, soon amended to fifteen, data elements ranging from such obvious elements as "Title" and "Creator" to such nuanced elements as "Identifier" (e.g., an unambiguous reference to a resource within a given context).[71] Starting in 2002, the Dublin Core Metadata Initiative took on the task of maintaining and updating Dublin Core metadata terms. Dublin Core was accepted as a national standard in 2007, with that original standard itself being updated in 2012.[72] Although not the only factor involved, Dublin Core was a step in the evolution of the role of "library cataloger" to that of "metadata librarian."

1997—MARC 21

Born of a joint effort to harmonize USMARC and Canadian MARC formats, MARC 21 spread to become an international standard intended to meet the needs of the twenty-first century.[73] MARC 21 includes separate formats for five data types: Bibliographic, Authority, Holdings, Classification, and Community.[74]

1998—FRBR

In the words of Barbara Tillet, "From 1992–1995 the IFLA Study Group on Functional Requirements for Bibliographic Records (FRBR) developed an entity-relationship model as a generalized view of the bibliographic universe, intended to be independent of any cataloging code or implementation."[75] The IFLA Study Group, of which Tillet was a member, began its work by asking if it were possible for bibliographic databases, including online library catalogs, to do a better job of helping users succeed in meeting their information needs. To this end, the IFLA Study Group identified "tasks that users perform while using information retrieval tools and interacting with bibliographic data."[76] The IFLA Study Group went on to develop an entity-relationship conceptual model built on the "Group 1" entities of *Work*, *Expression*, *Manifestation*, and *Item*, a quartet sometimes referred to as "WEMI." The FRBR conceptual model expanded in complexity as it took into consideration not only the Group 1 entities' relationships to each other but also their relationships to the "Group 2" entities of *Person* and *Corporate Body* and the "Group 3" entities of *Concepts*, *Objects*, *Events*, and *Places*. At its core, FRBR is about creating metadata that identifies a large and diverse number of relationships among data sources. As mind-boggling as these complex relationships may be, FRBR is nonetheless grounded in practical utility in that its ultimate goal is to enable information seekers "to find, identify, select, and obtain the resources they want."[77]

In 1998, IFLA published FRBR as *Functional Requirements for Bibliographic Records: Final Report*.[78] Key additions to this initial publication include:

- *Functional Requirements for Authority Data: A Conceptual Model* (2009)[79]
- *Functional Requirements for Subject Authority Data (FRSAD): A Conceptual Model* (2010)[80]

2009—Update to Paris Principles

IFLA updated the Paris Principles with the publication of "Statement of International Cataloguing Principles." The new statement, which itself would be further updated in 2014 and 2015, "replaced and explicitly broadened the scope of the Paris Principles from just textual resources to all types of resources, and from just the choice and form of entry to all aspects of bibliographic and authority data used in library catalogues."[81]

Metadata, the Semantic Web, and Linked Data

Library cataloging has always been about metadata, about creating data that provides information about other data, typically by adding context through the identification of such elements as creator, date of creation, format, source, place of origin, relationship to other information, subject, and so on. A manually typed, circa-1958 catalog card for Hannah Arendt's then-new book, *The Human Condition*, is a form of metadata just as a MARC record created for an InfoTrac CD-ROM released in 1989 is metadata or an EXIF file automatically generated by a smartphone camera in 2022 is metadata. Though metadata is a far from new phenomenon in libraries, the emergence of networked digital information changed, and greatly complicated, the ways in which library catalogers thought about and created metadata.

In 1999, Tim Berners-Lee spoke of his dream that there would someday be a "Semantic Web" on which, "Machines become capable of analyzing all the data on the Web—the content, links, and transactions between people and computers."[82] The Semantic Web, as imagined by Berners-Lee, would function as a global database, as "a web of things in the world, described by data on the Web."[83] Many librarians came to see that the precise linking of information objects made possible via the Semantic Web could become a means of allowing the vast quantities of structured bibliographic data created by library catalogers over the decades to serve not only the users of specific library catalogs but also all persons and machines on the Web. Although the idea of the Semantic Web was formulated before artificial intelligence (AI) had become commonplace, as Deepjyoti Kalita and Dipen Deka accurately observe from the perspective of the year 2020, "With the emergence of the philosophy of the Semantic Web, library catalogues can be an essential part of the artificial-intelligence-enabled Web."[84] In theory, the precision of the Semantic Web makes AI more intelligent by serving to reduce the all-too-familiar, frequently mocked instances of AI tools spectacularly misinterpreting the context of the information they present to their human end users.

Underpinning the Semantic Web is the concept of *linked data*, which Berners-Lee and his co-authors defined in 2009 as "data published on the Web in such a way that it is machine-readable, its meaning is explicitly defined, it is linked to other external data sets, and can in turn be linked to from external data sets."[85] Under Berners-Lee's vision of the Semantic Web, data should not merely exist as linked data but as *open linked data* (also known as *linked open data*) to which machines, including search engines, have unfettered access for retrieval and analysis. Whether open or not, the structure of linked data is based on the

> Resource Description Framework (RDF), "a flexible standard proposed by the W3C [World Wide Web Consortium] to characterize semantically both resources and relationships which hold between them."[86] Under the rules of RDF, codifying data requires an RDF statement to be written in an extensible markup language syntax known as RDF/XML. An RDF statement takes the form of a *triple* which consists of a subject, predicate, and object. The following are examples of triples:
>
> De Havilland Aircraft Company was an aircraft manufacturer.
> De Havilland Aircraft Company was a British company.
> De Havilland Aircraft of Canada is an aircraft manufacturer.
> De Havilland Aircraft of Canada is a Canadian company.
>
> Following the best practices of linked data, each element of a triple is identified by a Uniform Resource Identifier (URI) in such a way that a machine could not, for example, confuse the former British aircraft manufacturer with the current Canadian aircraft manufacturer, or confuse either of the two manufacturing concerns with the actress Dame Olivia de Havilland (1916–2020). By the same token, a machine tasked with searching the Web to create a database of current and former aircraft manufacturers would retrieve both companies and treat them as separate, though historically related, entities.
>
> The impact of the Semantic Web and linked data was such that librarians of the twenty-first century developed new cataloging standards specifically designed to leverage the power and efficiencies of both phenomena to an extent well beyond the limitations of older cataloging standards.

2010—RDA

In March 1994, the Joint Steering Committee for Revision of AACR (JSC) considered "holding an invitational meeting of cataloging experts to deal with issues facing the Anglo-American Cataloging Rules."[87] The resulting conference, held in Toronto in October 1997, slowly yet ultimately led to the replacement of the old cataloging rulebook with a new standard published in June 2010 as *RDA: Resource Description and Access*.[88] Commenting on the situation as RDA was being developed, Lynne C. Howarth and Jean Weihs write:

> *The cataloging community is clearly at a crossroad, navigating the transition from forty years of creating bibliographic records using the Anglo-American Cataloguing Rules within a print-dominant environment to a proposed new content standard that reaches beyond the library domain to a world of digital objects and multipurpose metadata.*[89]

Unlike the "print-dominant" *AACR2*, the born-digital RDA is based on the conceptual models of FRBR and two of its offspring: Functional Requirements for Authority Data (FRAD) and Functional Requirements for Subject Authority Data (FRSAD). The intention of RDA's developers was for it to serve as an international standard for the creation of descriptive metadata that can be easily shared and reused by cultural heritage institutions of all types.

The prospect of RDA aroused a level of controversy by which the uproar surrounding the publication of *AACR2* pales in comparison. In 2007, *American Libraries* published "RDA: Imminent Debacle," an opinion piece in which Michael Gorman, one of the editors of *AACR2*, lambastes not only RDA but the entire concept of metadata, writing, "It is hard to believe the world's libraries have taken metadata seriously."[90] In the November 2012 entry for her regular "Dollars and Sense" column in the technical-services trade publication *Technicalities*, Sheila S. Intner writes, "I think I can safely say that *RDA* is poised to go down the slippery slope to ridiculousness."[91] While such strongly negative opinions are atypical of the entire library community, even librarians holding more moderate positions on the issue expressed misgivings as to whether RDA will work or if the majority of the library profession will ever agree to apply it in practice. At the time, a running joke among many senior library catalogers had it that RDA stands for "Retirement Date Approaches." One practical problem with implementing RDA at the time of its release was that, while RDA was developed as a "FRBR-based content standard," the integrated library systems (ILS) then in use were "bound by a flat record structure that has no accommodation for the hierarchical model of FRBR."[92]

Resistance to RDA aside, in 2012 the Library of Congress formed a committee to lead the transition from MARC to RDA with the goal of convening advisory and test groups by the end of the year.[93] On March 31, 2013, RDA became the official cataloging standard of the Library of Congress and the British Library.[94] Other libraries followed suit to the extent that, by 2015, the RDA Toolkit numbered 2,840 subscribers and 8,866 users representing sixty-four countries.[95] A 2016 survey of U.S. academic libraries reported that, of fifty-nine responses received, "the overwhelming majority (57) have formally adopted the new Resource Description and Access (RDA) cataloging rules."[96] On the other hand, a 2019 survey to which 310 public libraries responded found that 17 percent are still using AACR2, 20.2 percent are using RDA, and 48.9 percent are using "a combination of the two standards in regular cataloging practice."[97] Starting in 2016, the RDA Steering Committee (formerly the Joint Steering Committee for the Development of RDA) undertook the RDA Toolkit Restructure and Redesign Project (popularly known as "3R") in an effort to improve RDA in response to user input.[98]

2011—BIBFRAME

In May 2011, the Library of Congress launched the Bibliographic Framework Initiative. Commonly known as BIBFRAME, the new initiative sought to move cataloging beyond the library silo and into the wider networked universe while, at the same time, embracing the interconnectedness made possible by the Semantic Web and open linked data. The influence of FRBR on BIBFRAME is apparent from the latter's three principal high-level entities: Work, Instance, and Item.[99] Although BIBFRAME was developed as a linked-data alternative to MARC, its developers never intended that the vast amounts of MARC data created by library catalogers over the decades be shunted aside. As the authors of the original BIBFRAME proposal write:

> *MARC 21 is the latest evolution of a library interchange format that exchanges this data in a relatively specialized market. Libraries generate, maintain and curate an enormous amount of high-quality data, however, that is valuable well beyond traditional library boundaries. In reflecting the MARC 21 format to a Linked Data model we expand the utility and value of this data as well as the community that Libraries and Cultural Heritage institutions serve.* [100]

In April 2016, the Library of Congress announced BIBFRAME 2.0, an update to the original standard.[101] BIBFRAME, though in many ways a work in progress to the present day, has been implemented by a number of public, academic, and national libraries as well as such organizations as the Digital Public Library of America.[102] One example of a large-scale implementation of BIBFRAME took place in 2018 when the HathiTrust Digital Library successfully converted MARC records into a BIBFRAME dataset comprising "descriptions for 15,596,172 items; 8,224,772 instances; and 7,276,088 works."[103] Marshall Breeding's "2023 Library Systems Report" noted that such major commercial providers of library products and services as Ex Libris and EBSCO had begun to use and support BIBFRAME, which Breeding flatly declared to be "the successor to MARC 21 for bibliographic data."[104] In summing up the many, sometimes chaotic, efforts to implement BIBFRAME and integrate MARC data into the Semantic Web, Ian Bigelow and Abigail Sparling advised:

> *All of these steps to maintaining bibliographic control in a BIBFRAME environment point to the need for community wide planning, standardization, and transparent communication. As always, innovation will still be necessary to ensure projects move forward in a way that serves libraries and library users, while leveraging the new systems and discovery potential linked data affords.* [105]

As true in the twenty-first century as it was in the nineteenth, the benefits of standardization can only be reaped where there exists cooperative planning and communication among all concerned.

2017—IFLA LRM

In August 2017, the IFLA Professional Committee endorsed the final version of the Library Reference Model (LRM) as an IFLA standard.[106] The new standard consolidates FRAD and FRSAD into a single standard.[107]

Cataloging the Web

The World Wide Web began in earnest when Tim Berners-Lee launched the first website on August 6, 1991; in the span of ten years, that single instance grew into an astonishing 29,000,000 websites.[108] During the Web's first decade, millions of individuals created personal websites. Schools and government agencies launched institutional websites. Commercial businesses began selling products and services over the Web. On January 30, 2000, the "Dot Com Super

Bowl" featured advertisements promoting fourteen different Web-based businesses, each of which paid more than $2,000,000 ($3,740,000 in 2024 dollars) to air its spot.[109]

Well before Berners-Lee created the first website or published the Hypertext Markup Language (HTML) for the world to use as it saw fit, a significant number of librarians had already been making productive use of such internet-based, pre-Web tools as FTP, Usenet, email, MOO (Multi-user Object Oriented) worlds, and the Gopher. The most enthusiastic of this new breed of librarians proudly rebranded themselves as *cybrarians*, a word the *Oxford English Dictionary* dates from 1991 and defines as, "A person who is practised [sic] at finding information on the internet on behalf of others, or who compiles or administers a library of reference material online."[110] Whether or not they styled themselves as cybrarians, librarians were among the first to recognize the Web's potential, creating library webpages and expounding on the Web's virtues before most of the general public was aware that the Web so much as existed. Typical of early works advocating the Web to librarians is an article entitled "Web Your Library" in which the librarian author describes the workings of the Web in painstaking detail before concluding that, while the Web "is not a fix for all our woes," it "represents a tool that libraries can creatively use to control and communicate an ever increasing, diverse number of information opportunities."[111] The mid-1990s saw the publication of the first book-length guides to creating library websites, notably library publisher Neal-Schuman's *Using the World Wide Web and Creating Home Pages: A How-to-Do-It Manual*,[112] and the ALA's *Building the Service-Based Library Web Site: A Step-by-Step Guide to Design and Options*.[113] Before the 1990s ended, libraries without websites were the rare exception rather than the rule.

As websites of all sorts proliferated, Web users required better tools to find their way around the rapidly growing "Information Superhighway." One such tool was the Web directory. Led by the commercial Yahoo! Directory (1994–2014) and the community-edited DMOZ (1998–2017), Web directories offered users lists of websites classified by topic in much the same way that library call-number schemes classified physical collections. As of March 1995, Yahoo! Directory was reported to have "organized close to 30,000 links."[114] Taking an alternate approach to helping users find their way around the Web were search engines, essentially huge databases of website URLs from which users retrieved relevant links by entering queries in a process analogous to searching library OPACs or bibliographic CD-ROM databases. Notable early examples of Web search engines include W3Catalog (1993–6), Lycos (1994-present), AltaVista (1995–2013), Google (1995-present), and Dogpile (1996-present).

Librarians recognized that their skills in cataloging and classifying information could be used to help users navigate the Web. While the high costs of creating and maintaining Web search engines put that option out of reach of librarians, the classification model employed by Web directories represented an approach to organizing information that was familiar to librarians and which they could implement at minimal costs. Many academic libraries created in-house web directories to provide their users with curated lists of links to librarian-approved websites. For example, an article published in 1995 describes how the University of Tennessee, Knoxville's Hodges Library website featured a subject directory organized on the basis of the LCC scheme.[115] A more ambitious example of a librarian-curated Web directory took the form of INFOMINE, a project launched by the University of California, Riverside Library in 1994. Described by its creators as "one of the first Web-based, academic virtual libraries," by 1996 INFOMINE included classified links to "close to five thousand annotated and indexed records with links to selected, university-level resources in most major academic disciplines."[116] By April 2000, INFOMINE had grown to become a "collection of close to 20,000 librarian selected and described scholarly and educational Internet resources."[117] While large-scale Web directories had their day, the speed and convenience of search engines meant that such directories, whether librarian-curated or not, eventually lost the battle for the hearts and minds of Web users. INFOMINE was finally shut down in November 2016, two years after the closing of Yahoo! Directory and one year prior to the closing of DMOZ. Even so, selective directories of Web resources continue to live on in the form of librarian-curated subject guides, though the links provided in such directories are more likely to number in the dozens than the tens of thousands.

An alternative approach to connecting library users with digital information involved creating formal catalog records for online information resources with the expectation that such records could be shared via bibliographic utilities for incorporation into local library OPACs. As early as 1991, the ALA's Machine-Readable Bibliographic Information Committee recognized that cataloging rules based on physical objects held in library collections were not keeping up with changing technology and so proposed to the Library of Congress the creation of "a set of data elements that might be useful in describing online information resources."[118] Eventually, the concepts underlying this early proposal would be expanded upon by such metadata initiatives as Dublin Core (1995), FRBR (1998), and RDA (2010). The year 1991 also saw the launch of the OCLC Internet Resources Project, a pioneering experiment to test the utility of the MARC record for cataloging internet resources.[119] In 1994, OCLC launched Building a Catalog of Internet Resources (also known as "InterCat"), a collaborative cataloging project which saw 231 librarian volunteers catalog some 4,700 internet resources.[120] The cataloging of internet resources by librarians grew so widespread that 1997 saw the launch of the *Journal of Internet Cataloging*, a publication described by its founding editors as being "created in an atmosphere of great excitement, uncertainty, experimentation, and risk."[121]

Yet another approach to cataloging the Web took the form of an experimental project undertaken in 2001 by the Research Libraries Group (RLG) with funding from the Andrew W. Mellon Foundation. In the words of RLG project officer Merrilee Proffitt, "The project goal was to create a new service based on the data from the RLG Union Catalog, aimed at reaching new Web audiences. The result was RedLightGreen."[122] As a Web-discovery platform more attuned to the needs of undergraduates than subject experts, RedLightGreen employed FRBR-derived principles to mine RLG's union catalog of 126 million records so as to "reduce a potentially overwhelming number of editions into a smaller, more manageable set of works that match a user's search terms."[123] In essence, the idea was for RedLightGreen to perform more like a curated, academically focused Google and less like a traditional library catalog. RedLightGreen lasted until the merger of RLG and OCLC in 2006, at which point users were directed to instead use OCLC's WorldCat.[124]

Reflecting on the early efforts to organize and catalog the internet, the authors of *The Organization of Information* write:

> In the mid-1990s, some librarians and LIS researchers enthusiastically and somewhat naively attempted to design projects to help organize the Internet—the whole Internet.... but it became clear rather quickly that full-scale library cataloging was not particularly well suited for describing what often turned out to be ephemeral web-based resources.[125]

To some extent, the ambitions of overly enthusiastic librarians may seem as naïve as the ambitions of the high-flying, high-tech Dot-Com-Super-Bowl advertisers, most of whom had gone out of business or been acquired by other companies within a year of their thirty seconds of football-fuelled fame.[126] But just as the bursting of the dot-com bubble did not mark the death of online commerce, the unfulfilled dreams of cataloging and organizing the entire internet were a beginning rather than an end. Scaling back their ambitions, librarians began to selectively create catalog records for credible Web-based information resources with a high potential for use by academics, focusing especially on resources that fell into well-defined academic subject areas or appeared in academically relevant formats, such as government documents.[127]

In 1999, OCLC launched the Cooperative Online Resource Catalog (CORC), "a database of metadata records for online resources and an experimental interface for creating those records, along with sharable pathfinders."[128] Well received by the library cataloging community, CORC lasted only three years before being replaced with cataloging tools that unified the cataloging of online resources with that of more traditional library holdings, rather than segregating the two as if they were incompatible forms of information.[129] For catalogers, what had come to matter less than "the application of a set of arcane rules" was the application of useful metadata to valuable information resources, whatever those resources might be or wherever they might be found. The evolution in how the library cataloging community viewed the nature of its work is perhaps nowhere better reflected than the change, in 2008, of the title of the *Journal of Internet Cataloging* to the *Journal of Library Metadata*. In the words of Jeffrey Beall, the new editor of the *Journal of Library Metadata*, "As electronic resources produced and made available by libraries have proliferated, so has the importance of managing these resources.... This new journal, then, hopes to serve as a means of sharing and documenting information about metadata in libraries."[130]

Forty-Plus Years, and Counting, of Library Automation

Published in March 1983, library consultant Joseph R. Matthews's seven-page article "The Automated Library System Marketplace, 1982: Change and More Change" would become the first in an annual series of articles on library automation that remains in publication after more than forty years.[131] The series appeared in *Library Journal* from 1983 through 2013 before changing venues to *American Libraries* in 2014. For nearly the first two decades of its existence, the authorship of each year's article varied; however, from 2002 to the present day, library consultant Marshall Breeding authored every entry in the series. Each article in the series focuses on the state of the library technology industry—expounding on such topics as business strategies, market shares, mergers, acquisitions, profits, and losses—while simultaneously providing real-time snapshots of how library technology itself was evolving.

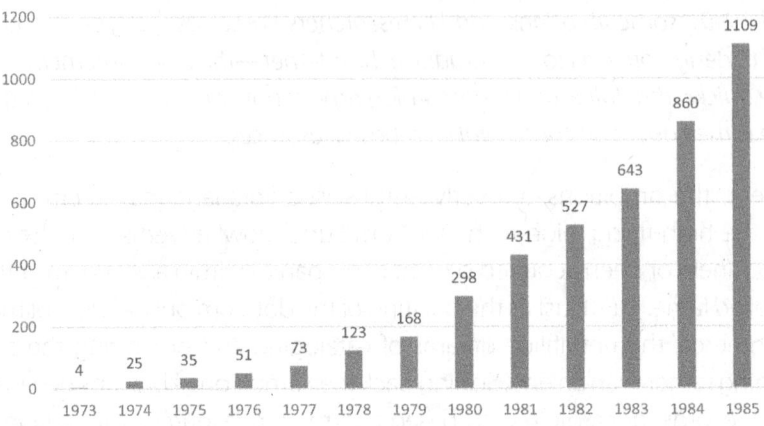

Figure 4.1 Cumulative number of installed library systems by year.
Source: Adapted from Joseph R. Matthews, "Growth & Consolidation: The 1985 Automated Library System Marketplace," *Library Journal*, April 1, 1986.

Reading the series from the oldest article to the newest provides a reasonably complete short course in the history of library technology from the days when the ILS was first entering the marketplace up to the present.

For anyone who is familiar with only the library catalogs of the twenty-first century, reading the articles published in the 1980s will be a revelation. The typical automated library catalog of the day consisted of vendor-supplied software running on a local server that may have taken the form of a mainframe computer (for very large libraries), a minicomputer, or a microcomputer (for very small libraries). Turnkey systems, for which the vendor-provided hardware, software, installation, and some level of support, were a popular option "because the majority of libraries have decided they do not want to take the risks associated with developing their own systems."[132] Because the ILS was new, many automated libraries of the early 1980s were still running stand-alone, single-purpose systems for such applications as circulation, cataloging, public access, and serials management (Figure 4.1).[133] Integrated system or not, access to the backend of a system by catalogers and other technical-services staff would have been via monochrome, text-only interfaces found on a limited number of dedicated machines on which the system vendor's proprietary software had been installed. On the front end, the interface for the OPAC would have been via monochrome, text-only dumb terminals located within the library building. One common metric for the capacity of early systems was the number of dumb terminals served. For the ninety-nine library automation systems newly installed in 1982, 34 percent served eight or fewer dumb terminals, while only 13 percent served forty-nine or more terminals.[134] The dumb terminal metric would become meaningless as remote access to OPACs came into play in the early 1990s. As reported in the 1991 library automation article, "With the continuing growth of campus and governmental local area networks (LANs), local library catalogs can no longer be considered self-contained entities serving a clearly defined audience."[135] As the 1990s went on, remote access beyond the boundaries of LANs would be facilitated thanks to refinements to the Z39.50 protocol and the gradual adoption of client/server technology.[136] Though dumb terminals may seem primitive from the viewpoint of twenty-first century, in the 1980s a large number of automated libraries had not gotten even that far. In 1984, 1,875 automated libraries employed computer-output-microform (COM) as the public-access interface to their catalogs.[137]

By 1990, the worldwide total of library systems installed in academic libraries added up to 1,000 systems, some of which served more than one library.[138] Just one year later, that total had risen to 1,523 libraries.[139] It would not be long until the card catalog had effectively disappeared from the academic library. All through the 1980s and into the 1990s, the OPAC tended to be regarded as a direct substitute for the physical card catalog, while ILS as a whole were conceived of as a new-and-improved way of doing things that libraries had been doing without the benefit of automation for decades. Instead of typing out cards, catalogers created (or copy cataloged) digital bibliographic records representing physical items owned by the library. These records were then uploaded into the local system for the benefit of information seekers who, it was assumed, would search the OPAC, jot down call numbers, and head into the stacks to retrieve physical items. One factor that worked to break down traditional views of the OPAC-as-card-catalog was the innovation of digital periodical indexes. Whereas the indexing of periodical articles had proven impossible in the physical card catalog, by the 1990s libraries were incorporating online and CD-ROM periodical databases into their OPACs, forever sundering the library's traditional separation of book catalogs and article indexes. In an accurate prediction of a future in which OPACs would provide access to not only books but also articles, locally produced databases, and more, the authors of the 1990 library automation article wrote, "For many libraries, the traditional automated library system will serve as a foundation (rather than the primary focus) for a larger network of information technologies and services."[140] In 1996, by which time it had become clear that the great disruptor known as the Web had come to stay, the changing role of library automation systems could be stated even more bluntly:

> *Systems modeled after traditional libraries no longer meet the needs of the Information Age. Library automation systems must go beyond managing collections within a single library. The new systems must be able to interact with other systems, such as the OPACs of other libraries, CD-ROM databases, online databases, information on the Internet, or other multimedia resources.*[141]

One key development in the transition of the OPAC from an automated card catalog into a tool for accessing networked information was the implementation of the MARC record's 856 field. Established in 1993, the 856 field allows information seekers to click on a link in an OPAC record and be directly connected to a corresponding online information resource.[142] Another innovation that allowed library OPACs to function more like Google and less like a card catalog was OpenURL, "a vendor-neutral standard for linking among online resources," the adoption of which was accelerated by library-system vendor Ex Libris' announcement in early 2000 of its new OpenURL-based SFX Reference Linking Software Solution.[143] The early 2000s also saw the development of electronic records management (ERM) systems designed to help libraries better manage and provide more seamless user access to the e-books, e-journals, and other electronic resources on which libraries were expending ever-increasing shares of their collection budgets.[144]

Despite efforts to make OPACs the first choice of information seekers, underfunded libraries found themselves fighting a losing battle with corporate giants like Google. It was not until

2006 that Breeding could report, "Simple Google-style search boxes are emerging; delivering well-ranked results remains a challenge."[145] Breeding's good news/bad news announcement came two years after the Beta release of Google Scholar and less than one year after Google, fresh off its $1.67 billion IPO, announced its intention to digitize and make freely available the full text of millions of books. While Google's initial ambitions in the digitization arena were never fully realized, its nonetheless considerable success stood in sharp contrast to the struggle of libraries, technology vendors, and publishers to devise effective means of providing access to in-copyright e-books in ways that met the needs of all concerned—library users included. Yet another library gambit to maintain relevance was the adoption of vendor-supplied discovery platforms—such as Serial Solutions' Summons, EBSCO Discovery Service, and Ex Libris' Primo—that provide Google-like search interfaces as well as direct access to a library's collection of electronic information resources.[146] Though no library technology vendor nor any librarian would care to admit it, their collective efforts to glamorize the OPAC added up to little more than putting lipstick on a pig. In 2019 Breeding frankly admits that the various vendor-provided OPAC discovery platforms are indistinguishable one from the other and that "these products have not made a dent in the reality that most researchers rely on Google Scholar or disciplinary indexes more than library provided discovery services."[147]

More successfully, system vendors expanded the capabilities of academic library systems far beyond the traditional limits of the library catalog by developing add-on applications that enabled libraries to more directly support research activities and curriculum. For example, in 2018 Ex Libris launched Esploro, a platform intended to help "universities to better manage, assess, and showcase their research programs."[148] Rosetta, another Ex Libris platform, positioned academic libraries to play a leading role in their campuses' digital preservation efforts.[149] An area where work remains to be done involves the development of out-of-the-box applications to harvest institutional repository metadata and seamlessly integrate it into the library OPAC.[150] In terms of supporting academic curriculum, the capacity of library systems was enhanced by "reading-list applications, discovery services for open educational resources, and support for application program interfaces (APIs) and protocols that connect the library with student information systems."[151]

Through the forty-plus years of the library-automation series, a theme that appears at times as subtext, at times more openly, is the often fraught relationship between librarians and library-system vendors. On a philosophical level, the fact that, over time, the number of library-system vendors dwindled down to a small number of large companies—many owned by venture capitalists—did nothing to warm the feelings of public-sector librarians toward for-profit vendors. As Breeding put it in 2021, "Business acquisitions spanning multiple decades have consolidated the library technology industry into one dominated by a handful of large companies."[152] Nor have librarians much welcomed the expansion of publishers into the turf of library technology, as when, for example, scholarly publisher Elsevier acquired library-system vendor Endeavor in 2001.[153] In 2017, Elsevier would top itself by spreading its corporate reach into institutional repositories through its acquisition of Bepress and into the field of altmetrics through its acquisition of Plum Analytics.[154]

On a more practical level, librarians and vendors could find themselves at odds when negotiating the long, costly, and sometimes adversarial RFP processes required to acquire a new system. Adversarial or not, once an RFP process ends and a vendor has been chosen, migrating from an existing library system to a new one can fray nerves on both sides of the transaction. Despite the fact that library bibliographic records are created in compliance with standards such as MARC, migrating bibliographic records that might number in the millions from one system to another requires extensive groundwork pre-migration and, very often, ongoing work post-migration to catch and clean up all the resultant errors. Even if the temptation of migrating to a new system holds out the carrot of better functionality and/or cost savings, libraries have a history of remaining with outdated legacy systems rather than shouldering the costs—in both dollars and staff wear-and-tear—of a migration. As libraries find themselves unable or unwilling to migrate, frontline librarians stuck with aging, increasingly outdated technology can come to see the system vendor through the same dismal lens with which tenants of an aging dwelling view their landlord. Being stuck with an outdated system, regardless of who is to blame, creates larger problems than simply being behind the technological curve. As Breeding accurately puts it, "Outdated automation systems can reinforce work patterns that no longer reflect priorities as core library activities change."[155]

Another reflection of librarians' unease over their relationship with system vendors is the development of open-source library systems, a movement that took root in the late 1990s and has continued to grow, if slowly, ever since. Developed in New Zealand in 1999, Koha was the first tangible manifestation of an open-source library system. In 2006, a significant milestone in the advancement of open-source library systems took place when PINES, a consortium of 252 public libraries in the state of Georgia, adopted the open-source, Georgia-based Evergreen ILS.[156] Because implementing an open-source system is a job beyond the capacity of many libraries, companies like ByWater Solutions and LibLime were formed to assist libraries in their migration to, and further development of, open-source systems.[157] The biggest development to date in open access library systems has been the 2017 launch of the FOLIO project, an open-source library service platform (LSP) backed by industry giant EBSCO.[158] To be sure, EBSCO's investment in FOLIO was not entirely altruistic, as "the current market of LSPs that are tightly bundled with their own discovery services . . . result in a competitive environment that disadvantages EBSCO Discovery Service."[159] By 2023, the staying power of FOLIO had been strongly endorsed following its adoption by the Library of Congress, the MOBIUS Consortium, and the National Library of Australia, among other libraries.[160]

The attraction of open-source as an alternative to vendor-provided systems lies in the possibility (but by no means the guarantee) of lower costs, coupled with the fact that open-source systems allow for the development of enhancements independent of any vendor involvement. The appeal of openness is powerful, as it promises a flexibility that was not possible with a traditional vendor-supplied system to which, upon adoption, a library might find itself wed for a decade or longer. When a library adopts and migrates to a proprietary ILS, it often means settling for technology that facilitates the way the library works *today*; on the other hand, adopting an open-source system holds out the possibility of acquiring technology that facilitates the way the library hopes to work in the *future*.

Roughly simultaneously with the growth of open-source systems was the movement to hosted library systems. For decades following the advent of automated library systems, mounting systems on local servers was the only option. While local servers permit libraries to maintain a high level of direct control over their systems, they also require libraries to hire specialized staff to tend to sometimes temperamental hardware and software. The trend of moving away from local servers began in the twenty-first century when vendors first offered software as a service (SaaS) as an alternative to local servers. Under the SaaS model, library systems run on a remote server owned and maintained by the vendor, thus relieving "the library from much of the complexities normally associated with managing a library automation system with lower overall costs."[161] Though SaaS was not immediately embraced by all, the eventual normalization of cloud-based computing throughout the technology industry meant, as Breeding asserted in 2010, "One of the overwhelming trends involves a shift away from libraries operating their own installations of library automation products to some flavor of hosted service."[162]

Even as open-source systems gained acceptance, not all stories were success stories. The open-source Kuali OLE system, developed with funding from the Andrew W. Mellon Foundation, was intended for the academic and research library marketplace.[163] By 2016 Kuali OLE had been adopted by only three academic libraries.[164] By 2019, Kuali OLE had been declared a failure.[165] Despite such setbacks, in 2023 Breeding reports, "In the US, about 10% of academic libraries and 17% of public libraries use an open source integrated library system (ILS). But the barriers to these products—real and perceived have largely collapsed."[166]

As the first quarter of the twenty-first century draws to a close, the ILS is giving way to the LSP, a technology which Breeding describes as "designed to manage complex, multiformat library collections with built-in knowledge bases that can efficiently manage large-scale collections of electronic resources."[167] Because LSPs are capable of supporting BIBFRAME and linked data to an extent beyond what was possible with the ILS, their deployment leads to the question of what role AI will play in the future of library technology. Though in 2024 Breeding reports that AI is not yet being incorporated into library systems, he predicts that "libraries can anticipate more prominent use of this technology in products within the next year or so."[168]

The Future of Cataloging and Technical Services

Whether the advent of AI will lead to library utopia, library apocalypse, or something in between is anyone's guess. At least for the present time, library systems continue to function in large part as the conduit between information seekers and the vast amounts of library metadata representing the intellectual output of generations of library catalogers and their technical-services affiliates. This means that the cataloging and technical-services workforces are, more than any other segment of the academic library organization, directly in the line of fire should some AI-dominated future of information technology prove profoundly disruptive. If, for example, AI is unleashed on a fully Semantic Web to the extent that any information on the Web is instantly "robo-cataloged," the career path of cataloging could disappear. In an article published in 1996, Martin Dillon and Erik Jul may have been the first to wonder if such a scenario might someday unfold:

> Is the practice of cataloging-where access is achieved for an object through a surrogate—no longer an approach worth applying or refining? Is there some evolutionary step we are missing, some new generation of access tool that no longer requires the kind of finicky extraction of descriptive properties from an object, and the formation from these extractions of a discrete record that, with added indicators of content, is then manipulated through a "catalog"?[169]

Less speculatively, and less apocalyptically, the cataloging profession has undeniably experienced profound change over recent decades. Besides the contraction of the cataloging workforce, catalogers have undergone an existential crisis so profound that they have repeatedly addressed the question, "What do we even call ourselves?" In 2000, Brad Eden addressed this issue in an article entitled, "Cataloger? Knowledge Manager?: What Do You Want to Be Called?"[170] By 2011, the number of job advertisements seeking "metadata/cataloging libraries" were increasing.[171] Job titles that included the phrase "metadata librarian," either alone or in combination with "cataloger," had become common enough by 2013 that the book *XML for Catalogers and Metadata Librarians* could be published with no need to explain, or apologize for, the title.[172] More radically, by 2022 the new job title of "Linked Data Librarian" was being discussed in the library literature.[173] A number of graduate library and information schools responded to cataloging's identity crisis by migrating from the teaching of "cataloging" to the teaching of "information organization" (IO).

Whatever job title they may hold, present-day catalogers face challenges that their predecessors could not have imagined. Circa 1995, recent library-school graduates stepping into their first jobs as catalogers would have been expected to be, at minimum, familiar with MARC; today, catalogers need to know MARC, which is still in use in many libraries, while also having familiarity with BIBFRAME, XML, RDA, and possibly other metadata schema. In response, library and information schools are increasingly incorporating metadata into their curricula. As Suzhen Chen and Margaret Joyce observe, "If there is a single term that recurs over and over in nearly every recent study written on IO education, it is metadata."[174] Opining on the importance of metadata for the future of libraries and librarians, Daniel N. Joudrey and Ryan McGinnis write that "whether they intend to work in cataloging or not, students will need a conceptual grounding in metadata concepts to navigate the changing information landscape—*especially* students who aim to work in cataloging."[175] The trick for library educators had become how to provide students with sufficient knowledge of past and present cataloging and metadata practices without bloating library graduate programs beyond anyone's tolerance.

Despite such challenges, metadata may well be where the future of cataloging lies. As this book's following chapter shows, academic libraries and archives are become increasingly involved in collecting, preserving, organizing, and providing access to the many varieties of information filling institutional repositories. As the importance of institutional repositories grows, the need for librarians who know their way around metadata is, barring some version of an AI apocalypse, only going to grow as well. More than traditional catalogers, academic libraries and archives will need metadata specialists who can organize information ranging from the digitized letters of a nineteenth-century college president to the born-digital emails of that president's twenty-first-century counterpart to a working climate researcher's massive set of data on polar icecaps. Similarly, it is not unreasonable to think that, as spending on physical materials continues its slow decline in academic libraries, the technical-services staff who once processed printed books and journals could be retrained to work with physical archival materials. If such scenarios unfold for the cataloging and technical-services workforce, it will testify to the prescience of those who added the word *futures* to the title of ALA's Core: Leadership, Technology, Futures, the present-day descendent of the RTS Division whose formation broke new ground all the way back in 1957.

Notes

1. In 1989 the Resources and Technical Services Division (RTSD) changed its name to become the Association for Library Collections and Technical Services (ALCTS). In 2020, ALCTS merged with the Library Information Technology Association (LITA) and the Library Leadership and Management Association (LLAMA) to form a new ALA division, Core: Leadership, Infrastructure, Futures.
2. Edwin B. Colburn, "The Resources and Technical Services Division," *Library Resources & Technical Services* 1, no. 1 (Winter 1957): 5–6, http://hdl.handle.net/11213/8710.
3. Joseph Lorence Cohen et al., "The Technical Services Division in Libraries: A Symposium," *College & Research Libraries* 10, no. 1 (January 1949): 56, https://doi.org/10.5860/crl_10_01_46.
4. Edwin B. Colburn, "The Value to the Modern Library of a Technical Services Department," *College & Research Libraries* 11, no. 1 (January 1950): 47–53, https://doi.org/10.5860/crl_11_01_47.
5. Louis Round Wilson and Frank A. Lundy, *Report of a Survey of the Library of the University of Notre Dame for the University of Notre Dame, November 1950-March 1952*, xiii, 195 p. (Chicago: American Library Association, 1952), 111, https://catalog.hathitrust.org/Record/001164891.
6. Gilbert William King, Herbert T. Spiro, and Allan D. Kotin, *Automation and the Library of Congress* (Washington, DC: Library of Congress, 1964), 1, https://catalog.hathitrust.org/Record/102186661.
7. Liz Mitchell, "Ron Diener, Systems Librarian: Hard-Nosed at Harvard," *American Libraries*, June 1976.
8. Frederick G. Kilgour, "Costs of Library Catalog Cards Produced by Computer," *Information Technology and Libraries* 1, no. 2 (May 31, 1968): 121–7, https://doi.org/10.6017/ital.v1i2.2929.
9. C. Sumner Spalding, ed., *Anglo-American Cataloging Rules. North American Text* (Chicago: American Library Association, 1967), 2.
10. Anne E. Bromley, "The Old Card Catalog: Collaborative Effort Will Preserve Its History," *University News*, December 9, 2010, https://news.virginia.edu/content/old-card-catalog-collaborative-effort-will-preserve-its-history.
11. Richard J. Schulz, "Recent History of the Princeton University Library Catalog," *University Archives* (blog), July 2011, https://universityarchives.princeton.edu/2011/07/recent-history-of-the-princeton-university-library-catalog/.
12. J. McRee Elrod, "Is the Card Catalogue's Unquestioned Sway in North America Ending?," *Journal of Academic Librarianship* 2, no. 1 (March 1976): 4–8.

13. Brady D. Lund and Daniel A. Agbaji, "What Scheme Do We Prefer? An Examination of Preference Between Library of Congress and Dewey Decimal Classification Among U.S.-Based Academic Library Employees," *Knowledge Organization* 45, no. 5 (2018): 383, https://doi.org/10.5771/0943-7444-2018-5-380.

14. Julián Aguilar, "Lawmakers Rebuke Library of Congress Over Dropping 'Illegal Alien' Language," *The Texas Tribune*, May 19, 2016, https://www.texastribune.org/2016/05/19/texas-congressmen-library-congress-keep-aliens-and/.

15. Policy and Standards Division, "Library of Congress Subject Headings: Module 5.2," Library of Congress, February 2017, https://www.loc.gov/catworkshop/lcsh/PDF%20scripts/5-2_Principles_of_heading_assignment_part2.pdf.

16. "Twenty-Percent Rule (LCSH)," Librarianship Studies & Information Technology, July 2, 2019, https://www.librarianshipstudies.com/2018/12/twenty-percent-rule-lcsh.html.

17. Melvil Dewey, "Co-Operative Cataloging," *American Library Journal*, November 30, 1876, https://catalog.hathitrust.org/Record/000494488.

18. William J. Welsh, "Report on Library of Congress Plans for Cataloging in Publication," *Library Resources & Technical Services* 15, no. 1 (1971): 25–8, http://hdl.handle.net/11213/8766.

19. Deborah A. Mohr and Anita Schuneman, "Changing Roles: Original Cataloging by Paraprofessionals in ARL Libraries," *Library Resources & Technical Services* 41, no. 3 (2011): 208.

20. Robert T. Ivey, "Perceptions of the Future of Cataloging: Is the Sky Really Falling?," *Cataloging & Classification Quarterly* 47, no. 5 (June 3, 2009): 467.

21. Lois Buttlar and Rajinder Garcha, "Catalogers in Academic Libraries: Their Evolving and Expanding Roles," *College & Research Libraries* 59, no. 4 (July 1, 1998): 313, https://doi.org/10.5860/crl.59.4.311.

22. Marybeth F. Grimes and Paul W. Grimes, "The Academic Librarian Labor Market and the Role of the Master of Library Science Degree: 1975 through 2005," *The Journal of Academic Librarianship* 34, no. 4 (July 2008): 333.

23. Roma Harris, "Information Technology and the De-Skilling of Librarians," *Computers in Libraries* 12, no. 1 (1992): 8–10.

24. Thomas H. Marshall and Jennalyn W. Tellman, "Processing Foreign Language Books without Catalog Librarians at the University of Arizona Library," *Against the Grain* 12, no. 3 (June 1, 2000): 28, https://doi.org/10.7771/2380-176X.3363.

25. Joan M. Leysen and Jeanne M. K. Boydston, "Supply and Demand for Catalogers," *Library Resources & Technical Services* 49, no. 4 (October 1, 2005): 259, https://doi.org/10.5860/lrts.49n4.250.

26. Clare B. Dunkle, "Outsourcing the Catalog Department: A Meditation Inspired by the Business and Library Literature," *Journal of Academic Librarianship* 22, no. 1 (January 1996): 33.

27. Marshall and Tellman, "Processing Foreign Language Books," 31.

28. Carmel C. Bush, Margo Sassé, and Patricia Smith, "Toward a New World Order: A Survey of Outsourcing Capabilities of Vendors for Acquisitions, Cataloging and Collection Development Services," *Library Acquisitions* 18, no. 4 (January 3, 1994): 397–416.

29. Michael Gorman, "The Corruption of Cataloging," *Library Journal*, September 1995.

30. Glen Holt, "Catalog Outsourcing: No Clear-Cut Choice," *Library Journal*, September 1995.

31 Douglas Cargille and Karen Cargille, "Sleeping with the Enemy: The Love/Hate Relationship between Acquisitions and Collection Development," *Library Acquisitions: Practice & Theory* 20, no. 1 (March 1996): 44.

32 Cargille and Cargille, "Sleeping with the Enemy," 43.

33 Lynn B. Williams, "Subject Knowledge for Subject Specialists," *Collection Management* 14, no. 3–4 (1991): 31–47.

34 Beverly P. Lynch, "The Development of the Academic Library in American Higher Education and the Role of the Academic Librarian," in *The Academic Library in the United States: Historical Perspectives*, ed. Mark L. McCallon and John Mark Tucker (Jefferson: McFarland & Company, Inc., Publishers, 2022), 51–2.

35 Fred J. Hay, "The Subject Specialist in the Academic Library: A Review Article," *Journal of Academic Librarianship* 16, no. 1 (March 1990): 12–13.

36 Dennis W. Dickinson, "Subject Specialists in Academic Libraries: The Once and Future Dinosaurs," in *New Horizons for Academic Libraries: Papers Presented at the First National Conference of the Association of College & Research Libraries, Boston, MA, November 8–11, 1978*, ed. Robert D. Stueart and Richard D. Johnson (New York: Saur, 1979).

37 Larry McMurtry, *Books: A Memoir* (New York: Simon & Schuster, 2008): 211.

38 Thomas A. Peters, "What's the Big Deal?," *Journal of Academic Librarianship* 27, no. 4 (July 2001): 303.

39 Ross Atkinson, "Contingency and Contradiction: The Place(s) of the Library at the Dawn of the New Millennium," *Journal of the American Society for Information Science and Technology* 52, no. 1 (2001): 4.

40 Kara M. Whatley, "New Roles of Liaison Librarians: A Liaison's Perspective," *Research Library Issues*, no. 265 (August 1, 2009): 29, https://doi.org/10.29242/rli.265.6.

41 Christine DeZelar-Tiedman, "Crashing the Party: Catalogers as Digital Librarians," *OCLC Systems & Services: International Digital Library Perspectives* 20, no. 4 (2004): 145–7, https://conservancy.umn.edu/server/api/core/bitstreams/acbe54e0-7631-4e84-a362-39a0fde1be20/content.

42 Dorothy Gregor and Carol Mandel, "Cataloging Must Change!," *Library Journal* 116, no. 6 (April 1, 1991): 44.

43 Gregor and Mandel, "Cataloging Must Change!," 47.

44 Gregor and Mandel, "Cataloging Must Change!," 43.

45 David A. Fiste and Christopher P. Thornton, "Bibliographic Services of the Future," *Technical Services Quarterly* 10, no. 3 (June 21, 1993): 31.

46 IFLA Study Group on the Functional Requirements for Bibliographic Records and Standing Committee of the IFLA Section on Cataloguing, "Functional Requirements for Bibliographic Records. Final Report," International Federation of Library Associations and Institutions, September 1997. As amended and corrected through February 2009, https://repository.ifla.org/handle/123456789/811.

47 Anthony Panizzi, *Catalogue of Printed Books in the British Museum. Volume I* (London: Printed by order of the Trustees, 1841), https://catalog.hathitrust.org/Record/001761602.

48 Charles Coffin Jewett, *Smithsonian Report on the Construction of Catalogues of Libraries, and Their Publication by Means of Separate, Stereotyped Titles, with Rules and Examples* (District of Columbia: Smithsonian Institution, 1853), https://catalog.hathitrust.org/Record/011531326.

49 Charles A. Cutter, *Rules for a Printed Dictionary Catalogue: Public Libraries in the United States of America, Their History, Condition, and Management, Part II* (Washington: Government Printing Office, 1876), https://catalog.hathitrust.org/Record/100771573.

50 *Catalog Rules Author and Title Entries*, American Edition (Chicago: American Library Association, 1908), https://catalog.hathitrust.org/Record/001162692.

51 Catalog Code Revision Committee of the American Library Association, *A.L.A. Catalog Rules, Author and Title Entries*, Preliminary American 2nd ed. (Chicago: American Library Association, 1941), https://hdl.handle.net/2027/mdp.39015033890123.

52 Catalog Code Revision Committee of the American Library Association, *A.L.A. Catalog Rules, Author and Title Entries*.

53 Library of Congress. Descriptive Cataloging Division, *Rules for Descriptive Cataloging in the Library of Congress* (Washington: U.S. Government Printing Office, 1949), https://catalog.hathitrust.org/Record/001162924.

54 "Statement of Principles Adopted by the International Conference on Cataloguing Principles. Paris, October 1961," International Federation of Library Associations and Institutions, 1961, https://web.archive.org/web/20140123232043/http://www.nl.go.kr/icc/paper/20.pdf.

55 Sally H. McCallum, "MARC: Keystone for Library Automation," *IEEE Annals of the History of Computing* 24, no. 2 (June 2002): 43.

56 "American National Standard for Bibliographic Information Interchange on Magnetic Tape" (New York: American National Standards Institute, 1971).

57 "Format for Bibliographic Information Interchange on Magnetic Tape" (Switzerland: International Organization for Standardization, July 1, 1973).

58 Spalding, *Anglo-American Cataloging Rules*, 1967.

59 "Statement of Principles Adopted by the International Conference on Cataloguing Principles."

60 C. Sumner Spalding, ed., *Anglo-American Cataloging Rules* (Chicago: American Library Association, 1970).

61 IFLA Study Group on the Functional Requirements for Bibliographic Records.

62 ISBD Review Group, "ISBD(M): International Standard Bibliographic Description for Monographic Publications," International Federation of Library Associations and Institutions, 2002, https://www.ifla.org/wp-content/uploads/2019/05/assets/cataloguing/isbd/isbd-m_2002.pdf.

63 Alan Hopkinson, "International Access to Bibliographic Data: MARC and MARC-Related Activities," *Journal of Documentation* 40, no. 1 (January 1, 1984): 16.

64 IFLA Working Group on Content Designators, International Federation of Library Associations and Institutions. Section on Cataloguing, and International Federation of Library Associations and Institutions. Section on Mechanization, *UNIMARC: Universal MARC Format/Recommended by the IFLA Working Group on Content Designators Set up by the IFLA Section on Cataloguing and the IFLA Section on Mechanization* (London: IFLA International Office for UBC, 1977).

65 "UNIMARC Committee–IFLA," International Federation of Library Associations and Institutions, https://www.ifla.org/units/unimarc-rg/ (accessed July 11, 2024).

66 Michael Gorman and Paul W. Winkler, eds., *Anglo-American Cataloguing Rules*, Second Edition (Chicago: ALA, 1978).

67 Robert L. Maxwell, *Maxwell's Handbook for AACR2: Explaining and Illustrating the Anglo-American Cataloguing Rules Through the 2003 Update* (Chicago: American Library Association, 2004), xvii.

68 Kathy Strand, "On My Mind," *American Libraries*, June 1980.

69 Susan K. Martin, "Managing Technological Change: A Learning Experience," *American Libraries*, February 1980.

70 Priscilla Caplan, *Metadata Fundamentals for All Librarians* (Chicago: ALA Editions, 2003), 76.

71 Bipin C. Desai, "Supporting Discovery in Virtual Libraries," *Journal of the American Society for Information Science* 48, no. 3 (March 1997): 194.

72 National Information Standards Organization, "ANSI/NISO Z39.85-2012, The Dublin Core Metadata Element Set" (NISO), https://doi.org/10.3789/ansi.niso.z39.85-2012 (accessed July 7, 2024).

73 Jackie Radebaugh, "MARC Goes Global–and Lite," *American Libraries*, February 2003.

74 Network Development and MARC Standards Office, "MARC Standards," Library of Congress, https://www.loc.gov/marc/ (accessed July 11, 2024).

75 Barbara Tillett, "A Conceptual Model for the Bibliographic Universe," Library of Congress, 2004, https://www.loc.gov/cds/downloads/FRBR.PDF.

76 Daniel N. Joudrey, Arlene G. Taylor, and Katherine M. Wisser, *The Organization of Information*, Fourth edition, Library and Information Science Text Series (Santa Barbara: Libraries Unlimited, an imprint of ABC-CLIO, LLC, 2018), 204–5.

77 Linda Gonzalez, "What Is FRBR?," *Library Journal*, April 16, 2005.

78 IFLA Study Group on the Functional Requirements for Bibliographic Records and Standing Committee of the IFLA Section on Cataloguing, *Functional Requirements for Bibliographic Records: Final Report*, vol. 19, UBCIM Publications-New Series (München: G.K. Saur, 1998), https://repository.ifla.org/bitstream/123456789/830/1/ifla-functional-requirements-for-bibliographic-records-frbr-en-1998.pdf.

79 IFLA Working Group on Functional Requirements and Numbering of Authority Records (FRANAR), "Functional Requirements for Authority Data: A Conceptual Model," 2009, https://www.ifla.org/wp-content/uploads/files/assets/cataloguing/frad/frad_2013.pdf.

80 Zeng Marcia Lei, Maja Žumer, and Athena Salaba, "Functional Requirements for Subject Authority Data (FRSAD): A Conceptual Model," International Federation of Library Associations and Institutions, June 2010, https://repository.ifla.org/bitstream/123456789/835/3/frsad-final-report.pdf.

81 IFLA Cataloguing Section and IFLA Meetings of Experts on an International Cataloguing Code, "Statement of International Cataloguing Principles (ICP)" (International Federation of Library Associations and Institutions, December 2016), https://www.ifla.org/wp-content/uploads/2019/05/assets/cataloguing/icp/icp_2016-en.pdf.

82 Tim Berners-Lee, *Weaving the Web: The Original Design and Ultimate Destiny of the World Wide Web by Its Inventor* (New York: HarperBusiness, 1999), 157–18.

83 Christian Bizer, Tom Heath, and Tim Berners-Lee, "Linked Data— The Story So Far," *International Journal on Semantic Web and Information Systems* 5, no. 3 (July 1, 2009): 2, https://doi.org/10.4018/jswis.2009081901.

84. Deepjyoti Kalita and Dipen Deka, "Searching the Great Metadata Timeline: A Review of Library Metadata Standards from Linear Cataloguing Rules to Ontology Inspired Metadata Standards," *Library Hi Tech* 39, no. 1 (March 12, 2020): 191.

85. Bizer, Heath, Berners-Lee, "Linked Data—The Story So Far," 2.

86. Tiziana Possemato and Mauro Guerrini, "Linked Data: A New Alphabet for the Semantic Web," *Italian Journal of Library and Information Science* 4, no. 1 (January 2013): 79–80, https://doi.org/10.4403/jlis.it-6305.

87. Ralph W. Manning, "The Anglo-American Cataloging Rules and Their Future," *Library Resources & Technical Services* 44, no. 3 (2000): 132.

88. Joint Steering Committee for Development of RDA, Canadian Library Association, and Chartered Institute of Library and Information Professionals, *RDA: Resource Description and Access* (Chicago: American Library Association, 2010).

89. Lynne C. Howarth and Jean Weihs, "Making the Link: AACR to RDA: Part 1: Setting the Stage," *Cataloging & Classification Quarterly* 45, no. 2 (October 31, 2007): 3–18.

90. Michael Gorman, "RDA: Imminent Debacle," *American Libraries*, December 2007.

91. Sheila S. Intner, "From the Sublime to the Ridiculous," *Technicalities*, November/December 2012.

92. Stuart Hunt, "RDA in Your ILS," *Catalogue and Index*, no. 169 (December 2012): 22–4, https://cdn.ymaws.com/www.cilip.org.uk/resource/collection/F71F19C3-49CF-462D-8165-B07967EE07F0/Catalogue_and_Index_issue_169,_December_2012.pdf.

93. Céline Carty, "RDA at ALA, Or, Attack of the Acronyms," *Catalogue and Index*, no. 169 (December 2012): 20–1, https://cdn.ymaws.com/www.cilip.org.uk/resource/collection/F71F19C3-49CF-462D-8165-B07967EE07F0/Catalogue_and_Index_issue_169,_December_2012.pdf.

94. Stuart Hunt, "RDA: An Innovation in Cataloguing," *Insights: The UKSG Journal* 26, no. 2 (July 1, 2013): 185, https://doi.org/10.1629/2048-7754.69.

95. James Hennelly, "Is RDA a Global Standard?," *American Libraries*, September 23, 2016, https://americanlibrariesmagazine.org/2016/09/23/rda-global-standard/.

96. Salman Haider, "Survey of Emerging Cataloging Practices: Use of RDA by Academic Libraries," Primary Research Group, 2016, 18, https://www.primaryresearch.com/Upload/ReportPdf/20160504_134351Survey_of_Emerging_Cataloging_Practices_Use_of_RDA_by_Academic_Libraries.pdf.

97. Roman S. Panchyshyn, Frank P. Lambert, and Sevim McCutcheon, "Resource Description and Access Adoption and Implementation in Public Libraries in the United States," *Library Resources & Technical Services* 63, no. 2 (April 24, 2019): 123–4.

98. Hennelly, "Catalog Locally, Share Globally: RDA's Cataloging Evolution Continues with the 3R Project," *American Libraries*, July 2021, https://americanlibrariesmagazine.org/2021/07/08/catalog-locally-share-globally/.

99. Joudrey, Taylor, and Wisser, *The Organization of Information*, 283.

100. Eric Miller, Victoria Muller Ogbuji, and Kathy MacDougall, "Bibliographic Framework as a Web of Data: Linked Data Model and Supporting Services" (Library of Congress, November 12, 2012), https://www.loc.gov/bibframe/pdf/marcld-report-11-21-2012.pdf.

101. "Overview of the BIBFRAME 2.0 Model (BIBFRAME-Bibliographic Framework Initiative)," Library of Congress, https://www.loc.gov/bibframe/docs/bibframe2-model.html (accessed July 19, 2024).

102 Madireng Monyela, "Library Catalogue on the Cloud: The BIBFRAME Approach," *Journal of Library Metadata* 23, no. 1–2 (April 3, 2023): 64–5.

103 Jacob Jett et al., "Applying BIBFRAME in Large-Scale Digital Libraries: The HathiTrust Research Center's Experience," *Proceedings of the Association for Information Science and Technology* 57, no. 1 (October 2020): e410.

104 Marshall Breeding, "2023 Library Systems Report: The Advance of Open Systems," *American Libraries*, May 2023, https://americanlibrariesmagazine.org/2023/05/01/2023-library-systems-report/.

105 Abigail Sparling and Ian Bigelow, "Control or Chaos : Embracing Change and Harnessing Innovation in an Ecosystem of Shared Bibliographic Data," *Italian Journal of Library and Information Science* 13, no. 1 (2022): 82, https://doi.org/10.4403/jlis.it-12735.

106 Pat Riva, Patrick Le Boeuf, and Maja Žumer, "IFLA Library Reference Model A Conceptual Model for Bibliographic Information," International Federation of Library Associations and Institutions, 2017, https://repository.ifla.org/bitstream/123456789/40/1/ifla-lrm-august-2017_rev201712.pdf.

107 Violet B. Fox, "Cataloging News," *Cataloging & Classification Quarterly* 56, no. 4 (June 2018): 387–8.

108 "Total Number of Websites," Internet Live Stats, https://www.internetlivestats.com/total-number-of-websites/ (accessed July 31, 2024).

109 Kathryn Kranhold, "The Real Action: Ad Bowl XXXIV: This Year's Line-Up Features A Heavy Blitz of Dot-Coms And Some Odd Cowboys," *Wall Street Journal*, January 28, 2000.

110 Oxford English Dictionary, "Cybrarian, n." (Oxford University Press, July 2023), Oxford English Dictionary, https://doi.org/10.1093/OED/1567651017.

111 Robert W. Pasicznuk, "Web Your Library," *Colorado Libraries*, Winter 1995.

112 Ray E. Metz, *Using the World Wide Web and Creating Home Pages: A How-to-Do-It Manual* (New York: Neal-Schuman Publishers, 1996).

113 Kristen L. Garlock and Sherry Piontek, *Building the Service-Based Library Web Site: A Step-by-Step Guide to Design and Options* (Chicago: American Library Association, 1996).

114 William A. Britten, "Building and Organizing Internet Collections," *Library Acquisitions: Practice & Theory* 19, no. 2 (1995): 246.

115 Britten, "Building and Organizing Internet Collections," 245–6.

116 Steve Mitchell and Margaret Mooney, "INFOMINE–A Model Web-Based Academic Virtual Library," *Information Technology and Libraries* 15, no. 1 (1996): 20.

117 Julie Mason et al., "INFOMINE: Promising Directions in Virtual Library Development," *First Monday* 5, no. 6 (June 2000), https://firstmonday.org/ojs/index.php/fm/article/view/763/672.

118 Caplan Priscilla, "Cataloging Internet Resources," *The Public-Access Computer Systems Review* 4, no. 2 (1993): 61, https://uh-ir.tdl.org/server/api/core/bitstreams/b9caf397-94f5-47bc-b012-bb4dba02ea56/content.

119 Martin Dillon and Erik Jul, "Cataloging Internet Resources: The Convergence of Libraries and Internet Resources," *Cataloging & Classification Quarterly* 22, no. 3–4 (September 30, 1996): 217.

120 Vinh-The Lam, "Cataloging Internet Resources: Why, What, How," *Cataloging & Classification Quarterly* 29, no. 3 (July 2000): 53.

121 Ruth C. Curter and Roger Brisson, "Editorial," *Journal of Internet Cataloging* 1, no. 1 (March 24, 1997): 1–2.

122 Merrilee Proffitt, "How and Why of User Studies: RLG's RedLightGreen as a Case Study," *Journal of Archival Organization* 4, no. 1–2 (April 11, 2007): 87.

123 Dylan Tweney, "Mining the Catalog," Storylines, January 15, 2003, https://dylan.tweney.com/2003/01/15/mining-the-catalog/.

124 Brad Eden, "FRBR Implementations," *Library Technology Reports*, November 2006, https://journals.ala.org/index.php/ltr/article/viewFile/4564/5373.

125 Joudrey, Taylor, and Wisser, *The Organization of Information*, 25–6.

126 Brian Morrissey, "The Dot-Com Super Bowl," *MediaWeek*, January 24, 2011.

127 Cecily Johns, "Cataloging Internet Resources: An Administrative View," *Journal of Internet Cataloging* 1, no. 1 (March 24, 1997): 17–23.

128 Steven Jack Miller and Tom Zillner, "CORC," *Information Technology & Libraries* 22, no. 1 (March 2003): 44.

129 Miller and Zillner, "CORC," 44.

130 Jeffrey Beall, "Editor's Introduction," *Journal of Library Metadata* 8, no. 1 (April 9, 2008): 1–3, https://doi.org/10.1300/J517v08n01_01.

131 Joseph R. Matthews, "The Automated Library System Marketplace, 1982: Change and More Change," March 15, 1983.

132 Joseph R. Matthews, "Unrelenting Change: The 1984 Automated Library System Marketplace," *Library Journal*, April 1, 1985.

133 Matthews, "The Automated Library System Marketplace," 1983.

134 Joseph R. Matthews, "Competition & Change: The 1983 Automated Library System Marketplace," *Library Journal*, May 1, 1984.

135 Frank R. Bridge, "Automated System Marketplace 1991," *Library Journal*, April 1, 1991.

136 Frank R. Bridge and Francine Fialkoff, "Automated System Marketplace 1993," *Library Journal*, April 15, 1993.

137 Matthews, "Unrelenting Change," 1985.

138 Bridge, "Automated System Marketplace 1991," 1991.

139 Frank R. Bridge, "Automated System Marketplace 1992," *Library Journal*, April 1, 1992.

140 Robert A. Walton and Frank R. Bridge, "Automated System Marketplace 1990: Focusing on Software Sales and Joint Venture," *Library Journal*, April 1, 1990.

141 Jeff Barry, Jose-Marie Griffiths, and Peiling Wang, "Jockeying for Supremacy in a Networked World," *Library Journal*, April 1, 1996.

142 Theresa Pepin and Jeff Barry, "The Competitive Edge: Expanded Access Drives Vendors," *Library Journal*, April 1, 1997.

143 Jeff Barry, "Automated System Marketplace 2001: Closing in on Content," *Library Journal*, April 1, 2001.

144 Marshall Breeding, "Automation Marketplace 2008: Opportunity Out of Turmoil," *Library Journal*, April 1, 2008, https://librarytechnology.org/document/13192.

145 Marshall Breeding, "Automated System Marketplace 2006: Reshuffling the Deck: Deal-Making Fueled Development of ILS and Non-ILS Products," *Library Journal*, April 1, 2006, https://librarytechnology.org/document/11996.

146 Marshall Breeding, "Automation Marketplace 2009: Investing in the Future," *Library Journal*, April 1, 2009, https://librarytechnology.org/document/13895.

147 Marshall Breeding, "Library Systems Report 2019: Cycles of Innovation," *American Libraries*, May 2019, https://americanlibrariesmagazine.org/2019/05/01/library-systems-report-2019.

148 Marshall Breeding, "Library Systems Report 2018: New Technologies Enable an Expanded Vision of Library Services," *American Libraries*, May 2018, https://americanlibrariesmagazine.org/2018/05/01/library-systems-report-2018.

149 Marshall Breeding, "2020 Library Systems Report: Fresh Opportunities amid Consolidation," *American Libraries*, May 2020, https://americanlibrariesmagazine.org/2020/05/01/2020-library-systems-report.

150 Amanda Y. Makula, "Come Together: Interdepartmental Collaboration to Connect the IR and Library Catalog," *The Serials Librarian* 76, no. 1–4 (June 14, 2019): 201–7.

151 Breeding, "2020 Library Systems Report," 2020.

152 Marshall Breeding, "2021 Library Systems Report: Advancing Library Technologies in Challenging Times," *American Libraries*, May 2021, https://americanlibrariesmagazine.org/2021/05/03/2021-library-systems-report.

153 Barry, "Automated System Marketplace 2001," 2001.

154 Breeding, "Library Systems Report 2018," 2018.

155 Breeding, "Library Systems Report 2019," 2019.

156 Marshall Breeding, "Automation Marketplace 2007: An Industry Redefined," *Library Journal*, April 1, 2007, https://librarytechnology.org/document/12576.

157 Marshall Breeding, "Library Systems Report 2016: Power Plays," *American Libraries*, May 2016, https://americanlibrariesmagazine.org/2016/05/02/library-systems-report-2016.

158 Marshall Breeding, "Library Systems Report 2017: Competing Visions for Technology, Openness, and Workflow," *American Libraries*, May 2017, https://americanlibrariesmagazine.org/2017/05/01/library-systems-report-2017.

159 Breeding, Library Systems Report 2018," 2018.

160 Breeding, "2023 Library Systems Report," 2023.

161 Breeding, "Automation Marketplace 2007."

162 Marshall Breeding, "Automation Marketplace 2011: The New Frontier," *Library Journal* 136, no. 6 (April 1, 2011 2011): 24–34, https://librarytechnology.org/document/15557.

163 Marshall Breeding, "Kuali OLE: The Open Source Library Services Platform," *Smart Libraries Newsletter*, September 1, 2013, https://librarytechnology.org/document/18671.

164 Breeding, "Library Systems Report 2016," 2016.

165 Breeding, "Library Systems Report 2019," 2019.

166 Breeding, "2023 Library Systems Report," 2023.

167 Marshall Breeding, "2024 Library Systems Report," *American Libraries*, May 2024, https://americanlibrariesmagazine.org/2024/05/01/2024-library-systems-report.

168 Breeding, "2024 Library Systems Report," 2024.

169 Dillon and Jul, "Cataloging Internet Resources," 232.

170. Brad Eden, "Cataloger? Knowledge Manager?: What Do You Want to Be Called?," *Information Technology* 11, no. 2 (2000): 5–7.

171. Margaret E. I. Kipp et al., "Emerging Trends in Knowledge Organization and Information Organization Course Curriculum," *Proceedings of the American Society for Information Science and Technology* 48, no. 1 (2011): 1–4, https://doi.org/10.1002/meet.2011.14504801079.

172. Timothy W. Cole and Myung-Ja K. Han, *XML for Catalogers and Metadata Librarians* (Santa Barbara: Libraries Unlimited, 2013).

173. Donna Ellen Frederick, "The Linked Data Librarian–An Emerging Speciality or the New Cataloguer [Sic]," *Library Hi Tech News* 39, no. 8 (September 2022): 5–11.

174. Suzhen Chen and Margaret Joyce, "Teaching a Cataloging/Metadata Course in a Changing World: Experience and Reflection," *International Journal of Librarianship* 4, no. 2 (December 29, 2019): 111, https://doi.org/10.23974/ijol.2019.vol4.2.132.

175. Daniel N. Joudrey and Ryan McGinnis, "Graduate Education for Information Organization, Cataloging, and Metadata," *Cataloging & Classification Quarterly* 52, no. 5 (July 4, 2014): 512–13.

5 Distinctive Collections Go Digital

Following the logic informing the old adage "The library is the heart of the campus," then distinctive collections (i.e., special collections and archives) must be considered the heart of the heart. Distinctive collections, in the form of special collections and archival collections, are home to a library's rarest and most valuable treasures. If an academic library possesses a manuscript letter signed by a significant historical figure, a career's worth of notebooks from the lab of a faculty member who earned election to the National Academy of Sciences, or a rare first edition of a printed book, these items will be housed in the library's distinctive collections. Often, the treasure-house aspect of distinctive collections is emphasized through the imposing design and architecture of the spaces they occupy, whether it be an elegantly furnished reading room located within a multi-function library building or, on some larger campuses, a freestanding building of monumental size and design. Although together they comprise the key components of an academic library's distinctive collections, there are significant differences between special collections and archives.

Special Collections

In the words of Meredith R. Evans, "Special collections in any generation or iteration are 'special' because of the rarity, scarcity, uniqueness, and distinctiveness of their holdings."[1] Though some special collections operate under the somewhat quaint rubric of *rare book library*, special collections may include not only published rare books but also such materials as maps, artwork, periodicals, media, ephemera, and manuscripts. Very broadly, the specialty of special collections are esoteric materials that require more custodial oversight than materials kept in open library stacks. Special collections may also actively collect and permanently house materials that are not particularly special if those materials relate to research areas of high interest to the parent institution. For example, within Brigham Young University's L. Tom Perry Special Collections, the Mormon & Western Publications Collection includes not only a wealth of rare, scarce, and unique materials relating to the Mormon faith and the American West but also readily available books and other published materials on those same topics that could be part of a circulating collection. In practice, in many libraries, the special-collections copies of readily available items are duplicated by copies available in the circulating collection.

Archives

Painting with a very broad brush, it is fair to say that archives differ from special collections in that archival collections consist primarily of unique, primary-source materials rather than published items. In addition, *academic* archives typically operate under a mandate to collect primary-source materials related to the history of the institution with which they are affiliated.

Robert P. Spindler provides a succinct definition of the role of academic archivists and the purpose of the collections they manage:

> Academic archivists are charged with responsibility for documenting the broad landscape of evidence, history, and culture associated with their institutions, and most university archives address this mandate by collecting, preserving, and making accessible both institutional publications and faculty research products.[2]

Distinguishing between special collections and archives is often complicated by the fact that within the organizational structures of some academic libraries, the campus archives exist as a subunit of special collections, possibly sharing both space and staff. Again using the Brigham Young University (BYU) Library as an example, within that library's organizational structure, the University Archives function as a subunit of the L. Tom Perry Special Collections. On campuses like BYU, the phrase *special collections* may encompass both special collections (narrowly defined) and archives.[3] Another source of confusion when talking about academic archives is that, in informal usage, the word *archives* may be used to indicate an archival collection as well as an archive functional unit: *The Ned Brooks Science and Genre Fiction archives are maintained by the campus archives.*

Academic archives are distinguished from special collections in that academic archives are the permanent home of unique institutional materials, including such examples as the official correspondence of past university administrators, the research and pedagogical records of retired faculty, oral histories collected from students, faculty, and staff, and historic photographs of campus buildings, events, and people. Records management—the legally mandated processing of official administrative and business records—is another institutional role that may be assigned to a campus archives unit, though some campuses instead assign records management to an organizationally distinct administrative unit. While it is true that academic archives are more focused on collecting unique materials than published works, archives may nonetheless contain published works acquired as parts of donated collections as well as such in-house publications as alumni magazines, yearbooks, and student newspapers. Academic archives may also collect and preserve a wide range of campus memorabilia and ephemera, such as event programs and tickets, athletic uniforms, campaign materials from student-body elections, flyers created by campus activists, plaques, trophies, certificates, and the like.[4] Beyond materials that relate directly to an institution's history, academic archives often collect materials relevant to the specific research interests of their home institutions, including the archival records of individuals, families, agencies, and corporations. For one example, the archives of the University of Idaho contain a wealth of material relating to forestry and mining—two research areas of great importance to the university and the State of Idaho. Less predictably, a third area of focus for the University of Idaho archives is jazz music.[5]

The Changing Perceptions of Distinctive Collections

The differing functions of special collections and archives aside, the rarity, scarcity, uniqueness, and distinctiveness of their holdings result in many commonalities between the two. For both special collections and archives, the materials they hold do not normally circulate and must be consulted on the premises under staff supervision. As a precaution against theft or damage, local policies often require potential users of distinctive collections to register and undergo a screening process before being allowed to access materials; once registered and screened, users may be required to deposit their possessions in lockers and are allowed to carry into the reading room only paper and pencils (no pens). In the interest of security, the storage areas for the materials held by distinctive collections are typically off-limits to the public. Denied the opportunity to browse, users of distinctive collections must page items they wish to consult sight unseen and are typically not permitted to consult more than a few items at a time. Distinctive collections that rely on remote storage facilities may even require users to submit requests for items they wish to consult several days in advance of a planned visit. On the one hand, there is justification for the security procedures practiced in distinctive collections. As books like Harvey Miles' *The Island of Lost Maps: A True Story of Cartographic Crime* make clear, the criminal threats to valuable special collections and archival materials are quite real.[6] On the other hand, the security procedures practiced in most reading rooms are not particularly effective in stopping determined thieves, including the antiques dealer whose long career of razoring valuable map plates out of special-collections books is chronicled in *The Island of Lost Maps*. Or the Minnesota thief whose cache of rare books stolen from libraries around the country numbered 30,000 volumes when he was finally arrested in 1990.[7]

Managers of distinctive collections may enforce additional policies and procedures that users see as a hindrance to their scholarly activities. For example, such technologies as laptops, digital cameras, scanning devices, and smartphones were long banned from the reading rooms of most distinctive collections, with policies slow to change even as these devices became common. A guide to using archives published in 2011 by the Society of American Archivists advises, "Many archives allow the use of cameras, laptops, and other personal digital devices, but restrictions may exist."[8] Even as late as 2024, statements such as, "Personal duplication/reproduction equipment is not allowed in the reading room without prior permission," still appear in reading-room policies.[9] Users also find it frustrating that opening hours for distinctive collections often add up to less than forty hours a week with no options for access on evenings, weekends, or holidays. Some reading rooms go so far as to close for the daily lunch hour. Even though scant opening hours are often the unavoidable consequence of inadequate budgets, they nonetheless render many distinctive collections inaccessible to potential users.

Overreachingly restrictive policies and procedures have inspired both those outside and inside the field of distinctive collections to level accusations of elitism. In the very first issue of *RBM: A Journal of Rare Books, Manuscripts, and Cultural Heritage*, special-collections librarian Daniel Traister calls out "the standard attitudes of my profession" for a tendency to value preservation over access:

> All of us know people who have been turned away from, had difficulties at, or experienced condescension, downright rudeness, or suspicion of their integrity, cleanliness, or general demeanor while trying to use—or simply not been encouraged to think about using—rare book and manuscript repositories. . . . [Special collections] exist, viewed from one not entirely

unreasonable perspective, not to bring readers and books together but, rather, to keep them as far apart as possible. Always, of course, with the best interests of the books in mind.[10]

In extreme cases, managers of distinctive collections may render the most special of treasures effectively inaccessible by locking them away in tightly controlled vaults. Though the intention of providing special care and handling is to protect distinctive materials, the degree of protection can edge closer to the approach of museums, where visitors may look but not touch, than to that of libraries, where users are expected to, as the word *user* implies, lay hands on the materials and get to work. Even more typical of museums than libraries is the fact that many distinctive collections charge not only copying fees but also permission fees for anyone who wants to reproduce distinctive materials in articles, books, films, or other public-facing media. A survey of 125 U.S. research library distinctive collections published in 2015 found, "Fifty-five percent of institutions charge use fees or permission fees, in addition to scanning fees, for publishing any content from their holdings."[11] In their defense, archival collections are land poor in that, while they may possess books, manuscripts, photos, and other materials that would sell for millions in the world's auction houses, they are often underfunded and lack the capital to carry out projects that would allow them to better care for, and make available to the public, their valuable (monetarily as well as scholarly) collections. From that perspective, charging a major Hollywood studio to use images from the campus archive in a big-budget film seems more than reasonable; on the other hand, charging an untenured assistant professor of gender studies for the right to reproduce a photograph in a scholarly book that will be lucky to sell 400 copies comes off more mean-spirited than not.

Like the treasures of museums, the treasures of library distinctive collections are often used as props for promoting the institutional brand. Of the five U.S. academic libraries that hold substantially complete copies of a Gutenberg Bible, four proudly and prominently mention that distinction on the homepages of their respective special collections.[12] Special treasures may also serve public relations and fund-raising purposes by being incorporated into heavily promoted exhibitions or shown off in private for the benefit of VIPs.

In calling out "my profession," Daniel Traister is careful to note that not everyone who works with distinctive collections is an obstacle to access. Similarly, Michael Garabedian characterizes "the kind of exclusivity sometimes associated with special collections libraries and the professionals who are responsible for the materials stored there" as the product of outdated "attitudes that many practitioners now deplore."[13] There is no doubt that, in the world of distinctive collections, attitudes of exclusivity and intellectual snobbery have gone increasingly out of fashion in the twenty-first century. For example, the mission statement of the University of Illinois Rare Books and Manuscript Library reads, in part:

> *Rare books and manuscripts, as a tangible part of the human record, are for everyone, engaging us with our shared histories. We preserve these cultural heritage materials to make them accessible to all who wish to connect with them, now and in the future. . . . The Rare Book & Manuscript Library is deeply committed to making our shared cultural heritage publicly available to all who wish to interact with it.*[14]

Hardly the sentiments of an organization determined to keep books and readers apart.

There are several reasons for the rejection of a tradition of elitism on the part of special-collections librarians and archivists in the twenty-first century. For simple self-preservation, managers of distinctive collections have come to see that their operations must serve a broader audience than a handful of privileged insiders if they are to stand any chance of successfully competing in campus budget battles. Furthering the retreat from elitism is the fact that any acts of exclusion that might be interpreted as racist, sexist, or classist are anathema on twenty-first-century campuses. Finally, the rise of digital technology has done more than any other force to democratize access to distinctive collections. In the digital age, academic special collections and archives have been able to extend their reach beyond the protective walls of grand reading rooms and the tight limits of bankers' hours by making parts, sometimes sizeable parts, of their collections both discoverable and accessible from anywhere at any time. Just as importantly, digital technology has helped to undermine the mindset that access must take a backseat to "the best interests of the books" by making it possible to share distinctive collections without the risk of loss or damage that comes with in-person use.

Digital Technology and Distinctive Collections: Access and Discovery

In the past, anyone who sought to make use of distant distinctive collections faced three obstacles: discovering exactly what distinctive materials existed, determining which libraries held those materials, and, finally, getting access to those materials. Though not a complete solution, digital technology has greatly enhanced discovery and access by reducing or, in the best cases, eliminating obstacles to access and discovery.

Discovering and Accessing Special Collections in the Analog Era

Imagine that a scholar in the year 1960 is searching for the kinds of materials held in special collections. After visiting every nearby special collection, the scholar would face the challenge of discovering and accessing materials held in distant special collections. In 1960, this scholar could consult bibliographies and footnotes in order to learn of the existence (though not necessarily the location) of books and other items not held by nearby libraries. Calling on personal networks of other scholars, librarians, and free-range bibliophiles could also be an aid to discovery and access. (A strategy still very much alive in the present day.) With luck, a scholarly colleague might be able to provide some assistance, pointing out that, say, all twenty numbers of *Bleak House* as it was serially published from March 1852 through September 1853 are held by the John Hay Library at Brown University. A scholar could also make bibliographic inquiries by sending letters (in 1960 a first-class stamp cost four cents, the equivalent of forty-three cents in 2024 dollars) or making (at the time very expensive) long-distance phone calls to likely special collections. The problem with relying on such resources as personal networks and long-distance communications as means of discovery was that these strategies often served to feed the elitism long associated with distinctive collections. A helpful response to an inquiry comes more readily to a scholar with the right connections and a high degree of privilege than to some unvetted, unconnected nobody. As a last resort, a scholar of an earlier era with time and money to spare could travel to distant special collections, hoping for the best.

One advantage scholars in 1960 had over those of previous generations is that they could consult *The National Union Catalog* (*NUC*), the first volumes of which were published in 1953, to discover what books were held by major U.S. and Canadian libraries. The limitation of *NUC* was that the cumbersome, multivolume set was never so comprehensive nor so up to date that a scholar at, say, the University of Missouri, Columbia, might not, after consulting *NUC*, travel all the way to the East Coast in pursuit of rare books that were, in fact, held by libraries in Kansas City or Saint Louis. Digital technology first enhanced the ability of scholars to discover remote materials, whether held in special or circulating collections, through the development of such bibliographic utilities as OCLC (1967) and RLIN (1975). Though for many years access to bibliographic utilities was largely limited to library catalogers, the launch of OCLC's FirstSearch in 1991 made it possible for non-librarians to independently search the collective holdings of thousands of libraries in order to confirm the existence and locations of millions of books and other items. The early 1990s also saw the connecting of local online public access catalogs (OPACs) to the internet, making it possible for scholars to use tools like the Gopher Protocol and, slightly later, web browsers to search the catalogs of libraries around the world. In addition, digital technology amplified the power of discovery via personal interactions, with email, listservs, Usenet groups, and websites facilitating fast and cheap communication among scholars and librarians as well as the wide sharing of specialized knowledge of books and other sources of scholarly information, the more esoteric of which might otherwise prove difficult, if not impossible, to discover.

Knowing that an item exists and which libraries hold it is all well and good, but there remains the last-mile problem of laying hands on a wanted item. Because special collections do not participate in interlibrary-loan agreements, it was long the case that anyone who wanted access to a book that was distinctive enough to be held in a special collection had no choice other than to travel to a place where that book was held and seek permission to consult it. The access situation greatly improved as the digitization projects of the early twenty-first century began bringing the full text of millions of books and other items online. Looking back again to the year 1960, few scholars of that time would have been lucky enough to enjoy ready access to a special collection in which they could have compared, side-by-side, the first editions of the six or nine (depending on how you count) revisions of *Leaves of Grass* that Walt Whitman saw into print between 1855 and 1889; today, anyone with access to the internet can freely view high-quality digital copies of every 1855-through-1889 first edition of Whitman's magnum opus. From a preservation perspective, older rare books such as the first editions of *Leaves of Grass* are ideal targets for digitization because making them available online provides access to irreplicable physical books without incurring any risk of damage or loss. From an operational perspective, older books like *Leaves of Grass* represent low-hanging fruit for digitization because their public-domain status means they are free of any copyright restrictions.

Some of the oldest and rarest of rare books became available online after being singled out for boutique-level digitization by the libraries holding them, as when the Ransom Center at the University of Texas digitized its copy of the Gutenberg Bible beginning in 2002.[15] However, a far greater number of public-domain books were digitized and made available online as a result of being swept up in such mass-digitization initiatives as the Google Books Project. In addition to books, millions of public-domain sound recordings, photographs, periodical articles, and other items housed in not-especially-accessible special collections have been made freely and widely available thanks to digitization. One notable, pioneering example of digitization projects that go beyond the book is Making of America, a joint project of Cornell University and the University of Michigan that got underway in the fall of 1995. By 2018, at which time Making of America transitioned to being served via HathiTrust, the project had digitized and made available the full texts of 100,000 journal and magazine articles dating from the period of 1850 to 1877.[16] A similar example is the University of California, Santa Barbara Cylinder Audio Archive, a digital collection of over 10,000 cylinder recordings that anyone can download or stream for free.[17]

In an essay published in 2002, a few years before the largest mass-digitization projects had gotten underway, Peter B. Hirtle accurately predicts that digitization will inevitably disrupt the nature of special collections, bluntly declaring, "*Electronic access will replace most uses of printed paper copies,*" and, "*The use of paper originals will decrease.*"[18] (Emphasis Hirtle.) Hirtle also observes that digitization will make special collections materials less special, rhetorically asking how important it will be for a library to own a seventeenth-century edition of a book like Leonard Mascall's *Booke of the arte and maner, howe to plant and graffe all sorts of trees* "when thirty-four different editions are available in digital facsimile form via Early English Books Online?"[19]

It's Not the Same, Now, Is It?

There is no getting around the fact that no digital copy of a physical object will ever be the exact equivalent of the object from which it was created. In fact, it is, to some extent, more accurate to describe the reproductions manifesting on computer screens as digital *surrogates* rather than as digital *copies*. Some see digital surrogates as inferior to analog originals. For example, it is well known that many music aficionados assert that analog recordings are superior to digital recordings, while very many readers report a preference for paper books over e-books.

That differences between digital surrogates and physical objects can sometimes hinder the pursuit of knowledge is illustrated by Paul Duguid's anecdote of observing, with some alarm, a researcher in an academic archive methodically sniffing each letter in a collection of eighteenth-century manuscript letters. It turns out there was a logical explanation for this seemingly bizarre behavior. In times past, letters sent during cholera outbreaks were treated with vinegar in hopes of preventing the spread of cholera via the mail. The letter sniffer, a medical historian, was trying to pinpoint the dates of a long-ago cholera outbreak by detecting on any of the letters the lingering scent of vinegar.[20] To state the obvious, nobody is going to detect the scent of vinegar, smoke, perfume, or any other odor by accessing a digital surrogate. Another shortcoming of digital surrogates is that when they are displayed on a screen it is often impossible to get an accurate sense of the size and substance of the physical object from which the surrogate was created. Is the original of the page image shown on screen a page from a printed book small enough to slip into the pocket of a Civil War uniform coat, or is it a page from an elephant folio that would cover a significant chunk of real estate if cracked open on a library table? Is the paper represented in the digital surrogate thin and cheap or thick and costly? If the original paper on which the text was printed was held up to the light, would it reveal chain lines and watermarks that are not visible in the digital image?

In the defense of digitization, the process can sometimes increase the readability of printed documents, in some cases revealing details that cannot be seen on paper.[21] It is also true that the ability to access, analyze, and combine digital surrogates has generated new ways of conducting research, such as the entire field of digital humanities, that were not possible with print.[22]

The point here is not to engage in the eternal debate about digital versus analog, as each has its advantages and disadvantages. What is not debatable is that, for most users in most circumstances, digital surrogates are perfectly adequate, with their ease of access more than compensating for any shortcomings compared to a physical object. Alternatively, it is also a fact that, in some special circumstances, digital surrogates are not good enough. It is for this latter reason that the preservation of physical books and other materials housed in special collections remains just as important today as it was in the past. Digitization has been a boon to access, but the idea that physical objects can be casually tossed into the shredder once they have been digitized is, fortunately, the stuff of dystopian fiction rather than the practice of librarians and archivists.

Discovering and Accessing Archival Collections in the Analog Era

For that same hypothetical scholar from the year 1960, discovering and accessing faraway archival collections would have presented a challenge similar to that presented by discovering and accessing faraway special collections. As Janice E. Ruth explains:

> *Especially before the advent of online catalogs and finding aids, researchers learned of pertinent [archival] collections by word-of-mouth from colleagues, by scanning footnotes and bibliographical references, by addressing numerous letters and telephone inquiries to multiple repositories, and by undertaking time-consuming and expensive research trips.*[23]

The 1962 publication of the first volumes of *The National Union Catalog of Manuscript Collections* (*NUCMC*) somewhat improved the discoverability of archival materials, just as the launch of *The National Union Catalog* (*NUC*) a decade earlier had somewhat improved the discoverability of published books. Scholars with access to the massive set of *NUCMC* volumes, which were published from 1962 to 1993, could consult them to get leads on where to find archival and manuscript materials. Following the pattern in which the contents of the *NUC* printed volumes were eventually integrated into the OCLC bibliographic utility, the contents of *NUCMC* were, in 1986, integrated into the RLIN bibliographic utility which, in 2007, was itself integrated into OCLC. Before those integrations could happen, however, there was much work to be done.

What made the discovery of, and access to, archival collections especially challenging in the pre-digital age is that the mostly unpublished, mostly unique materials held in archival collections have never been cataloged like individual books nor indexed like the contents of periodicals. Nor are archival collections normally organized by subject or format. Instead, archival practice is based on the principle of *provenance*, a term which refers both to the origins of a collection as well as to its custody and ownership prior to its accession by an archive. A related archival concept derived from the principle of provenance is that of the *fonds*, which the Society of American Archivists defines as "the entire body of records of an organization, family, or individual that have been created and accumulated as the result of an organic process reflecting the functions of the creator."[24] The word *collection* is often used interchangeably with *fonds*, though the two words have slightly different meanings. One attempt to explain the difference between collections and fonds proposes that collections are "physical or material" accumulations while "fonds are conceptual entities whose membership need not be physically brought together."[25]

For an example of a collection (that might also be described as a fonds), consider the archival records of William Oxley Thompson (1855–1933), a scholar and academic administrator who served as president of the Ohio State University from 1899 to 1925.[26] Held by the Ohio State University Archives, the materials that comprise the Thompson collection range widely, touching on such topics as agricultural education, military training, the influenza epidemic of 1918, laboratory equipment, and college athletics. Under the principle known as *respect des fonds*, all the diverse materials in the Thompson collection are treated as a unified whole on the grounds that every item in that particular collection is a byproduct of the activities of the Ohio State University Office of the president during Thompson's tenure. Because the items in the Thompson collection share an *archival bond*, they must never be intermingled with any other collection. Yet another archival principle, that of *original order*, requires that the materials within a collection maintain the hierarchies and patterns of organization employed by the original creators of those materials. This means that even if the "organic process reflecting the functions of the creator" resulted in the materials being organized in idiosyncratic ways that create confusion for anyone trying to use them at a later date, that pattern of organization will nonetheless be maintained when archivists process the collection. Adding to the complexity of working with archives is the fact that any single collection may contain materials in a variety of formats, including letters, reports, diaries, sound recordings, artworks, maps, photographs, published materials, ephemera, and born-digital objects. Within any one format in a collection, the media for that format may itself vary. For example, a single collection might include sound recordings in such formats as wax or metal cylinders, vinyl discs (of various sizes and playback speeds), magnetic tapes (including reel-to-reel, eight-tracks, and cassettes), and digital discs, the latter of which may themselves come in a variety of physical formats (e.g., MiniDisc, LaserDisc, CD-ROM), with each of these physical formats containing a variety of possible file formats (e.g., WAV, WMA, MP3).

Rather than taking on the impossible task of cataloging or indexing every item in a collection at the level of detail that would be provided to a book or other individually published item, the archivists who process archival records instead create archival finding aids. According to the Society of American Archivists, a finding aid:

> *places archival resources in context by consolidating information about the collection, such as acquisition and processing; provenance, including administrative history or biographical note; scope of the collection, including size, subjects, media; organization and arrangement; and an inventory of the series and the folders. Finding aids could also describe a single level or a single item.*[27]

Finding aids are hierarchical, starting with a high-level description of an entire collection and working downward through such components of the collection as subgroups, series, subseries, files, and, in rare cases, individual items. Once again turning to the Thompson collection as an example, the archivists who processed those materials created a type-written archival finding aid that provides historical context for the collection as a whole as well as a hierarchical list of its contents. For example, the finding aid for the Thompson collection includes the description "Football: OSU, 1905" for the contents of Box 3/Folder 37.[28] Though the processing archivists could have gone into more detail if they felt the contents of Box 3/Folder 37 warranted the extra time and attention required to add more detail, limiting the description to a terse "Football: OSU, 1905" means that the only way for a scholar to know exactly what and how much information Folder 37 contains is to lay hands on it and have a look.

Archival Finding Aids in the Digital Era

Whereas the development of the MARC record in the 1960s led to a revolution in the sharing of information and collaboration among book and serial catalogers, archivists would not have "a standard to follow in creating data records either manually or on a computer system" until the Library of Congress's release of the USMARC Archival and Manuscripts Control (MARC AMC) format in 1983.[29] In that same year, the standardization goals reflected in MARC AMC were furthered by the Library of Congress's publication of *Archives, Personal Papers, and Manuscripts (APPM)*, which the Society of American Archivists described as "a content standard for developing a catalog of archival materials, mainly at the collection level, with consistent descriptions and access points that can be integrated into bibliographic catalogs."[30] With these tools at their disposal, archivists were at last in a position to enhance the discoverability of their collections to such an extent that, from 1983 through 1998, archivists "created and distributed to the RLIN and OCLC databases nearly 800,000 collection-level catalog records providing important access to archival and manuscript holdings scattered throughout the United States."[31] A related development in the standardization of digital archival collections was the International Council on Archives' 1994 adoption of an international standard for the description of archives: the General International Standard Archival Description (ISAD-G).[32] In 2005, the Society of American Archivists would publish *Describing Archives: A Content Standard (DACS)*, effectively a U.S. version of ISAD-G.[33]

On a more ad hoc basis, the discoverability of archival collections was enhanced by the transition from typewriters to word processors, a development which greatly facilitated the creation, updating, and expansion of archival finding aids. Even more impactfully, archivists leveraged the power of the internet by posting digital versions of finding aids where anyone might access them. Initially, archivists posted finding aids as plain-text files accessible via the Gopher Protocol; later, they posted them as HTML files accessible via web browsers. Information seekers were thus able to use tools like OCLC FirstSearch and various web search engines to discover thousands of archival collections and access untold numbers of previously hidden archival finding aids. Though MARC AMC and files posted in either plain-text or HTML enhanced the discoverability of archival collections, none of these formats had all the features required to create the wished-for union catalog of archival finding aids capable of fully conveying the complex intellectual organization of archival collections. Even with MARC AMC, researchers still had to resort to printed finding aids to access full, detailed descriptions of archival collections. What was needed was a solution archivists had been discussing since the 1980s, the development of "'relational' archival systems that enable creating and maintaining each of these fundamental components of description separately and bringing them together dynamically upon user request."[34] In pursuit of such a solution, staff at the UC Berkeley Library working under the direction of Daniel Pitti set out in 1993 to develop a new standard that would maintain complex hierarchical relationships while also supporting "element-specific indexing and retrieval."[35]

Because Standard Generalized Markup Language (SGML) was capable of reflecting hierarchical relationships, the Berkeley team used SGML to develop FindAid, a Document Type Definition (DTD) released in March 1995. FindAid established rules for marking up and encoding archival documents so that they could be "searched, retrieved, displayed, and exchanged" on any platform.[36] Building on the work of the Berkeley team, the EAD Working Group of the Society of American Archivists published in 1998 the first iteration of Encoded Archival Description (EAD) in both SGML and XML, the latter a normalized version of SGML that eventually became the standard. As noted by Daniel Pitti, XML both "provides reasonable assurance that the data will endure changes in hardware and software" and "also enables multiple uses of the data."[37] Described by the Library of Congress as "the international metadata transmission standard for hierarchical descriptions of archival records," EAD was essential for migrating archival description onto the internet, developing national standards for the description of archival content, and "the emergence of a professional consensus that archival description existed to be shared widely and shared well."[38] EAD was updated several times over the years, with EAD3 being released in 2018. Another standard that played an important role in bringing finding aids online was Encoded Archival Context—Corporate bodies, Persons, and Families (EAC-CPF). Adopted by the Society of American Archivists in 2011, EAC-CPF is an international standard that "primarily addresses the description of individuals, families and corporate bodies that create, preserve, use and are responsible for and/or associated with records in a variety of ways."[39]

Because implementing EAD and getting finding aids online requires technical expertise and incurs costs, its adoption was never universal. Following the initial release of EAD, the technical obstacles to adoption were lessened by the creation of EAD authoring tools, web-based templates, and database conversion protocols.[40] The 2006 launch of two open-source platforms—the Archivists' Toolkit and Archon—allowed archivists to create and publish digital finding aids without the need to develop high levels of technical expertise with EAD. Starting in 2009, work began on combining Archivists' Toolkit and Archon to create ArchivesSpace, a new open-source platform which was released on September 30, 2013.[41] Regularly updated, by 2019 ArchivesSpace was described as "the most influential adopted system at this time," and lauded for providing the benefit of "the ability to post finding aids without encoding them in EAD, but also to have access to EAD when needed, thus providing the best of both worlds to the archivist."[42] With EAD and the creation of tools like ArchivesSpace, increasing numbers of archives were able to put their finding aids online. A survey of 313 U.S. institutions published in 2019 shows that, prior to 1999, only sixteen archives had put finding aids online; by 2017, that total had increased to 229.[43] According to that same survey, of the responding institutions that had put finding aids online, 60 percent indicated that they used EAD to do so.[44]

Archival Collections Go Online

When CD-ROM bibliographic databases started appearing in libraries in the late 1980s, it was a natural progression for users to go from being delighted at having convenient access to millions of bibliographic citations to wanting digital access to the full text of the articles those citations represented. Similarly, accessing an online archival finding aid to learn that Ohio State's Thompson archive includes a folder having something to do with OSU football in 1905 is fine, but even better is being able to instantly access digital surrogates of the archival materials themselves, including multiple years of OSU football team rosters, player photographs, game programs, and related primary-source documents.[45] Archivists were quick to grasp a fundamental truth about the advantage of getting their collections online, with Gwynneth Malin declaring in 2002: "Digital collections increase the visibility of archival collections."[46] Another early indication of the archival profession's awareness of the value of getting their collections online was the election of Peter Hirtle as the president of the Society of American Archivists in 2002. The co-director of the Cornell Institute for Digital Collections and associate editor of *D-Lib Magazine*, Hirtle was very much the model of a modern digital archivist.

Among the first U.S. digital archival collections was American Memory, a Library of Congress initiative which began life in 1990 as a demonstration project consisting of 210,000 digitized photos, films, audio recordings, photographs, and books distributed to forty-four U.S. test sites in the form of LaserDiscs and CD-ROMs. In 1995, American Memory became one of the first archival projects to go online when it became a key part of the Library of Congress's National Digital Library Program (NDLP).[47] Like American Memory, most of the early archival digitization projects came to exist as a result of grant funding. For example, in the spring of 1997, as part of the NDLP, the Library of Congress and the Ameritech Foundation awarded grants to ten libraries—including the academic libraries of Brown, Harvard, Duke, North Dakota State, the University of Chicago, the University of Texas, and the University of North Carolina—for the digitization of archival materials.[48]

The total amount of archival content available online continued to grow through the end of the twentieth century and beyond. By 2020, it would have been easier to count the number of academic archives that had not put at least some content online than to tally up those that had. For the largest academic archival collections, the total of digitized items numbered in the millions. By 2024, the Harvard Digital Collections numbered more than six million items;[49] the Michigan Library Digital Collections numbered 32,869,262 text page images plus 4,516,704 non-text images;[50] and the University of Florida Digital Collections numbered 1,144,759 items.[51] Emerging along with all the digitized academic archival collections were a number of very large digital archival collections created and curated by such nonacademic institutions as the U.S. National Archives and the New York Public Library. One of the most notable large-scale digital archival initiatives of the early twenty-first century was the Digital Public Library of America (DPLA), the idea for which grew out of a meeting held at Harvard University in October 2010.[52] DPLA went online in April 2013, with Founding Executive Director Dan Cohen describing DPLA as "a single place to discover and explore our country's libraries, archives, and museums—a portal—and so will bring entirely new audiences to formerly scattered collections."[53] By 2024, the DPLA hub was providing access to nearly fifty million "images, texts, videos, and sounds from across the United States," including, for just a few examples, 141,608 items from the Kentucky Digital Library; 61,404 items from the Orbis Cascade Alliance; and 1,151,823 items from Digital Commonwealth.[54]

Whether the source is a hub such as DPLA or a digital archive affiliated with a single institution, a user's ability to simultaneously retrieve archival items by typing words into a search box tends to instill a *disrespect des fonds* by obscuring both archival hierarchical relationships and provenance. In the words of Robin L. Chandler, "The digital environment presents an opportunity for users to deconstruct and reassemble finding aid information for their own purposes. This represents a dramatic change in the archivist's conception of the finding aid."[55] If, for example, users are searching for primary-source materials on depictions of wild horses in the American West, those users are typically more concerned about how well the items retrieved meet their information needs than they are about whether an item happens to come from the Jon Bilbao Papers at the University of Nevada, Reno Digital Archive or the J. Willis Sayre Collection of Theatrical Photographs at the University of Washington. Bradley D. Westbrook displays a clear understanding of how digital archival collections are actually used when he compares virtual collections of archival materials assembled by information seekers to the sports teams assembled by participants in fantasy leagues: "As the fantasy basketball team can be made up of players that have never played together on the same team or even in the same era, the virtual collection can be made up of digital items that have never existed together in the same collection."[56]

One way of looking at users virtually gathering and reassembling archival materials it to see it as doing no harm. Just as the real-world professional athletes who are drafted into fantasy teams are not actually displaced from their positions with the real-world teams that pay their salaries, the real-world archival items reassembled into virtual collections by information seekers are not actually removed from the archives in which they are housed and preserved. Organic provenance and hierarchical relationships remain fundamentally intact no matter the extent to which information seekers mix and match items gathered from various archival collections. Even more than allowing information seekers to reassemble archival collections to meet their specific information needs, the liberating power to rearrange digital collections is seen by Katja Müller as "a means to undo the colonial dominance of organization knowledge."[57] On the other hand, most information seekers who reassemble virtual archival collections could benefit from fuller understandings of the provenance of, and hierarchical relationships among, the archival items their searches retrieve. In the words of Cory Lampert, "there is a recognition that users may require context to best use the digital collection and that each digital object should refer to the hierarchy of archival arrangement as well as the provenance of the original collection."[58]

Why Archival Digitization Is Not Fast, Cheap, or Easy

Despite the archival profession's early and widespread awareness of the importance of making their collections accessible via online interfaces, and the large amount of archival resources that have gone, and are still going, online, the job of putting archival collections online has never been cheap, fast, or easy. The proof of this is the fact that only a small part of the archival collections that could be online have actually gone online. In 2021, Terrance J. McDonald, Director of the Bentley Historical Library at the University of Michigan, estimated that a meager one percent of the world's archival collections have been digitized.[59] There is, to put it mildly, plenty of challenging and costly work left to be done.

Copyright, Donor, and Privacy Restrictions

The wholesale digitization of archival collections becomes complicated when collections include such copyrighted materials as published books and articles, unpublished manuscripts, audio recordings, images, film, and video. For example, if an emeritus professor of ethnomusicology donates to the campus archives a collection of audio/video recordings documenting a decade of her course lectures on the history of rock-and-roll, any songs she may have played during those lectures are almost certainly copyrighted. So too are such elements of her lectures as images of album cover art, photographs of rock stars, and film footage of performances. The question for archivists tasked with managing such a donation is, "Under copyright law, what are we allowed to digitize and make available online and what must be redacted?" The answer depends on one's interpretation of the Fair Use Doctrine of the U.S. Copyright Act, and perhaps the only thing that everyone agrees on about the Fair Use Doctrine is that its interpretation is a messy and contentious area of law. Even if legal counsel were to advise the campus archivist that the Fair Use Doctrine clearly applies in the case of the donated rock-and-roll lectures, such a legal opinion does not rule out the possibility of lawyers representing copyright holders issuing take-down demands and threatening legal action.

An example of how copyright hindered digitization can be seen in the case of the University of North Carolina at Chapel Hill's efforts to digitize the papers of politician Thomas E. Watson. Though the university had permission to digitize any materials created by members of the Watson Family, the collection also included third-party manuscript materials that could not be digitized without either obtaining permission from the rights holder or until after the creator of the materials had been dead for seventy years.[60] With an archival collection of even moderate size, the time involved in identifying all the third-party authors, seeking permission or verifying death dates, and continually making additional manuscript materials available as copyrights expire adds up to significant costs. While the family of Thomas E. Watson in the above example was willing to grant permission to use copyrighted manuscript materials, not all donors are so cooperative. Donors may set embargoes dictating when materials may be digitized and made available online. Donors may also try to restrict who may access materials and/or how materials may be used. In a case dating from 2007, the heirs of Irish author James Joyce cited copyright in an attempt to deny a scholar writing a book about Joyce's daughter the right to quote from or share online manuscript letters otherwise publicly available in various academic archives. The scholar sued Joyce's heirs, with the case ultimately being settled out of court in favor of the scholar.[61]

Privacy protection raises yet another obstacle to making archival collections openly available online. When archival collections contain such personally identifiable information (PII) as social security numbers, financial information, home addresses, and the like, archivists' desire to provide access must take a back seat to the duty to not reveal personal information that may embarrass or create financial hardship for innocent third parties. Even more to the point, revealing some types of PII, such as medical or student records, is expressly prohibited by law. Especially when collections are large, archival staffs small, and budgets tight, the burden of identifying and screening out PII can become unmanageable.[62]

The Basic Costs of Digitization

Even without the burden of copyright, donor restrictions, and privacy concerns, the basic labor and technology costs of digitizing archival materials and making them available online have ensured that vast amounts of archival materials that could be shared online remain undigitized. While innovations such as sheet-feed scanners, robotic scanners, and increasingly capable optical character recognition (OCR) software have helped speed up the digitization of archival materials, archivists continue to face the costly logistics of locating the materials to be scanned, moving them from storage to the scanning location, pulling materials from boxes and folders, scanning them, and finally re-boxing and returning everything to storage. Once the initial digital images have been created, they may need to be edited with software such as Photoshop and saved in formats ranging from high-resolution master images to low-resolution thumbnail images that show up in initial search results. Paying human beings to conduct visual quality control of scanned output adds yet another layer of cost to digitization projects, though a cost-benefit analysis conducted at the Triangle Research Libraries Network suggests that scanning error rates are low enough that human-mediated quality control is not worth the cost.[63]

As archivists began digitizing in earnest, they found that the costs of digitizing physical items vary greatly depending on the amount of special handling required. Running unbound printed pages through a sheet-feed scanner is on the low end of the cost scale. Fragile items that require special handling to avoid damage add to the cost of digitization, as do such difficult-to-scan items as handwritten manuscripts, manually typed documents, and low-resolution copies such as those produced using spirit duplicators. Similarly, digitizing anything printed in a large or unusual format incurs added costs. When Google was scanning millions of printed books, staff were instructed not to unfold for digitization any oversized pages depicting maps, charts, or other images, as doing so would have added to the total cost of the project.[64] Many non-text items, such as sound recordings, 3D objects, and reel films, are costly to digitize. For one example, as of 2024, it cost the University of North Texas (UNT) Libraries $7,500 to digitize one month of film from its historical collection of daily news broadcasts aired by the Fort Worth, Texas NBC affiliate. Because the UNT Libraries hold over sixty years of these broadcasts, the total cost of digitizing the collection will approach $6,000,000—if and when the project is ever completed.[65] Finally, some materials are costly to digitize because they are hazardous. Among the most familiar hazards is that posed by silver-nitrate film stock. Used in the United States up until 1951, highly flammable silver-nitrate film "burns at higher temperature than gasoline" and "is very similar to gunpowder."[66] Poisonous materials may also make their way into archival collections; for example, plant specimens collected prior to the mid-1960s may have been treated with highly toxic mercuric chloride.[67]

Born-Digital Archives Are Not Born Free

At the same time that academic archivists were facing the challenge of creating digital surrogates for physical archival materials, they found themselves facing the separate, though related, challenge of managing born-digital materials worthy of archival curation and long-term preservation. While born-digital materials allow archivists to skip the work of converting analog materials to digital formats, the archiving of born-digital materials nonetheless incurs significant costs. In the not-so-distant past, archiving the official correspondence generated by, say, the campus Registrar was a relatively straightforward process: at some point, perhaps with the retirement of the Registrar, a somewhat limited number of printed letters and administrative documents generated by the activities of the Registrar would be pulled from the office file cabinets, transferred to the campus archives, and placed in Hollinger boxes. In the twenty-first century, the output from the Registrar would be dominated by digital content in the form of emails and documents in various digital formats. Over the years, these emails and electronic documents may or may not have been saved, and, if saved, may have ended up sitting on a forgotten hard drive or campus server, never to be forwarded to the archives. And even if all those Registrar-generated emails and documents are forwarded to the archives, the fact that some contain personally identifiable information means that an archivist cannot simply upload the lot and make them available to all comers. To complicate the situation even further, just as official campus communications were transitioning from analog to digital formats, so too was much of the campus-generated gray literature. While neither every cell phone video of students celebrating commencement nor every email emanating from the computer of a campus apparatchik is necessarily worthy of a place in the campus digital archives, at least some of those fugitive born-digital items constitute a significant enough part of the record of a campus's life and times that failing to capture them means failing to fully document the history of the campus. Beyond the challenge of getting a handle on the campus's born-digital output, archivists' workloads were made even heavier by the challenge of capturing for posterity all the preservation-worthy born-digital items that government agencies, businesses, and private individuals were creating in volumes unheard of in the analog era.

Perhaps the greatest challenge to archiving born-digital content arose with the launch and spread of the World Wide Web. Though far from all of the world's over one billion (as of 2024) websites can be said to have made a significant contribution to the growth of human knowledge, over the decades millions of websites have provided content of enough scientific, historic, or cultural significance to be worthy of archival curation and long-term preservation. In a prescient article published in 1998, Peter Lyman and Brewster Kahle begin by declaring the World Wide Web to be nothing less than a "cultural artifact." They then go on to discuss the issues involved in archiving websites, framing their ideas on who might do the work and how it might be done as "an attempt to create a common agenda for action."[68] Taking action to archive websites is complicated by both the sheer volume of information involved as well as by the highly dynamic nature of websites, the contents of which can be added to, revised, or deleted at dizzying rates. Even more disturbingly, entire websites can also disappear quickly and without warning. This was seen in 2022 when many Afghan websites came under threat in the wake of the Taliban regaining control of the country.[69] As it turned out, Brewster Kahle's greatest contributions to the preservation of websites were more concrete than simply calling for "a common agenda for action." In 1996, two years before publishing the article with Lyman, Kahle founded the Internet Archive; in 2001, Kahle's Internet Archive launched the Wayback Machine, a tool that allows users to search for and access archived snapshots of, as of 2024, over 866 billion web pages dating back to 1996.[70] These impressive achievements were followed, in 2006, by the Internet Archive's launch of Archive-It, a service that provides partner libraries, archives, and other cultural-memory institutions with "tools, training, and technical support for capturing and preserving dynamic web materials, as well as a platform for partners to share their collections, with multiple search, discovery, and access capabilities."[71] One example of a web-archiving project making use of Archive-It is the University of California, Los Angeles's *UCLA Online Campaign Literature Archive*, a project which archived websites relating to Los Angeles and California elections for the years 1998 to 2017.[72] This and many other targeted web-archiving projects, whether affiliated with Archive-It or not, have helped to preserve websites and content that might have otherwise vanished without a trace.

Outsourcing as a Cost-Saving Option

One potentially cost-saving alternative to in-house digitization has been to outsource the work, either to for-profit companies such as Crowley Digitization Services or to nonprofit organizations such as the Northeast Document Conservation Center.[73] The pros and cons of outsourcing digitization were under discussion at least as early as the 1996 publication of Anne Kenney and Stephan Chapman's *Digital Imaging for Libraries and Archives*.[74] In 1999, Roy Tennant published an article in *Library Journal* in which he notes that outsourcing digitization allows libraries and archives to: (1) avoid the cost of investing in digitization hardware and software, (2) overcome any lack of local expertise in digitization, and (3) save time spent training local staff to carry out digitization projects.[75] The common academic library strategy of training student employees to carry out digitization can be deceptively costly, as even though the hourly pay of students is low, the high rate of turnover among student employees renders the constant training of newly hired students a never-ending and costly burden.

A related alternative to in-house digitization has been the digital archival collections created by various commercial and nonprofit organizations. A commercial example is seen in the digital collections of AM. Formerly known as Adam Matthew Digital, AM and its forerunners have, since 1990, specialized in creating digital collections of primary-source materials relating to the arts, humanities, and social sciences. By 2024, the AM Primary collection consisted of over 100 databases on topics ranging from "China: Trade, Politics and Culture, 1793–1980" to "Jewish Life in America, c1654–1954."[76] AM fulfills an outsourcing role by partnering with archives and libraries to digitize their archival materials in order to make them commercially available online.[77] Gale Primary Sources is another for-profit company that partners with libraries and other cultural heritage institutions to create digital archives.[78] In the nonprofit sector, ArtStor has specialized in providing metadata-enhanced images for research and study, offering over two million images in 300 collections.[79] Similarly, the nonprofit David Rumsey Map Collection has provided access to over 130,000 digital maps and images.[80] Specialist digitizers like AM, Gale, ArtStor, and David Rumsey can achieve levels of efficiency that few in-house digitization services can match, making accessible millions of items that might have otherwise remained undigitized and largely invisible to potential users.

Despite the success of many outsourcing ventures, institutions have nonetheless tended to prefer in-house digitization. A 2014 Library of Congress survey to which 436 institutions responded found that, in 2010, external vendors comprised only 11 percent of staff devoted to digital preservation, while by 2014 that figure had slightly increased to 14 percent.[81] The situation has not changed much since then, with the authors of a 2023 systematic review of the literature concluding that "studies conducted in the USA also show a complete inclination toward in-house digital preservation activities instead of going for outsourcing."[82]

Whether outsourced or done in-house, for most archives the cost of digitization meant prioritizing which collections were digitized and which were not. As the Council on Library and Information Resources acknowledged in a report published in 1998, before setting out to digitize anything, archivists had to first ask the difficult question, "Does the intellectual quality of the source material warrant the level of access made possible by digitizing?"[83] Though asking this question is unavoidable, the subjectivity of the phrase "intellectual quality" inevitably leads to a host of uncomfortable questions about whose archival stories were made widely available online versus whose stories remained in less discoverable, less accessible analog formats.

Creating Metadata for Digital Archives

As seen in the example of the William Oxley Thompson collection, traditional archival practice focuses on the assignment of high-level descriptive metadata, starting at the collection level and rarely dipping down so low as the item level. At the level of a collection as a whole, *descriptive metadata* typically provides the following meaning and context:

- The name of the collection
- Who was involved in the creation of the collection
- When the materials in the collection were created

- Where the collection is physically located
- What the materials in the collection are generally about, their scope and content, and how they are related to each other.

Imagine that a researcher walks into the Ohio State University Archives and asks to access the Thompson archival collection. The archivist shows the researcher a finding aid containing descriptive metadata relating to the collection.[84] The finding aid directs the researcher to a box in which the researcher comes across a folder labeled "Football: OSU, 1905." Within that folder is a black-and-white photograph. Even though that photograph is not labeled or annotated in any way, from visual clues in the photograph plus the context provided by the collection's high-level metadata, it is a safe assumption that it is a photograph of the Ohio State University football team of 1905 and not, say, a photograph of the 1905 Stanford University rugby team. (Starting in 1905, several leading U.S. colleges on the West Coast temporarily replaced football, which was deemed too dangerous, with rugby.)[85]

When archival collections were exclusively analog, providing metadata that stopped several levels above individual items was considered adequate for all but exceptional cases. As archival collections went online, some archivists felt that digital archival items required item-level metadata on the grounds that digital items could be discovered in ways (e.g., via Google searches) that obscured their archival context. As the author of a comparative study of archival practices concludes, "It is clear that without item-level metadata, resources are much harder to find which can discourage and turn away users."[86] As desirable as the end result may be, the problem with assigning item-level metadata is that doing so is slow and costly.

In fact, the problem of the slow pace of archival processing began long before the advent of digital technology. For years, huge amounts of archival materials had been coming into archives far faster than those materials could be processed given the resources available to beleaguered, chronically underfunded archivists. In many archives, backlogged physical materials would sit unprocessed for years, even decades, inaccessible to potential users, quite possibly deteriorating as they sat. If backlogs of physical materials were not a problem enough, twenty-first-century archivists found themselves facing floods of born-digital materials ranging from websites to emails to digital photos and videos. Well aware of the growing problems processing archivists faced, in 2005 Mark Greene and Dennis Meissner published a seminal article entitled, "More Product, Less Process: Revamping Traditional Archival Processing." Although in their article Greene and Meissner mention the amount of time archivists spend on such mundane tasks as removing paper clips, staples, and rubber bands, their focus is much more on resource management than on the minutia of archival processing. Whether the archival materials being processed are digital or physical, Greene and Meissner's point is "that processing projects squander scarce resources because archivists spend too much time on tasks that do not need doing, or at least don't need doing all the time."[87] Following the article's publication, the phrase "More Product, Less Process," often shortened to MPLP, became a battle cry for archivists frustrated by the prohibitively high costs and intolerable delays incurred in getting physical collections digitized and online. By following the MPLP philosophy of applying only as much metadata as required—but no more—archivists found they could reduce costs, save time, and get archival resources online where they could be discovered and used. Ideally, once online and discoverable by information seekers, the descriptive metadata assigned to an archival item stands a chance of being enhanced through crowdsourcing.[88] Picking up on the widespread acceptance of MPLP by digital archivists, Greene published a follow-up article in 2010 in which he directly connects the dots between MPLP and archival digitization, writing:

> *Rather than falling prey to the supposed dichotomy between "Googlization" (ultramass digitization) and "boutique" digitization (most of what we are currently doing—unique items on a very small scale), we should be planted on a middle ground: digitizing larger quantities of unique material.*[89]

In 2011, Greene and Meissner again joined forces to publish "More Application While Less Appreciation: The Adopters and Antagonists of MPLP," in which they make the case that MPLP has been widely and successfully adopted while acknowledging that not everyone in the archival community approves of this approach. In defense of MPLP, Greene and Meissner point out that the strategies put forward in their earlier article are "baseline performance recommendations: things that you must do, but not the only things that you might do" and emphasize that MPLP does not prohibit in-depth processing in those cases where it is called for.[90]

The photograph of the Ohio State University 1905 football team provides a good example of MPLP. OSU archivists uploaded a digital version of the photograph to the Flickr photo-sharing website.[91] The metadata attached to the digital photo is adequate, if minimal; however, there are links from the photograph back to the Ohio State University Archives for the use of anyone seeking more information about the photograph or archival records relating to OSU football. From an information seeker's point of view, it is better to access a photograph without full, item-level metadata attached than to not access a photograph at all.

Descriptive metadata is only one type of metadata commonly applied to digital archival collections. The other forms of metadata include:

- Administrative Metadata
  - An overarching term for metadata required for internal management of digital archival materials, including preservation, technical, rights, and other forms of metadata.
- Preservation metadata
  - Metadata relating to the preservation of digital materials over time. The function of preservation metadata is to document any preservation actions that have already been taken and to include any other information that contributes to maintaining the integrity of the information over time.
- Rights Metadata
  - Metadata describing who is allowed to use the materials, if and how they may be reproduced, and the purposes for which reproductions can be used. A Creative Commons license is one example of rights metadata.
- Use Metadata
  - A form of administrative metadata that logs how often materials are used and, in some cases, who is using them.

- Structural Metadata
    - Structural metadata is information about the individual items that together create a whole. For example, structural metadata identifies the order in which the individual pages from a single document should appear.

In spite of MPLP, as more digital archival items were made available online, creating metadata became one of the key roles of archivists. The additional work of creating and assigning all that metadata introduced, in turn, a new and costly line item into archival budgets. According to Steven Jack Miller, creating metadata is the most time-consuming part of creating digital collections, consuming from "one-half to two-thirds of the time of the entire project."[92]

Achieving the Full Potential of Digitized Archival Materials

Today, almost every document we create and the output from almost every research-related project, is a digital object. Not everything has to be kept forever, but materials with scholarly or historical value should be retained for future generations. Preserving digital objects is more challenging than preserving items on paper. Hardware becomes obsolete, new software replaces old, storage media degrades.

—Bernadette Houghton[93]

Access to Digital Archives

In the world of digital archives, there are dark archives, dim archives, and light (a.k.a. open) archives. The purpose of dark archives is to store and preserve, but not to provide access to, digital content. The contents of dark archives are available to an archive's curators, but the public are denied access not only to protect content from external threats but also due to such factors as copyright restrictions, donor-imposed embargoes, and privacy concerns. Dim archives fall between dark archives and light (open) archives in that they allow access to some digital materials while blocking access to others. In the interest of preservation, both dark and dim archives serve as crucial sources of last resort for the recovery of digital materials that might otherwise be lost. As necessary as dark and dim archives are for long-term storage and preservation, the greater goal of archiving digital materials is to house them in light (open) archives where they are available for use; otherwise, those materials might as well remain in analog form. Digitization of thousands of open archival collections has democratized access by eliminating the barriers of "competing responsibilities and limited time and funds to dedicate to travel" that are cited "as major challenges to accessing collections" by respondents to a 2023 survey of 3,300 archives users.[94]

For digital archives to achieve their full potential for meeting the needs of information seekers, archival materials must not merely exist in digital form; they must also be discoverable, accessible, and persistent. Being discoverable and accessible are of manifest importance to information seekers. If digital archival materials cannot be discovered using online search tools or, once discovered, cannot be accessed without making a trip to a physical archive, what is the point of digitizing them? The discoverability of online information, including archival materials, was enhanced by the January 2001 release of the first version of the Open Archives Initiative Protocol for Metadata Harvesting (OAI-PMH), a protocol that "provides the basis for an information discovery environment that relies on transferring metadata en masse from one server to another in a network of information systems." Service providers harvest OAI-PMH compliant metadata and then "organize it so that users can then easily search large databases of related information that's come from many different sources."[95] OAI-PHM has, arguably, done more than any other initiative to de-silo archival content for the benefit of users around the world.

Preserving Digital Archives

In addition to access, one benefit of the digitization of physical collections is their preservation should they fall victim to the ravages of time or any number of natural or human-caused disasters. For a non-U.S. example, in 2012 thousands of manuscripts were smuggled out of the Mamma Haidara Library in Timbuktu to save them from destruction during the Mali War. These manuscripts were then digitized to preserve their content in case they were to fall victim to some future calamity.[96] Even after physical items have been digitized, and even when items are born digital, the preservation of those digital objects presents a challenge if they are to persist over time. Both because the costs of digitization are high enough that no organization can afford to redo work that has already been done and because, in some cases, lost materials may not be recoverable at any price, digital archival materials must be formatted and maintained so that they do not disappear due to the phenomenon of *bit rot* (a.k.a. *bitrot*), a catchall term describing both the tendency for digital content to deteriorate over time as well as for it to become inaccessible "when the infrastructure (the hardware and software) required to access, interpret, view, and use this information is no longer available or executable."[97] In *The Theory and Craft of Digital Preservation*, Trevor Owens identifies three processes for bit preservation: (1) managing multiple copies of the data, (2) "the management and use of fixity of information to ensure that you can account for all your digital information," and (3) ensuring that data cannot "be inadvertently or maliciously corrupted, damaged, or deleted."[98] Unlike text printed on acid-free paper that can remain legible for centuries if left undisturbed on a bookshelf or in a desk drawer, digital content is more like a potted plant that must be carefully and consistently tended if it is to survive for more than what amounts to a heartbeat in the archival time scale.

The international standard for long-term preservation of digital archival materials, ISO Standard 14721:2003, was initially published in 2003 as "Space Data and Information Transfer Systems: Open Archival Information System Reference Model."[99] Commonly known by the acronym OAIS, the standard (which was updated in 2012) defines six functional entities required for long-term preservation of digital objects, including digital archival materials. These entities are:

- Ingest
- Archival Storage
- Data Management

- Administration
- Preservation Planning
- Access[100]

To apply these six functions in a highly automated way, archivists turned to digital assets management systems (DAMS). James L. Hilton was among those who understood early on the importance and potential of DAMS when he wrote in 2003, "I have a friend who predicts that building a digital asset management system into the infrastructure—a system that allows searches, customization, and editing from the desktop—will be the digital equivalent of bringing indoor plumbing to the campus."[101] Another early proponent of DAMS, Alan McCord, provides a succinct description of what a DAMS does when he writes, "A DAMS infrastructure can ingest digital assets, store and index assets for easy searching, retrieve assets for use in many environments, and manage the rights associated with those assets."[102] For example, a DAMS might automatically make a backup of a WAV sound file to be ingested into a dark or dim archive for long-term preservation while simultaneously creating a copy in a smaller MP3 format for information seekers to access online. A DAMS can also be used to facilitate rights management (i.e., who can use an item and for what purpose) and to apply policies for long-term preservation as well as to apply version control when a scholar deposits multiple updates of a digital document in a single institutional repository.

A number of DAMS were developed in the early decades of the twenty-first century. CONTENTdm, Emu, and LUNA are all examples of proprietary DAMS, while Greenstone, Omeka, and Collective Access are examples of open-source DAMS. Some library management systems, such as those produced by Innovative Interfaces and Ex Libris, offer content management modules that function as DAMS. One of the most significant developments in the history of DAMS was the development of FEDORA (Flexible Extensible Digital Object Repository Architecture), which originated as a research project in 1997.[103] Over the years, FEDORA has gone through a number of versions and has been integrated in whole or in part into a number of popular DAMS, including Islandora, DSpace, and Samvera (formerly known as Hydra).

Whether processed through a DAMS or not, digital content cannot be uploaded to just any convenient local or cloud-based server if it is to persist over the years. The gold standard for long-term preservation of, and access to, digital content is the *trusted digital repository*, which the Research Libraries Group (RLG) and OCLC defined in 2002 as "one whose mission is to provide reliable, long-term access to managed digital resources to its designated community, now and in the future."[104] Starting in 2007, OAIS compliance, as specified under the *TRAC Standard*, defined the standard for determining whether or not a digital repository can be certified as trustworthy.[105] The *TRAC Standard* was later used as the basis for a new standard, *Audit and Certification of Trustworthy Digital Repositories: Recommended Practice*, which was formally adopted as ISO 16363 in 2012.[106]

Trusted digital repositories (TDRs) employ a combination of policies, strategies, and actions to ensure the authenticity, integrity, and persistence of data over time. Trusted digital repositories process descriptive metadata to ensure that the authentic identities of digital objects are not lost while processing preservation data both to track previous preservation actions and schedule future actions. One strategy employed by TDRs is reformatting and transferring files to different media to avoid obsolescence of both file formats and physical media. Fixity checking, a strategy which involves the creation, validation, and management of checksums, ensures that digital objects have not changed over time and allows those found to have changed to be restored to their original state. TDRs may fully leverage the LOCKSS (Lots of Copies Keep Stuff Safe) strategy by storing backup copies of digital objects on geographically remote servers. One such cooperative effort to preserve scholarly research data through the use of distributed repositories was the Digital Preservation Network (DPN). The idea for the DPN came out of a 2012 meeting of university presidents, librarians, and CIOs who saw the data being created on their campuses as being "vulnerable to natural disaster, political uncertainty, and business performance issues."[107] DPN launched in 2016, storing data in five geographically dispersed locations and relying on a membership model to fund its operations. While the DPN preservation strategy was sound enough, the funding model failed. DPN closed up shop at the end of 2018.[108]

Once digital archival materials have been created, processed, and uploaded to a server (whether a TDR or otherwise) from which they can be accessed, there still remains the issue of paying the cost of long-term storage and maintenance. For several decades, the cost of storage dropped significantly. According to data collected by computer scientist John C. McCallum, the cost in 1990 of storing one terabyte of data on a hard drive was $3,200,000 ($7,924,000 in 2020 U.S. dollars); by 2020, that cost had dropped to $16 per terabyte ($20 in 2024 dollars).[109] The growth of cloud-based storage also helped reduce costs, as storing data in large repositories shared by multiple users is almost always less costly than storing it on local servers. As welcome as the drop in storage costs has been, storage costs eventually bottomed out so that libraries and others wishing to store ever-larger amounts of data long-term will need to look to emerging technologies if they are to keep up with demand.[110]

Storing digital materials over the long term in a preservation-oriented environment, such as a trusted digital repository, typically incurs annual charges that run higher than the cost of simply uploading materials to a non-OAIS compliant hard drive. For example, in 2024, the nominal price for storing one terabyte of data for one year in the University of California's Merritt Digital Preservation Repository was $150 per year.[111] As with many institutional repositories serving the higher-education community, the storage costs levied by the Merritt Digital Repository are paid by institutions rather than by individual faculty or students. Because annual fees cannot, in the long term, be covered by research grants, some repositories charge one-time fees for data storage. In 2024, figshare+ charged a one-time fee of $3,500 to store up to one terabyte of data.[112] Regardless of the financial model used, managing the ongoing costs of long-term storage remains a problem to be solved. In the words of computer scientist David S. H. Rosenthal, chief scientist of the LOCKSS project, "The fundamental problem is not storing bits safely for the long term, it is paying to store bits safely for the long term."[113]

Archives, Libraries, and Ever-Bigger Data

Academic librarians and archivists have been involved in the world of digital data almost from the beginning. As early as 1962, academic librarians and archivists were playing a role in the creation and development of the Inter-university Consortium for Political Research (ICPR), one of the earliest, if not the first, efforts to collect and freely share research data in digital forms. (In 1975, the ICPR became the ICPSR when the word *social* was added to its name.) The ICPSR is particularly notable for its pioneering digitization projects, the earliest of which involved manually transferring data from printed formats to machine-readable punch cards. On most campuses affiliated with ICPSR, it became common for an academic librarian or archivist to serve as the official campus representative to the ICPSR, a role which included facilitating the retrieval of external research data from the ICPSR for the use of local researchers as well as the transfer of locally produced research data to the ICPSR where it could be archived and shared.[114] So important were ICPSR liaisons that the term *data librarian* was initially coined to describe the librarians and archivists who assumed that role.[115] At roughly the same time that librarians and archivists were becoming involved with the ICPSR, the profession at large was becoming involved in the creation and management of significant amounts of data as a result of such innovations as the MARC record (1965), the bibliographic utility (1967), and the online library catalog (1975). The need for librarians who knew their way around digital technologies and data was such that, by 1967, thirty-five U.S. colleges and universities were offering library-related courses in data processing or systems analysis.[116]

Given the long-standing role of academic librarians and archivists as curators of data, it is not surprising that campus researchers looked to the library for help as they increasingly began creating their own large data sets and, as a result, began recognizing the necessity of preserving and sharing their data. Academic libraries responded to researchers' needs for help curating their data by hiring data librarians and developing groundbreaking data services. A study of sixty Association of American Universities member institutions found that, in 2019, forty-six (76.7 percent) had a data librarian on staff, and fifty-six (93 percent) were providing data services to their campus communities.[117] For many years before libraries began hiring data librarians, however, on many campuses the people with the most hands-on experience managing large amounts of digital data were digital archivists. After all, even if the materials digital archivists work with may have started life as 35 mm slide photographs, copies of handwritten letters, or vinyl sound recordings, the end product of digitization is digital data, pure and simple.

Among grant-funded faculty and researchers, the need for help in managing their data grew more acute in 2013, the year in which a number of large U.S. federal agencies, including the National Science Foundation, the National Institutes of Health (NIH), and the National Endowment for the Humanities, "began requiring the submission of a data-management plan as a component in all or certain kinds of grant proposals."[118] Not all of the workload of managing research data and complying with the new data-management mandates fell to academic libraries, but some of it certainly did. One example of librarians and archivists coming to the aid of the research community was the creation of the DMP Tool, a project that started in 2011 when six academic libraries plus two non-library cultural-memory organizations collaborated to create a free online tool designed to help researchers quickly create data-management plans that were compliant with emerging federal funding mandates.[119] Around this same time, academic libraries increasingly worked directly with campus researchers, primarily faculty and graduate students, to teach frontline researchers how to properly create and manage their own research data so that it could be ingested and shared without the need for time-consuming, and therefore costly, reformatting.

The advent of Data Carpentry workshops in 2014 marked a major step forward in empowering researchers to effectively manage their own data. Often sponsored by the local campus library with the involvement of library and archives staff, Data Carpentry workshops take the form of two-day training events at which attendees acquire such data-creation and data-management skills as working with spreadsheets, cleaning data, using SQL (structured query language), and programming in R.[120] The growing need for data librarians was reflected in the 2019 establishment of the Research Data Management Librarian Academy (RDMLA), "a free, online Research Data Management Librarian Academy (RDMLA) aimed primarily for practicing librarians and information professionals, but also for researchers to gain knowledge about research data management (RDM) principles and best practices."[121] Data visualization was another service provided to researchers under the auspices of academic libraries, with *American Libraries* naming the job of Data Visualization Librarian as one of "5 Library Jobs on the Rise" in 2020.[122]

A specialized data-intensive arena into which academic libraries found themselves entering into, starting in the 1990s, was that of geographic information systems (GIS). Articles about the role that academic libraries could play in GIS started appearing in the literature in the late 1990s, with one advocate advising academic librarians that instead of focusing on the then-emerging digital map-making technologies, "GIS should be regarded as the means of accessing, managing, and querying geospatial data, rather than as an end result."[123] Library involvement with GIS began with the appearance of CD-ROM map discs in the wake of the 1990 U.S. Census, then evolved to take the form of projects to digitize printed maps and geographic images, and hit its stride with the development of full-fledged GIS software packages such as ESRI's ArcGIS product. Library support for GIS spread so broadly by 2020 that the author of a literature review and survey of U.S. librarians could confidently assert that "academic libraries have almost universally implemented some level of support for GIS."[124]

Archives and Digital Humanities

Though the digital humanities may seem cutting edge in the twenty-first century, the field began to emerge before most of its present-day practitioners were born. One of the most notable pioneering digital-humanities projects got its start in the 1940s, when Italian Jesuit priest Father Roberto Busa began what would become a thirty-year project to create *Index Thomisticus*, a concordance to the complete works of Thomas Aquinas created using IBM mainframe computers.[125] In 1987, a key advancement in the practice of digital humanities was set in motion with work leading to the Text Encoding Initiative (TEI), a Document Type

Definition (DTD) that became the standard for marking up digital texts.[126] As a way of studying, teaching, and publicly sharing the work of humanists, the field of digital humanities only began to spread broadly after personal desktop computers, the internet, and the Web came onto the academic scene. As a phrase, *digital humanities* covers so much ground that even its most dedicated practitioners and advocates find it difficult to define. In 2012, the authors of the MIT Press book *Digital_Humanities* crafted a definition that gets to the heart of the matter: "Digital humanities refers to new modes of scholarship and institutional units for collaborative, transdisciplinary, and computationally engaged research, teaching, and publication."[127]

The collaborative and transdisciplinary nature of the digital humanities demands a team-based approach that is radically different from the traditional image of a lone humanities scholar researching and writing in solitude. Archivists and librarians were welcomed as members of digital-humanities teams not only because their traditional skill sets related to discovering and organizing information were valued but also due to the simple fact that most digital-humanities projects incorporate the types of images, videos, audio recordings, and historical documents housed in archives and libraries. An outstanding example of what a collaborative digital-humanities team can achieve is seen in *The Valley of the Shadow*, an early digital-humanities project that tells the story of one northern and one southern community during the years before, during, and after the Civil War.[128] Though work on *The Valley of the Shadow* began at the University of Virginia in 1993, the website remains a vital resource to the present day, in part due to having been processed for preservation by the University of Virginia Library in 2007. A different example of how digital humanists leverage technology is seen in the HathiTrust Research Center, which launched in 2011 to enable "large-scale analysis of works in the HathiTrust Digital Library (HTDL) to facilitate nonprofit research and educational uses of the collection."[129] Examples of works resulting from substantial use of the HathiTrust Research Center include scholarly books published by the University of Chicago Press and the Columbia University Press; peer-reviewed articles published in such journals as *Public Services Quarterly*, *The Journal of American History*, and *Digital Humanities Quarterly*; and a number of conference publications and research datasets.[130]

Digitization as a Win for Distinctive Collections

Despite their reputation as tradition-bound and, in the worst case, elitist, distinctive collections were arguably more transformed by digital technology than any other part of the academic library. For special collections, the fact that anyone with access to the internet can read high-quality digital surrogates of rare, often valuable books that were once nearly inaccessible to all but a privileged few made it easier to protect vulnerable materials without denying access. For archives, digitization brought attention to their physical collections by making them easily accessible to millions of information seekers who might never have set foot in a physical archive. Yale University archivist William E. Landis's early prediction that digitization of archives would draw a different clientele than "the research-intensive users with whom many of us have the most experience" proved prescient.[131] A less predictable consequence of large-scale digitization has been the blurring of the distinction between libraries, archives, and museums, all of whose contributions to the digital whole begin to look very much alike from the perspective of the end user. This blurring is reflected in the coining of such new rubrics such as "LAM (Libraries, Archives, and Museums)," "culture memory institutions," and "cultural heritage institutions," all of which serve to house once-discrete institutions under a single big tent. Although vast amounts of materials remain undigitized and the challenges of long-term storage remain to be fully solved, the use of digital technology to de-silo and democratize distinctive collections must be seen as one of the greatest triumphs in the history of distinctive collections in particular and libraries as a whole.

Notes

1. Meredith R. Evans, "Modern Special Collections: Embracing the Future While Taking Care of the Past," *New Review of Academic Librarianship* 21, no. 2 (May 4, 2015): 117.
2. Robert P. Spindler, "Electronic Publishing and Institutional Memory," in *College and University Archives: Readings in Theory and Practice*, ed. Christopher J. Prom and Ellen D. Swain (Chicago: Society of American Archivists, 2008), 53.
3. In this chapter, the term *special collections* is used in the narrower sense unless otherwise indicated.
4. In archival parlance, items such as clothing, plaques, scientific apparatus, and other objects are known as *realia*.
5. "Description of the Collections," University of Idaho Library, https://www.lib.uidaho.edu/special-collections/description.html (accessed January 31, 2024).
6. Miles Harvey, *The Island of Lost Maps: A True Story of Cartographic Crime*, 1st ed. (Westminster: The Crown Publishing Group, 2010).
7. "Cache of Stolen Rare Books Said to Number Some 30,000," *American Libraries* 21, no. 5 (May 1990): 391.
8. Laura Schmidt, "A Guide to Effective Research," Society of American Archivists, 2011, 8, https://files.archivists.org/pubs/UsingArchives/Using-Archives-Guide.pdf.
9. "Archives Reading Room," Georgia Tech Library, https://library.gatech.edu/archives/archives-reading-room (accessed April 15, 2024).
10. Daniel Traister, "Is There a Future for Special Collections? And Should There Be?: A Polemical Essay," *RBM: A Journal of Rare Books, Manuscripts, and Cultural Heritage* 1, no. 1 (March 1, 2000): 60, https://doi.org/10.5860/rbm.1.1.181.
11. Michelle Light, "Controlling Goods or Promoting the Public Good: Choices for Special Collections in the Marketplace," *RBM: A Journal of Rare Books, Manuscripts, and Cultural Heritage* 16, no. 1 (March 1, 2015): 50, https://doi.org/10.5860/rbm.16.1.435.
12. Based on an examination of library websites in February 2024.
13. Michael Garabedian, "'You've Got to Be Carefully Taught': American Special Collections Library Education and the Inculcation of Exclusivity," *A Journal of Rare Books, Manuscripts, and Cultural Heritage* 7, no. 1 (2006): 55–6, https://doi.org/10.5860/rbm.7.1.257.
14. "About: Mission Statement," University Library: Rare Book and Manuscript Library, https://www.library.illinois.edu/rbx/about (accessed February 1, 2024).

15. "The Digitization of the Ransom Center's Gutenberg Bible," Harry Ransom Center, July 22, 2003, https://www.hrc.utexas.edu/press/releases/2003/digital-gutenberg.html.
16. "Cornell University Library Making of America Collection," Cornell University Library, https://collections.library.cornell.edu/moa_new/index.html (accessed March 8, 2024).
17. "About the UCSB Cylinder Audio Archive," University of California, Santa Barbara Library (University of California, Santa Barbara. Library. Department of Special Collections, November 16, 2005), https://cylinders.library.ucsb.edu/overview.php.
18. Peter B. Hirtle, "The Impact of Digitization on Special Collections in Libraries," *Libraries & the Cultural Record* 37, no. 1 (2002): 45–6.
19. Hirtle, "The Impact of Digitization," 47.
20. John Seely Brown and Paul Duguid, *The Social Life of Information* (Boston: Harvard Business School Press, 2002), 172–3.
21. E. Michael Attas, "Enhancement of Document Legibility Using Spectroscopic Imaging," *Archivaria* 57 (May 2004): 131–45.
22. Hirtle, "The Impact of Digitization," 44.
23. Janice E. Ruth, "The Development and Structure of the Encoded Archival Description (EAD) Document Type Definition," *Journal of Internet Cataloging* 4, no. 3–4 (November 27, 2001): 29.
24. Society of American Archivists, "Fonds," Dictionary of Archives Terminology, https://dictionary.archivists.org/entry/fonds.html (accessed February 27, 2024).
25. Geoffrey Yeo, "The Conceptual Fonds and the Physical Collection," *Archivaria* 73 (April 25, 2012): 43, https://archivaria.ca/index.php/archivaria/article/view/13384.
26. "Ohio State University, Office of the President (William Oxley Thompson) Records," Special Collections Registry, https://library.osu.edu/collections/rg.3.e/administrative-information (accessed February 9, 2024).
27. Society of American Archivists, "Finding Aid," Dictionary of Archives Terminology, https://dictionary.archivists.org/entry/finding-aid.html (accessed February 15, 2024).
28. "Guide to the Ohio State University, Office of the President (William Oxley Thompson) Records, 1870–1975, Bulk 1870–1933 RG.3.E," Ohio State University Libraries: University Archives, https://library.osu.edu/finding-aids/ead/UA/RG.3.E.xml (accessed February 9, 2024).
29. Diana Madden, "An Overview of the USMARC Archival and Manuscripts Control," *SA Archives Journal* 33 (June 1991): 47.
30. Society of American Archivists, "Archives, Personal Papers, and Manuscripts (APPM)," Society of American Archivists, https://www2.archivists.org/node/10163 (accessed February 28, 2024).
31. Ruth, "The Development and Structure of the Encoded Archival Description," 31.
32. Elizabeth Shepherd and Charlotte Smith, "The Application of ISAD(G) to the Description of Archival Datasets," *Journal of the Society of Archivists* 21, no. 1 (April 2000): 55.
33. Beth M. Whittaker, "Insights and Questions from the New Archival Descriptive Standard," *Library Resources & Technical Services* 51, no. 2 (April 2007): 98–105.
34. Daniel Pitti, "Encoded Archival Description (EAD)," in *Understanding Information Retrieval Systems: Management, Types, and Standards*, ed. Martha J. Bates (Boca Raton: CRC Press, 2012), 696.
35. Sharon Gibbs Thibodeau, "Development of the Encoded Archival Description DTD," Official Site, Library of Congress, 2002, https://www.loc.gov/ead/eaddev.html.

36 Ruth, "The Development and Structure of the Encoded Archival Description," 34–6.

37 Pitti, "Encoded Archival Description," 690.

38 Mike Rush and Bill Stockting, "Encoded Archival Description Tag Library Version EAD3 1.1.1," Library of Congress, 2019, https://www.loc.gov/ead/EAD3taglib/EAD3.html.

39 Society of American Archivists, "Encoded Archival Context–Corporate Bodies, Persons, and Families (EAC-CPF)," Society of American Archivists, May 2022, https://www2.archivists.org/node/23669.

40 Thomas J. Frusciano, "'Ten Years After': The Next Wave of EAD Implementation," *Journal of Archival Organization* 5, no. 3 (May 14, 2008): 2.

41 "History," ArchivesSpace, https://archivesspace.org/about/history (accessed March 6, 2024).

42 Jennifer G. Eidson and Christina J. Zamon, "EAD Twenty Years Later: A Retrospective of Adoption in the Early Twenty-First Century and the Future of EAD," *The American Archivist* 82, no. 2 (September 2019): 324, https://doi.org/10.17723/aarc-82-02-02.

43 Eidson and Zamon, "EAD Twenty Years Later," 312.

44 Eidson and Zamon, "EAD Twenty Years Later," 317.

45 "Ohio State Football Collection Guide," Ohio State University Libraries: University Archives, https://library.osu.edu/ohio-state-football-collection-guide (accessed March 7, 2024).

46 Gwynneth Malin, "'Digitize This!': The Impact of Digital Collections on Archival Description," *Journal of Archival Organization* 1, no. 4 (September 2002): 74.

47 Guy Lamolinara, "Metamorphosis of a National Treasure," *American Libraries*, March 1996.

48 Michael Rogers, "Ten Sites Chosen for Digitization," *Library Journal* 122, no. 9 (May 15, 1997): 25–6.

49 "Harvard Digital Collections," Harvard Library, https://library.harvard.edu/digital-collections (accessed March 11, 2024).

50 University of Michigan Library, "Usage and Size Statistics (Digital Collections)," https://staff.lib.umich.edu/content/usage-and-size-statistics-digital-collections (accessed March 11, 2024).

51 "Statistics," University of Florida Digital Collections, https://ufdc.ufl.edu/stats (accessed March 11, 2024).

52 "Digital Public Library of America," Digital Public Library of America, https://dp.la/ (accessed March 10, 2024).

53 Matt Enis, "Q&A: Dan Cohen on His Role as the Founding Executive Director of DPLA," *Library Journal*, April 1, 2013.

54 "Digital Public Library of America," Digital Public Library of America.

55 Robin L. Chandler, "Building Digital Collections at the OAC: Current Strategies with a View to Future Uses," *Journal of Archival Organization* 1, no. 1 (January 2002): 94.

56 Bradley D. Westbrook, "Prospecting Virtual Collections," *Journal of Archival Organization* 1, no. 1 (January 2002): 73–80.

57 Katja Müller, *Digital Archives and Collections: Creating Online Access to Cultural Heritage*, vol. 11, Anthropology of Media (New York: Berghahn Books, 2021), 4, https://doi.org/10.2307/j.ctv29sfzfx.6.

58 Cory Lampert, "Ramping Up," *Digital Library Perspectives* 34, no. 1 (January 1, 2018): 47.

59 Terrence J. McDonald, "Digitization by the Numbers," *Collections: A Publication of the Bentley Historical Library*, Summer 2021, https://bentley.umich.edu/news-events/magazine/digitization-by-the-numbers/.

60 Maggie Dickson, "Due Diligence, Futile Effort: Copyright and the Digitization of the Thomas E. Watson Papers," *The American Archivist* 73, no. 2 (Fall/Winter 2010): 627, https://doi.org/10.17723/aarc.73.2.16rh811120280434.

61 Robert E. Spoo, "Archival Foreclosure: A Scholar's Lawsuit Against the Estate of James Joyce," *American Archivist* 71, no. 2 (Fall/Winter 2008): 544–51, https://doi.org/10.17723/aarc.71.2.gq50902754j2388w.

62 Zachary Stein, "Privacy in Public Archives: Managing Personally Identifiable Information in Special Collections," *RBM: A Journal of Rare Books, Manuscripts, and Cultural Heritage* 22, no. 2 (2021), https://doi.org/10.5860/rbm.22.2.85.

63 Joyce Chapman and Samantha Leonard, "Cost and Benefit of Quality Control Visual Checks in Large-Scale Digitization of Archival Manuscripts," *Library Hi Tech* 31, no. 3 (May 2013): 405–18.

64 Janet Gertz, "Is Your Google Book Incomplete? We May Be Able to Help," *The Long View: Columbia University Libraries* (blog), April 28, 2017, https://blogs.cul.columbia.edu/longview/2017/04/is-your-google-book-incomplete-we-may-be-able-to-help/.

65 "NBC 5/KXAS (WBAP) Television News Collections," UNT University Libraries, https://library.unt.edu/special-collections/archives-manuscripts/kxasnbc-5/ (accessed February 23, 2024).

66 "Identifying and Handling Nitrate Film," The Association of Moving Image Archivists, December 2008, https://www.amianet.org/wp-content/uploads/Resource-Nitrate-Identifying-and-Handling.pdf.

67 W. Brent Webber, Lorie Jayne Ernest, and Srikanth Vangapandu, "Mercury Exposures in University Herbarium Collections," *Journal of Chemical Health & Safety* 18, no. 2 (April 2011): 11–14.

68 Peter Lyman and Brewster Kahle, "Archiving Digital Cultural Artifacts: Organizing an Agenda for Action," *D-Lib Magazine* 4, no. 7/8 (July 1998), https://doi.org/10.1045/july98-lyman.

69 Liladhar R. Pendse, "Saving Afghanistan's At-Risk Websites: A Race to Archive Digital and Cultural Content under Threat of Erasure by the Taliban," *American Libraries*, January/February 2022, https://americanlibrariesmagazine.org/2022/01/03/saving-afghanistans-at-risk-websites.

70 "Wayback Machine," Internet Archive, https://web.archive.org/ (accessed April 24, 2024).

71 "About Us," Archive-It, 2014, https://archive-it.org/learn-more/.

72 "UCLA Online Campaign Literature Web Archive," Archive-It, https://www.archive-it.org/collections/5903 (accessed April 24, 2024).

73 Carrie Smith, "Saving Your Media: Digitization of Audio, Print, and Film," *American Libraries*, April 2017, https://americanlibrariesmagazine.org/2017/03/01/saving-your-media-digitization.

74 Anne R. Kenney and Stephen Chapman, *Digital Imaging for Libraries and Archives* (Ithaca: Department of Preservation and Conservation, Cornell University Library, 1996).

75 Roy Tennant, "Outsourcing Digitization," *Library Journal* 124, no. 15 (September 15, 1999): 34.

76 "Our Collections," AM, https://www.amdigital.co.uk/discover/collections (accessed March 21, 2024).

77 Jennifer Kemp, "The Birth of a Database," *Library Journal*, June 1, 2014.

78 Chris Houghton and Sarah Ketchley, "From Provider to Partner: How Digital Humanities Sparked a Change in Gale's Relationship with Universities," *Insights: The UKSG Journal*, October 16, 2019, 1–9, https://insights.uksg.org/articles/10.1629/uksg.482.

79 "About Artstor," Artstor, https://www.artstor.org/about/ (accessed April 5, 2024).

80 Cartography Associates, "About," David Rumsey Map Collection, https://www.davidrumsey.com/about/about (accessed April 7, 2024).

81 Library of Congress, "2014 DPOE Training Needs Assessment Survey" (Washington, DC: Library of Congress, December 18, 2014), https://blogs.loc.gov/thesignal/2015/01/report-available-for-the-2014-dpoe-training-needs-assessment-survey/.

82 Rafiq Ahmad, Muhammad Rafiq, and Muhammad Arif, "Global Trends in Digital Preservation: Outsourcing versus in-House Practices," *Journal of Librarianship and Information Science* 56, no. 4 (May 25, 2023): 10.

83 Dan Hazen, Jeffrey Horrell, and Jan Merrill-Oldham, "Selecting Research Collections for Digitization" (Washington, DC: Council on Library and Information Resources, August 1998).

84 "Guide to the Ohio State University, Office of the President (William Oxley Thompson) Records, 1870–1975, Bulk 1870–1933 RG.3.E."

85 Brian M. Ingrassia, *The Rise of Gridiron University: Higher Education's Uneasy Alliance with Big-Time Football* (Lawrence: University of Kansas Press, 2012), 61–3.

86 Grace Therrell, "More Product, More Process: Metadata in Digital Image Collections," *Digital Library Perspectives* 35, no. 1 (February 11, 2019): 2–14.

87 Mark Greene and Dennis Meissner, "More Product, Less Process: Revamping Traditional Archival Processing," *The American Archivist* 68, no. 2 (September 1, 2005): 209, https://doi.org/10.17723/aarc.68.2.c741823776k65863.

88 Edward Benoit III, "#MPLP Part 2: Replacing Item-Level Metadata with User-Generated Social Tags," *American Archivist* 81, no. 1 (Spring/Summer 2018): 38–64, https://doi.org/10.17723/0360-9081-81.1.38.

89 Mark A Greene, "MPLP: It's Not Just for Processing Anymore," *The American Archivist* 73, no. 1 (Spring/Summer 2010): 194, https://doi.org/10.17723/aarc.73.1.m577353w31675348.

90 Dennis Meissner and Mark A. Greene, "More Application While Less Appreciation: The Adopters and Antagonists of MPLP," *Journal of Archival Organization* 8, no. 3–4 (2010): 176.

91 The Ohio State University Archives, *1905_football_team*, February 9, 2015, photo, https://www.flickr.com/photos/ohio-state-university-archives/27161742836/.

92 Steven Jack Miller, *Metadata for Digital Collections: A How-to-Do-It Manual*, Second Edition, How-To-Do-It Manuals Series (Chicago: ALA Neal-Schuman, 2022).

93 Bernadette Houghton, "Trustworthiness: Self-Assessment of an Institutional Repository against ISO 16363–2012," *D-Lib Magazine* 21, no. 3/4 (March 2015), https://doi.org/10.1045/march2015-houghton.

94 Chela Scott Weber, "Digitization and Access in Archives," *Hanging Together* (blog), October 25, 2023, https://hangingtogether.org/digitization-and-access-in-archives/.

95 Marshall Breeding, "Understanding the Protocol for Metadata Harvesting of the Open Archives Initiative," *Computers in Libraries* 22, no. 8 (September 2002): 24, https://search.ebscohost.com/login.aspx?direct=true&db=lxh&AN=7280939&site=ehost-live.

96   Joshua Hammer, "The Brave Sage of Timbuktu: Abdel Kader Haidara," National Geographic | Innovators, April 21, 2014, https://www.nationalgeographic.com/culture/article/140421-haidara-timbuktu-manuscripts-mali-library-conservation.

97   Marc Kosciejew, "Digital Vellum and Other Cures for Bit Rot," *Information Management Journal* 49, no. 3 (June 5, 2015): 21.

98   Trevor Owens, *The Theory and Craft of Digital Preservation*, 1st ed. (Baltimore: Johns Hopkins University Press, 2018), 105–6.

99   "ISO 14721:2003," ISO, https://www.iso.org/standard/24683.html (accessed May 9, 2024).

100   Brian Lavoie, "The OAIS Reference Model," *OCLC Newsletter*, February 2000, https://www.oclc.org/research/publications/2000/lavoie-oais.html.

101   James L. Hilton, "Digital Asset Management Systems," *EDUCAUSE Review*, April 2003, https://er.educause.edu/-/media/files/article-downloads/erm0327.pdf.

102   Alan McCord, "Digital Asset Management Systems" (EDUCAUSE2002, Atlanta, Georgia: EDUCAUSE, 2002), 6, https://events.educause.edu/annual-conference/2002.

103   Sandra Payette and Carl Lagoze, "Flexible and Extensible Digital Object and Repository Architecture (FEDORA)," in *Research and Advanced Technology for Digital Libraries*, ed. Christos Nikolaou and Constantine Stephanidis, vol. 1513, Lecture Notes in Computer Science (Berlin, Heidelberg: Springer Berlin Heidelberg, 1998), 41–59.

104   Research Libraries Group and OCLC, "Trusted Digital Repositories: Attributes and Responsibilities: An RLG-OCLC Report" (Mountain View, California: Research Libraries Group, May 2002), 5, https://www.oclc.org/content/dam/research/activities/trustedrep/repositories.pdf.

105   OCLC, Center for Research Libraries, and National Archives and Records Administration, "Trustworthy Repositories Audit & Certification: Criteria and Checklist" (OCLC and the Center for Research Libraries, 2007).

106   Houghton, "Trustworthiness."

107   Mary Molinaro, "The Digital Preservation Network (DPN) Has Launched and Is Accepting Content," *D-Lib Magazine*, April 3, 2016, https://www.dlib.org/dlib/march16/03inbrief.html.

108   Roger C. Schonfeld, "Why Is the Digital Preservation Network Disbanding?," *The Scholarly Kitchen* (blog), December 13, 2018, https://scholarlykitchen.sspnet.org/2018/12/13/digital-preservation-network-disband/.

109   "Historical Cost of Computer Memory and Storage," Our World in Data, https://ourworldindata.org/grapher/historical-cost-of-computer-memory-and-storage (accessed May 1, 2024).

110   Wasim Ahmad Bhat, "Long-Term Preservation of Big Data: Prospects of Current Storage Technologies in Digital Libraries," *Library Hi Tech* 36, no. 3 (June 4, 2018): 539–55.

111   California Digital Library, "Merritt Digital Preservation Repository Policies & User Guidelines," California Digital Library, https://cdlib.org/services/uc3/merritt/merritt-policies-and-procedures/ (accessed May 2, 2024).

112   "Publish Big Data," Figshare+, https://knowledge.figshare.com/plus (accessed May 2, 2024).

113   David Stuart Holmes Rosenthal, "The Medium-Term Prospects for Long-Term Storage Systems," *Library Hi Tech* 35, no. 1 (March 20, 2017): 11–31.

114 Erik W. Austin, "ICPSR: The Founding and Early Years," ICPSR, https://www.icpsr.umich.edu/web/pages/about/history/early-years.html (accessed May 2, 2024).

115 Carolyn L. Geda, "Training the Professional Data Librarian," *Drexel Library Quarterly* 13, no. 1 (January 1977): 100–8.

116 Robert M. Hayes, "Data Processing in the Library School Curriculum," *American Libraries* 61, no. 6 (June 1967): 662–9.

117 Elise Gowen and John J. Meier, "Research Data Management Services and Strategic Planning in Libraries Today: A Longitudinal Study," *Journal of Librarianship and Scholarly Communication* 8, no. 1 (April 18, 2020): 1–19.

118 Anne R. Diekema, Andrew Wesolek, and Cheryl D. Walters, "The NSF/NIH Effect: Surveying the Effect of Data Management Requirements on Faculty, Sponsored Programs, and Institutional Repositories," *Journal of Academic Librarianship* 40, no. 3/4 (May 2014): 322.

119 "About," DMP Tool, https://dmptool.org/about_us (accessed May 2, 2024).

120 Sarah Pugachev, "What Are 'The Carpentries' and What Are They Doing in the Library?," *Portal: Libraries & the Academy* 19, no. 2 (April 2019): 209–10.

121 Jean P. Shipman, Rong Tang, and Bonnie Lawlor, "The Collaborative Creation of a Research Data Management Librarian Academy (RDMLA)," *Information Services & Use* 39, no. 3 (July 2019): 243–7.

122 Terra Dankowski, "5 Library Jobs on the Rise," *American Libraries*, June 2022, https://americanlibrariesmagazine.org/2022/06/01/5-library-jobs-on-the-rise/.

123 Melissa Lamont, "Managing Geospatial Data and Services," *The Journal of Academic Librarianship* 23, no. 6 (November 1997): 469.

124 David Cowen, "The Evolution of GIS Services in Academic Libraries," *E-Perimetron* 16, no. 4 (2021): 201, https://www.e-perimetron.org/Vol_16_4/Cowen.pdf.

125 Dolores M. Burton, "Automated Concordances and Word Indexes. Part 1: The Fifties," *Computers & the Humanities* 15, no. 1 (February 1981): 1–14.

126 Judith R. Ahronheim, "Descriptive Metadata: Emerging Standards," *Journal of Academic Librarianship* 24, no. 5 (September 1998): 397.

127 Anne Burdick et al., *Digital_Humanities* (Cambridge, MA: MIT Press, 2012), 122.

128 "The Story Behind the Valley Project," Valley of the Shadow, https://valley.lib.virginia.edu/VoS/usingvalley/valleystory.html (accessed May 7, 2024).

129 "HathiTrust Research Center," HathiTrust Digital Library, https://www.hathitrust.org/about/research-center/ (accessed May 6, 2024).

130 "HTRC Research Impact," HathiTrust Research Center, May 7, 2024, https://htrc.atlassian.net/wiki/spaces/COM/pages/159973402/HTRC+Research+Impact.

131 William E. Landis, "Nuts and Bolts: Implementing Descriptive Standards to Enable Virtual Collections," *Journal of Archival Organization* 1, no. 1 (January 2002): 84.

6 Reference, Instruction, and Facilities

The Challenge of Meeting Changing User Expectations in the Digital Age

While it is correct to say that digital technology transformed academic libraries, it is equally correct to say that academic libraries transformed themselves in response to the changing expectations of academic library users brought on by the spread of digital technology into everyday life. Most obviously, library users in the digital age came to expect instant access to the entire universe of information (or close to it) at any time, from any place. Rather than access to collections, however, this chapter will focus on changed user expectations about library services—primarily reference and instruction—as well as changed user expectations for library facilities.

Reference Service

In the academic library, reference service has long been centered on the model of a staffed reference desk located in a high-traffic area of the library adjacent to a non-circulating, print-format reference collection. While reference service may seem as if it has always been an integral part of the academic library, this service was not commonly provided in academic libraries until the late nineteenth or, in some cases, the early twentieth century. Protecting valuable book collections was more important than making books available for use, and reference service was not in much demand when the typical academic library collection was tiny and access to it tightly controlled. When it came to providing quality reference service, U.S. public libraries were far in advance of academic libraries until well into the twentieth century. For example, in the early years of the twentieth century, it was an open secret among Harvard students and faculty that seeking out a librarian was not the best way to get help in navigating the nooks and crannies of Harvard's many libraries; instead, the person to consult was one John Shea (1881–1959), a legendary Harvard Library employee "with, at best, a sixth grade education" who nonetheless demonstrated an uncanny talent for knowing what was in the collection and where it could be found.[1] It would not be until 1915 that, in the interest of providing better service to students, Harvard undertook the first formal organization of its library circulation and reference departments, quite naturally hiring an expert reference librarian from a major public library to lead that effort.[2]

The leading virtue of the reference-desk model has always been that anyone with a need for information—whether it be the location of the nearest dictionary or in-depth guidance on researching a doctoral dissertation—is welcome approach and ask for assistance. The kinds of human-to-human interactions that take place at a reference desk have only grown more valued in a world in which empathetic human expertise has been increasingly replaced by indifferent machines. Michael Gorman speaks for many librarians when he writes that "technology can enhance but will never supplant human-to-human reference service. Further, if the latter were to disappear, it would be a severe, and possibly fatal, blow to the whole concept of library service."[3] In an article published in *College & Research Libraries* in 1958, American literary scholar James D. Hart expresses a similar point of view from the perspective of an experienced library user and researcher, writing, "Whether in libraries great or modest, the reference librarian is the living link between the text and the reader."[4]

As a profession, reference librarians have long prided themselves on their ability to establish emphatic, non-judgmental connections with library users in order to help fulfill any and all information needs. To this end, reference librarians have traditionally employed the *reference interview*, a technique established in the early twentieth century "in which librarians ask questions in order to get a clearer, more complete picture of what users want to know—all with the goal of linking the user to appropriate resources."[5] When presented with complex, challenging inquiries, academic reference librarians may arrange one-on-one follow-up consultations outside of the time constraints and distractions of a busy reference desk. They may also triage a challenging inquiry by seeking input from librarian colleagues or other experts with greater in-depth knowledge of the topic in question. Reference librarians tend to see themselves as teachers, often taking pains to clearly demonstrate the process for finding information rather than robotically dispensing answers to questions. What starts as an ordinary reference-desk transaction may lead to an ongoing intellectual partnership from which both the librarian and information seeker benefit. This phenomenon is testified to not only in the anecdotes of academic reference librarians but also by the vast number of scholarly books, theses, and dissertations whose preliminary pages include heartfelt thanks to one or more helpful and empathetic reference librarians.

Taking a less charitable view of the institution of the reference desk are the many librarians who have questioned the model's effectiveness. In an article published in 1983, Thelma Freides, at that time the head of Readers Services at Purchase College, concluded that the reference desk "works best for directional questions and requests for specific factual information. It is not well designed for dealing with questions requiring interpretation or exploration."[6] A few years later, Barbara J. Ford proposed that, among the library profession's many time-worn traditions, "The reference desk, as the center and 'given' of reference service, is one of the traditions that should be examined."[7] In 1995, the librarian-authors of an article published in the *Journal of Academic Librarianship* went even further when they asserted that the reference desk "does not need to be rethought or reformed, it needs to be eliminated."[8] Five years later, Jerry D. Campbell, then dean of the libraries at the University of Southern California, called out reference librarians for their "frenetic efforts to defend the honor of face-to-face reference—even when study after study repeatedly confirms its pitiful success rate."[9] These representative critics of the reference desk are hardly voices in the wilderness. The author of the 2013 article "Shall We Get Rid of the Reference Desk?" cited forty-five librarian-authored articles that argue in favor of either entirely eliminating or radically reimaging the traditional reference desk.[10]

An operational drawback of the reference desk is that it mimics the hospital emergency-room model in which the highest-paid employees stand by to provide a level of assistance that very often may not be required. From the viewpoint of a budget-conscious administrator, it makes no more economic sense for a librarian to tell an undergraduate where the bathroom is located than it does for a surgeon to hand a patient an aspirin. While there are many articles reaching conclusions similar to that of a 2011 review article which contends that "given the generic nature of the vast majority of enquiries received, it is not cost-effective for librarians to provide reference desk services," very little research has been done on the actual costs of operating a reference desk.[11] A study conducted at Stetson University in 2009 is quite possibly the only published document to put dollar costs on reference service, reporting a cost of $7.00 ($10.46 in 2024 dollars) for every question answered.[12] Even if the cost-per-question is only a few dollars, those costs add up over the course of a year in which thousands of questions are answered.

Costs aside, the inescapable fact is that academic library reference desks have been experiencing a significant, long-term decline in the number of reference transactions reported. For one specific example, a study conducted at the Edinboro campus of Pennsylvania Western University finds that the number of reported reference-desk transactions fell from 11,593 in 1999 to 1,062 in 2019, a 90.84 percent decrease.[13] This decrease was not a result of the Covid-19 pandemic, as the Edinboro campus reported similarly low numbers for several years prior to 2019.[14] A nearly 91 percent decrease, though extreme, is not an anomaly, as broader studies of U.S. academic libraries show that reductions in the number of reference-desk transactions have been widespread. Data compiled by the American Library Association's Office of Research and Statistics show an almost 50 percent drop in academic library reference transactions from 1994 (n= 111,649,668) to 2008 (n= 56,148,040).[15] Along similar lines, the U.S. Department of Education's National Center for Education Statistics (NCES) biennial survey *Academic Libraries: 2000* shows that, for the 3,527 U.S. colleges and universities responding, the number of reference transactions per a typical week was 1,582,386.[16] The NCES biennial survey for 2012 shows a yearly total of 28,856,409 reference transactions for the 3,793 U.S. colleges and universities reporting.[17] Adjusting for the differences in weekly (2000) versus yearly (2012) reporting, the NCES data show an approximately 62 percent decrease in the number of reference transactions from 2000 to 2012. It is worth noting that these same two NCES annual surveys show that, from 2000 to 2012, academic library gate counts increased by 36.14 percent, indicating that reference-desk transactions dropped despite a more than one-third increase in library foot traffic. The discontinuation of the NCES biennial survey after 2012 means that more recent data on reference-desk transactions are available only via the less-comprehensive Association of College and Research Libraries (ACRL) annual survey. Understanding that the ACRL data is not directly comparable with the NCES data, the ACRL annual survey draws a more mixed picture from 2015 to 2019, with the average number of in-person reference transactions at bachelor's- and master's-level institutions remaining largely level over those years, the number at doctoral-level institutions decreasing by approximately

27 percent, and the number at associates-level institutions increasing by approximately 50 percent.[18]

The reason for the overall drop in reference-desk transactions is no mystery. With the spread of digital technology into everyday life, library reference services found themselves in competition with digital sources that could provide answers to questions library users would have once brought to the reference desk. By 2010, finding answers to questions ranging from the specific gravity of bromine to the addresses of self-service laundries in Warsaw, Poland, to the winner of the 1946 Academy Award for Best Picture was no longer a matter of visiting a library or even sitting down at a computer—it had become a matter of reaching for a smartphone. By 2020, artificial intelligence was playing a role in generating all those answers popping up on smartphones. For more in-depth inquiries, information seekers who might have once come to the reference desk for help finding scholarly books and journal articles could readily retrieve such documents online. Whether or not all these self-service information seekers, including the increasing numbers of students enrolled in online degree programs, were finding the most credible or the most appropriate information without the help of reference librarians remains an open question.

Changing User Expectations: Circulation, Interlibrary Loan, and Reserve Collections

Library circulation was one of the first library services to be automated, with examples of successful systems dating back to the 1960s.[19] Thanks to automated circulation systems, borrowers no longer had to write their names on circulation cards for every item they borrowed, while staff no longer had to stamp, file, and keep track of hundreds, if not thousands, of cards. Eventually, automated circulation systems became capable of independently emailing to library users such communications as recall notices, warnings of approaching due dates, and notifications that items were overdue—all functions which had previously been carried out by human library employees. At the same time that automated circulation systems were becoming more efficient, the circulation workload in academic libraries was dropping. According to data from the National Center for Educational Statistics (NCES), for the 1997–98 academic year, academic libraries reported an overall average of twenty circulations per full-time student enrolled in U.S. degree-granting, post-secondary institutions; for 2011–12, that average had dropped to ten circulations per student. ACRL data for all circulation transactions, physical and electronic, show the numbers going up and down from 2015 to 2023, with the number of circulations for 2023 (620,488) coming in at 19.9 percent lower than the number for 2015 (774,710).[20] Tellingly, those same ACRL data show digital items accounting for 98.4 percent of all circulations reported in 2023.

Like circulation services, interlibrary-loan (ILL) services also became increasingly automated during the twenty-first century. Instead of filling out a paper form at the ILL desk, academic library users could submit requests online, often directly from a bibliographic record retrieved during a search in an online public access catalog (OPAC) or a periodical index. At the same time, the delivery of articles requested via ILL transitioned from printed pages sent via postal mail to files delivered electronically.

In the area of library reserve services, by 1992 the Association of Research Libraries (ARL) was already exploring ways to replace physical items placed on reserve with digital surrogates.[21] The long-standing academic library practice of placing physical items on reserve never disappeared, though with so much information available in digital formats, including a growing number of OER (Open Educational Resources) textbooks, the need to place physical items on reserve lost some of its former urgency. In any case, savvy students who did not worry much about legal niceties discovered they could, in many cases, use BitTorrent technology to avoid both the wait at the reserve desk and the bill at the campus bookstore.

Library Instruction

In the interest of providing historical context, the following section considers the tradition of library instruction that was firmly in place by 1990. The subsequent section focuses on the ways in which the spread of digital technology disrupted traditional library instruction.

The Library Instruction Backstory

Chronicling what may be the earliest example of library instruction in a U.S. academic library, an account dating from the 1820s tells of a Harvard librarian who occasionally lectured undergraduates about rare books found in the library collection.[22] While the nineteenth century provides subsequent examples of library instruction, the record is spotty. Chapter IX of 1876's *Public Libraries in the United States*, entitled "Professorships of Books and Reading," consists of two essays arguing in favor of colleges and universities appointing professors of books and reading, but both essays focus on teaching students to develop refined tastes in reading rather than offering any ideas on how librarians might teach students the sort of library-research skills a budding scholar could put to practical use.[23] Multiple sources indicate that in 1881 the University of Michigan became what was probably the first U.S. academic institution to offer a for-credit library course.[24] Another pioneering example of library instruction comes from Oberlin College Library, where from 1899 to 1927 Azariah Smith Root developed and taught "his own program of library instruction" consisting of three courses—"The Use of Libraries," "Elementary Bibliography," and "History of the Printed Book."[25]

In 1898, Emma Louise Adams surveyed forty normal-school libraries regarding their instruction efforts. Of the twenty replies Adams received to the question, "What instruction is given students in the use of reference books?", one library reported providing no instruction, nine reported "informal or individual instruction," and ten reported such activities as assigning students to compile subject bibliographies and "informal talks by librarians or heads of departments."[26] A similar survey of instruction in U.S. academic libraries from 1876 to 1910 reports, "Some twenty institutions gave credit courses in library research and forty offered non-credit courses in library use."[27] In 1908, the University of Illinois Library published *Handbook of the Library*, a fifty-four-page guidebook informing students of everything librarians thought students might want to know about the library, including library rules, the location of various collections, and a list of the periodical indexes available in the library.[28] The *Handbook* also informs students of the existence of a weekly, two-credit class on the use of the library. A discussion held at a meeting of the American Library Association Annual Meeting in June 1913 saw what may have been the first use of the phrase *bibliographic instruction*.[29] In a 1934 article on the topic of library instruction in teachers' colleges that is, to some extent, a continuation of Adams' 1898 survey, Mabel Harris disappointedly concludes that no "complete and thoroughly thought-out plan for bibliographic instruction in teachers colleges has yet been made."[30] Summing up the historical situation from the perspective of 1982, Frances L. Hopkins writes, "A bibliography of articles on academic library instruction published between 1876 and 1932 documents the decline from instruction in use of library materials for research to instruction in access procedures."[31]

The heyday for library instruction did not finally come about until after the Second World War, a time of significant changes to U.S. higher education. One change students experienced over the postwar decades was finding themselves increasingly taking courses from faculty who expected students to demonstrate curiosity, ask meaningful questions, engage in active learning, and show initiative through participation in such activities as self-directed learning and group projects. Though not necessarily true for every course on every campus, the old pedagogical approach in which students sat like empty vessels waiting to be filled with facts straight from the textbook faded away, especially during the 1960s and thereafter. Taking their cue from the ongoing transition to more participatory forms of learning, librarians adopted a teach-a-student-to-fish approach to instruction. An orientation tour of the library building followed by a recitation of library rules was no longer good enough. Not only should all students be taught the transferable skills required to identify, locate, organize, and cite information, but they should learn to become critical thinkers capable of evaluating the credibility and appropriateness of information.

From a more practical perspective, academic librarians of the postwar period recognized that, without the benefit of instruction, most students would never be able to successfully navigate increasingly large and complex academic library collections that not only consisted of growing numbers of books and journals but also were incorporating ever-larger amounts of information in such unintuitive packaging as microfilm/fiche, audio/visual media, and, starting as early as the 1970s, digital formats. From an administrative perspective, library instruction came to be seen as providing a good return on investment. Especially after U.S. higher-education enrollment surged due to the effects of the baby boom, the model of one librarian instructing classroom-sized groups of students offered a more sustainable model than that of providing one-on-one assistance to every student who walked through the library doors.

Early in the postwar period, the library literature began reporting on teaching collaborations between librarians and instructional faculty, with the first-year English composition course often serving as the locus for such collaborations. For instruction librarians, first-year English composition was seen as an ideal course to target because the students were motivated to learn about the library in order to complete the research paper that is typically a requirement in such courses. In an article published in 1952, an English instructor and a librarian at Flushing, New York's Queens College reported on a teaching collaboration that involved the librarian meeting with the students in a first-year composition course twice during the semester. The first meeting introduced students to "the use of such research tools as the card catalogue, encyclopedias, general and special bibliographies, union lists, and periodical indexes," while the second meeting focused on reviewing the initial library work done by the students.[32] The library instruction provided at Queens College in 1952 outlines a model of instruction that would be loosely followed for decades to come, though the opportunity of a second meeting between librarian and students would be more the exception than the rule.

The use of the phrase *bibliographic instruction* (often initialed as *B.I.*) gained traction in the 1970s, a decade that saw librarians publishing increasing numbers of articles, books, conference papers, and other documents on the topic of instruction. The 1970s also saw the "First Annual Conference on Library Orientation" at Eastern Michigan University, an event which led to the founding of the LOEX library-instruction clearinghouse in 1971.[33] In 1977, the ACRL added the Bibliographic Instruction Section to its roster.[34] By the end of the 1970s, a new term of art, *information literacy*, was entering the library lexicon.[35] While the phrases *bibliographic instruction* and *information literacy* are related and are, at times, used interchangeably, they are not identical. In general, information literacy is broader in scope than the more library-focused bibliographic instruction. By 1996, bibliographic instruction had fallen so far out of favor that the ACRL Bibliographic Instruction Section rebranded itself as the "Instruction Section."[36]

By the 1980s, most academic libraries had at least one librarian charged with coordinating instruction efforts, while larger academic libraries employed multi-person instruction units. For academic librarians, some greater or lesser amount of teaching became a requirement for all but the most specialized of positions. In addition to being expected to teach, academic librarians were often expected to promote instructional services to teaching faculty, though this was not always an easy sell. Often enough, instruction librarians encountered teaching faculty who believed they could teach library-research skills better than any librarian. As evidenced by the somewhat heated exchanges between prominent librarian John Cotton Dana (1856–1929) and Vassar College historian Lucy Maynard Salmon (1853–1927), the faculty-versus-librarians debate dates back to at least the 1910s.[37] John Cotton Dana notwithstanding, some library leaders took up Salmon's side of the debate. William M. Randall, whose resume includes a stint as director of the University of Georgia Library, believed that librarians should focus on tending to the catalog while, "The task of bringing about a contact between the books and the students is left largely to the faculty of the institution and to the least mature and experienced members of the library staff."[38] Instruction librarians also found, and continue to find, their outreach efforts thwarted by faculty who either assume their students already know how to use libraries or who simply see library instruction as unimportant. Even faculty who value library instruction may find it too painful to sacrifice even an hour of class time to a librarian guest-lecturer.

In a paper presented at the ACRL's 1997 national conference, Risë L. Smith identified an eminently practical problem that had long hampered academic librarians' efforts to promote information literacy:

> *Integrating information literacy throughout the undergraduate curriculum is limited as long as librarians insist on doing the instruction themselves. Despite idealistic instructional goals, most libraries simply do not have enough staff to offer instruction extensively throughout a curriculum.*[39]

While Smith was not the first librarian to highlight this capacity issue, nor was her proposed solution—that academic librarians should teach faculty how to integrate information literacy into their courses—previously unheard of, Smith clearly expressed a line of thinking championed by the movement known as "information literacy across the curriculum." In pursuit of their goal of information literacy across the curriculum, advocates called on librarians to, first, broaden the traditional librarian-faculty relationship from a nearly exclusive focus on library collections to one that brought information literacy into the conversation and, second, to integrate "information literacy instruction across a program, rather than attempting to piece together a successful approach from a series of individual relationships."[40] Writing in 2005, a time by which information literacy had come to be "enshrined in the criteria of the regional accrediting bodies," William Miller and Steven Bell make the argument that faculty are better positioned than librarians to teach information literacy because students heed the words of their primary instructors more readily than the words of a librarian who does not wield the power of a grade.[41] Selling the importance of information literacy to students themselves could be as hard as selling it to faculty. After all, why would anyone need to be taught how to do research when it was as easy as typing a keyword or two into Google? The extent to which students suffer from unwarranted overconfidence in their levels of information literacy provides a compelling example of the Dunning-Kruger Effect at work.[42]

One of the biggest challenges academic librarians have faced as teachers is that they are often limited to one-shot instruction sessions in which they are granted an hour, or less, to teach everything there is to know about using libraries, evaluating information, and applying it to papers, presentations, and other academic work. To overcome this challenge some academic libraries took the route of offering librarian-led, for-credit information-literacy courses. Although for-credit library courses date back to the University of Michigan example from 1881, they have always been more the exception than the rule. In a survey of U.S. academic libraries conducted in 1995 to which 631 institutions responded, about 30 percent reported offering a librarian-led for-credit course while only 2 percent of respondents reported that the course was required.[43] A similar survey conducted in 2014, to which 691 institutions responded, found that, "In all, 19 per cent of the institutions in the survey have IL credit courses taught by librarians."[44] While for-credit courses can be satisfying for librarians to teach and beneficial for students to take, any library offering such courses may face a number of obstacles. At some institutions, the fact that librarians lack faculty status can be a barrier to teaching for-credit courses, while library administrators may see the cost of freeing up enough hours for a librarian to teach a semester-long course that reaches only twenty-five (plus-or-minus) students as a poor return on investment. Because for-credit library courses are almost always elective, student enrollment in the course may drop too low to justify offering it consistently. Librarians have at times made eloquent arguments in favor of making a library-based course in information literacy a requirement for undergraduates.[45] Eloquence notwithstanding, convincing disciplinary faculty and campus administrators to shoehorn yet another required course into existing baccalaureate degree programs means entering into an academic battle that few librarians will win.

A significant burden librarians bear in trying to get information literacy into the curriculum in any form—for-credit or otherwise—is the challenge of assessing the outcomes of their instructional efforts. Sadly, instruction librarians have not always been up to the challenge of producing meaningful assessment of instruction, with nobody being harder on librarians for this shortcoming than librarians themselves. In 1982, a trio of researchers funded by the Council on Library Resources wrote of academic library instruction that "there is a good deal of talking about evaluation, but few seem to be doing anything about it."[46] Ten years later, Tom Eadie, in the role of truth-telling curmudgeon, scolded his fellow librarians with the harsh observation that most of what passed for assessment among instruction librarians focused on student satisfaction rather than what, if anything, students actually learned.[47] Similarly, the number of assessment-free "How We Done Good" articles in the literature of library instruction became something of a running joke within the profession. Which is not to say that librarians did not get better at assessing instruction over the years or that librarians have not done a lot of work, some of it quite good, on assessing the outcomes of their teaching. However, when carrying out assessment in real-world academic settings, librarians face a number of obstacles: too few working librarians are trained in assessing instruction, librarians' contact with the students they would like to assess is often limited to one-shot instruction sessions, and librarian efforts at instructional assessment often lack administrative support. Under such limitations, librarians often must make do with imperfect assessment tools. A pre-test/post-test type of assessment might show that students are better at searching for periodical articles after an instruction session with a librarian than they were before. Assessment by citation analysis might show that students use a wider variety of sources following library instruction. A GPA correlation might show students who attended a library-instruction session have higher GPAs than students who did not. The problem with these drive-by assessments is that none fully address the crucial question that librarians, along with others in the academy, want answered: *To what extent, if any, does librarian-led instruction enhance student learning and outcomes?*

Library Instruction Post-1990

The year is 1990. Twenty or so first-year writing students, their instructor, and a librarian are gathered in a library-instruction room. The librarian has fifty minutes to familiarize the students with the standard library-research process, a well-established sequence of steps taking the novice researcher from such general sources as encyclopedias and other reference books to such specific sources as scholarly books and articles. The standard library-research process is not new in 1990. What is new is the instructional technology on display: a monochromatic, flat-panel LCD computer projector connected to a desktop computer. This cutting-edge piece of technology allows the students to watch the librarian demonstrate a search of the library OPAC. The students, however, do not get to try out a search for themselves. They only watch. Whatever they may have learned or not learned from their time with the librarian, once the students are turned loose to do research, they will rely almost entirely on whatever sources of information they can find within the walls of the campus library.

By the year 2015, students working on their first college research paper would undergo a much different experience. For one thing, their principal challenge will have evolved from, "How do I find enough information for a research paper?" to "How do I make any sense of all this information?" For another, most of the information the students discover and access during their research will not be found among the carefully selected information resources contained within the walls of the campus library. The students of 2015 will likely start researching their topics by turning to a web search engine. If they start with Google Scholar, there is a good chance that the bulk of the hits they retrieve will lead to information from the higher end of the credibility continuum. If they start with a general-purpose search engine, they will retrieve some highly credible information sprinkled with the lowest forms of misinformation, disinformation, troll bait, and weaponized partisan content. Even those students whose level of information literacy enables them to spot the difference between a peer-reviewed scholarly article and a piece of state-sponsored disinformation may find themselves tripped up by a seemingly credible article from a predatory journal.

One way in which twenty-first-century academic library instructors leveraged new technology in order both to address a complex information universe and avoid the limitations of the traditional one-shot instruction session was to employ the flipped-classroom model. Under the flipped-classroom model, students would be given such assignments as completing a virtual tutorial or watching an instructional video prior to their session with a librarian. Class time would then be used to review the pre-class assignments, answer questions, and discuss what had been learned.[48] With or without flipping the classroom, by 2015 the standard library-research process taught circa 1990 had come to seem as quaint as filling a fountain pen from a library-supplied inkwell.

If for no other reason, 2015 stands as a watershed year in the history of library instruction because this was the year the ACRL released its *Framework for Information Literacy for Higher Education* (*ACRL Framework*).[49] The distant ancestor of the *Framework* is "Guidelines for Bibliographic Instruction in Academic Libraries," a one-page document published in 1977, "In order to assist college and university libraries in the planning and evaluation of effective programs to instruct members of the academic community in the identification and use of information resources."[50] *ACRL Framework*'s most immediate ancestor is the ACRL *Information Literacy Competency Standards for Higher Education* (*ACRL Standards*).[51] Published in January 2000, *ACRL Standards* acknowledges the increasingly important role of digital technology in the discovery and processing of information, though the document's five standards, twenty-one performance indicators, and dozens of outcomes are more reflective of the relatively tame information environment of an analog past than of the wild-west digital future waiting beyond the turn of the millennium.

By 2013, a critical mass of the academic library-instruction community had come to believe that the *ACRL Standards* was showing its age. The task force charged with drafting a new document chose to entirely replace the *ACRL Standards* rather than merely updating them, declaring:

> The **Framework** offered here is called a framework intentionally because it is based on a cluster of interconnected core concepts, with flexible options for implementation, rather than on a set of standards or learning outcomes, or any prescriptive enumeration of skills.[52]

The pedagogical foundations of the *ACRL Framework* come out of Jan H. F. Meyer and Ray Land's Threshold Concept Theory. In simple terms, Meyer and Land's theory is that every discipline has threshold concepts, and that although learners may initially find threshold concepts to be "troublesome," it is through engaging with them that "A new way of understanding, interpreting, or viewing something may thus emerge—a transformed internal view of subject matter, subject landscape, or even world view."[53] The six concepts comprising the backbone of the *ACRL Framework* are:

- Authority Is Constructed and Contextual
- Information Creation as a Process
- Information Has Value
- Research as Inquiry
- Scholarship as Conversation
- Searching as Strategic Exploration

Realizing they were making a radical departure from a standards-based approach to information literacy, the authors of *ACRL Framework* widely shared several drafts of their work-in-progress and provided many opportunities for input from the academic library community.[54] In the months and years following the February 2015 release of the final version of *ACRL Framework*, many academic librarians embraced the document, seeing it as a timely, progressive approach to information literacy, one well-suited to an information environment that had grown too large, too politicized, and too complex for the rigidity of a standards-based approach. Although applying the concepts of the *ACRL Framework* in the classroom presented new challenges, librarians devised innovative techniques for aligning their teaching with the new model. For one example, librarians at California State University, Chico, devised choose-your-own-adventure flip books as a way of integrating *ACRL Framework* into user-centered learning experiences.[55] For a very different example, instruction librarians at the University of New Mexico developed an instructional model specifically based on the *ACRL Framework's* core concept of "Information Creation as a Process." They then paired this instructional model with their own "research clinics" variation on the flipped classroom.[56]

As much as some academic librarians embraced the *ACRL Framework*, it also drew fire from critics. In January 2015, a group of New Jersey academic librarians drafted "An Open Letter Regarding the Framework for Information Literacy for Higher Education" in which they outlined a number of issues with the *ACRL Framework* and asked that the old *ACRL Standards* be revised and used in conjunction with the *ACRL Framework* rather than being completely discarded.[57] Speaking on behalf of frontline academic librarians as a whole, and community-college librarians in particular, Kim Leeder Reed wrote of the *Framework* that "the document is an ambitious and highly theoretical approach to the concept of information literacy that (by design) lacks any direct, practical application."[58] Similarly, Christine Bombaro, speaking from the perspective of a frontline instruction librarian, criticized the *ACRL Framework* on multiple grounds, pointing out "contradictions between the *Framework* and the Threshold Concept theory," presenting cogent arguments as to the ways in which the *Framework* is impractical and elitist, and calling out the ACRL for failing to educate librarians on how to implement the *ACRL Framework* in the classroom.[59]

The controversy over the *ACRL Framework* is reflective of the many information-related conflicts of the twenty-teens. If the *ACRL Framework* had been printed on paper, the ink would have barely been dry by the time the phrase *fake news* was suddenly everywhere. Seemingly overnight, separating the teaching of information literacy from the worldwide hyper-politicization of information in all its forms had become impossible. The situation was, by most measures, made worse by the politicization of any and all information related to the Covid-19 pandemic. In such a fraught information environment, it is not surprising that some librarians balked at the relativism of the *ACRL Framework*. As fundamentally true as it is to say, "Authority Is Constructed and Contextual," how was an instructor, quite possibly limited to a single meeting with students, supposed to convey so nuanced a concept without sending some of those students down a relativist rabbit hole where any given source of information becomes just as credible as any other? Equally perilous was taking a less relativistic, more didactic approach. Introducing IFLA's "How to Spot Fake News" checklist represents a sound approach for familiarizing students with a set of practical skills for evaluating information.[60] However, such a checklist approach oversimplifies the true complexity of evaluating information, potentially leading students to internalize such easy truisms as, *Articles from scholarly journals are the best sources of information*, while glossing over scholarly communication's laundry list of systemic problems, including flawed peer-review processes, misuse of impact factors, instances of plagiarism, the use of falsified data, and unethical uses of artificial intelligence.

By 2020, the digital innovations that had made discovering information faster and easier than ever before had simultaneously raised the bar for teaching information literacy higher than ever before. At the same time, these digital innovations presented academic librarians with both a new opportunity and a new challenge. The new opportunity was the possibility of extending both one-on-one reference transactions and group instruction beyond the limits of the library walls. The new challenge was exactly how to go about doing that.

Reference and Instruction beyond the Library Walls

Historically, an obstacle for those seeking out the key library services of reference and instruction has been the requirement that the recipient go to where those services are being dispensed rather than having the services come to them. This obstacle has proven especially daunting to distance learning students who may reside far from their home campuses. For instruction, there was no practical option for students of the past other than to be where the instruction was being provided at the time it was being provided. For reference service, library users had for many years the long-distance options of the telephone and postal mail, though the telephone is not well suited for anything more complex than ready-reference questions, and the slowness of postal mail deadens the productive interactivity that can occur during a real-time reference transaction.

The situation began to change significantly in the early 1990s, a time by which librarians were increasingly aware that improvements in the internet's ease of use and its growing popularity with the general public were transforming the "Information Superhighway" into a viable tool for informing and interacting with library users. Even with such growing awareness, the phrase *virtual reference* was a neologism in 1993, and in that same year Wright State University set off a minor buzz when it posted a job advertisement for something called an "Internet Services Reference Librarian."[61] From the 1990s and into the twenty-first century, academic libraries adopted a number of digital technologies for the purpose of providing virtual reference and instruction. The following sections touch on the most significant of these:

- Email Reference
- Web-Based Library Guides
- Digital Chat Reference
- Virtual Library Tour and Tutorials
- Web Video
- Social Media
- Texting
- Videoconferencing

Email Reference

The concept of providing reference service via email was proposed as early as the mid-1980s.[62] According to the NCES survey of academic libraries, by 1996, 40 percent of U.S. academic libraries offered reference service by email.[63] By 2012, that figure had risen to 77 percent of all U.S. academic libraries and was even higher among libraries serving baccalaureate institutions (86.4 percent), master's institutions (93.7 percent), and doctoral/research institutions (97.2 percent).[64]

Web-Based Library Guides

Before the coming of the Gopher or the Web, academic librarians routinely created *pathfinders*, a catchall term for a variety of guides designed to help library users locate information and use libraries more effectively. Printed on paper, pathfinders were costly to produce, challenging to distribute to their intended audiences, and subject to going out of date as quickly as new books and other information resources were added to a library's collection. The Gopher was the first innovation that allowed academic librarians to easily post—and library users to easily access—online equivalents of paper-format pathfinders. The University of California, Santa Cruz Library's InfoSlug, which provided information about the UCSC Library and campus as well as links to information resources from around the internet, was an early example of a Gopher-based, librarian-curated Campus-Wide Information System (CWIS).[65] Posting pathfinders and other librarian-produced information resources on a CWIS (and, eventually, on the Web) eliminated the cost of printing on paper as well as the challenges of distributing and updating physical documents. Unlike physical materials, online documents also exhibited the desirable properties of being asynchronous (accessible at any time) and ubiquitous (accessible from any place).

The menu-driven, plain-text Gopher was quickly sidelined by the Web. For librarians, the Web allowed the creation of library guides that were more attractive, informative, and interactive than Gopher-based documents. After listing a number of advantages of web-based subject guides, the author of an article advocating their use notes, "The guide itself is value-added in its overarching structure and arrangement of individual hypertext links, reflecting human intelligence and expertise in its evaluative criteria, subjective interpretations, classification decisions, and annotative descriptions."[66] As innovative as the early web-based library guides might be, the process of creating them followed the handmade, labor-intensive model of paper-format pathfinders. The amount of time librarians were putting into creating web-based guides led to questions about whether the extent to which users made beneficial use of such guides justified the amount of work involved in their creation and maintenance.[67] Such concerns were somewhat assuaged by the introduction of labor-saving content-management systems, the most notable of which was Springshare's LibGuides. Introduced in 2007, LibGuides allowed librarians to more easily "create dynamic subject guides that include social features like tagging, bookmarking, RSS feeds, user ratings, and comments."[68] The results of a survey published one year after LibGuides' launch attest to its instant popularity: of the 188 responding libraries (of which 179 were academic), 69 percent were using LibGuides.[69] LibGuides had the virtue of making it easy for librarians to borrow (with the consent of the creator) content from other LibGuides rather than needing to create all content from scratch. According to Springshare's own publicity, by 2024 there were over 500,000 shareable LibGuides worldwide.[70] The efficiencies provided by content-management systems allowed librarians to create not only dynamic versions of traditional library pathfinders but also new genres of specialized guides, including course-specific guides, dynamic lists of databases, and guides to unique digital collections. The value of web-based library guides would be further enhanced by their direct integration into campus learning-management systems.[71]

Digital Chat Reference

During the first quarter of the twenty-first century, digital chat technology was widely adopted by businesses, government agencies, and nonprofits as a tool for providing virtual customer service. In library settings, the original concept of digital chat technology was simple: information seekers and reference librarians used a shared digital chat technology to engage in reference transactions via plain-text messages. The first experiments with chat reference typically consisted of a library providing limited hours of service through one of the early, somewhat crude instant-messaging programs, specifically Internet Relay Chat (launched in 1988), ICQ (launched in 1996), and AOL Instant Messenger (launched in 1997). A typical example of such an approach is described in "Our Experiment in Online, Real-Time Reference," a 2001 article about Bowling Green State University Library's implementation of its home-grown chat reference service.[72] As more sophisticated commercial chat software, such as LSSI's Virtual Reference Desk, came on the market, librarians were able not only to chat but also to "demonstrate Web sites, provide useful links, and 'escort' patrons through elaborate searches."[73] An added benefit of sophisticated chat-reference software was its ability to keep accurate statistics on how many questions were asked, track the amount of time spent answering each question, and create permanent knowledge bases of questions asked and answered.

Early on, librarians realized the greatest potential of chat reference lay in the development of collaborative services in which librarians from multiple institutions shared the workload. In 2000, the Library of Congress initiated Collaborative Digital Reference Service (CDRS), a pilot project involving sixteen U.S. and international libraries in a test of the feasibility of an around-the-clock, chat based reference service; by early 2001, the pilot was receiving technical support from OCLC and had grown to include sixty libraries.[74] In 2002, CDRS was phased out to be replaced by the QuestionPoint 24/7 Reference Cooperative, an OCLC-managed service available to libraries via subscription.[75] End-user access to QuestionPoint was provided by a widget that member libraries embedded on their websites. Once a user clicked on the widget and submitted a question, it might be answered by a librarian on the user's campus, a librarian affiliated with a different library, or by a member of a team of librarians directly employed by QuestionPoint. Because libraries in the cooperative were geographically dispersed, around-the-clock reference service was possible without the management headaches and expense of assigning librarians to graveyard shifts. For example, librarians working afternoons or early evenings in the United States routinely answered questions from students working late at night in the United Kingdom. In 2004, QuestionPoint expanded with the acquisition of 24/7 Reference, a chat based service launched in 2000 that had grown a customer base of 500 libraries by the time of its acquisition.[76] By 2008, 2,200 libraries were subscribed to QuestionPoint.[77] In June 2019, the for-profit business Springshare purchased QuestionPoint from OCLC, migrating QuestionPoint users to Springshare's own LibAnswers, a digital-reference platform launched in 2009. At the time of the purchase, OCLC's subscriber base had dropped to 980 libraries while LibAnswers' subscriber base had grown to 1,400 libraries.[78]

As with in-person reference, little research has been done on the actual cost of providing reference service via digital chat. An article published in 2003 reports per-question costs ranging from $12.00 to $15.00 ($21.00 to $26.00 in 2024 dollars) when libraries outsourced chat reference through Library Systems and Services.[79] A 2013 analysis of the consortial digital reference services provided by the ten academic libraries in the University of California System calculated that, when taking into account the cost of subscribing to OCLC QuestionPoint plus salary costs (less benefits), answering a single chat-reference question cost $8.20 ($11.25 in 2024 dollars).[80]

Virtual Library Tours and Tutorials

By 1995, librarians at Texas A&M University had launched what may have been the first web-based virtual library tour.[81] While early virtual library tours employed text, maps, and other images with the goal of orienting learners to a specific library building, later virtual tours incorporated such elements as instructional videos (live-action or animated), hands-on learning activities, learning games, and interactive quizzes. The tools and techniques employed by the most fully developed virtual library tours caused them to blend into the next stage in the evolution of library digital-learning objects: virtual library tutorials. Compared to tours, tutorials are generally less place-bound and more focused on achieving universal information-literacy outcomes. Tutorials can also be tied to specific courses, with librarians and instructors collaborating to verify participation and assess student learning.[82]

Early on, creating a library virtual tour or tutorial was beyond the capabilities of most academic libraries. The process eventually became easier, in part thanks to the growing librarian-authored literature covering both the practical and theoretical aspects of developing effective virtual tours and tutorials. An early book-length how-to for creating virtual library tutorials is *Designing Effective Library Tutorials: A Guide for Accommodating Multiple Learning Styles* (2012).[83] Another early book on the topic is *Creating Online Tutorials: A Practical Guide for Librarians* (2015).[84] The University of Arizona's open-source Guide on the Side (released in July 2012), Springshare's LibWizard (released in February 2016), and Articulate 360 (released in November 2016) all helped to streamline the creation of highly interactive tours and tutorials in much the same way that content-management tools streamlined the creation of web-based guides.[85]

To take advantage of new and emerging technologies for instructing and serving users via the Web, the early 2000s saw academic libraries increasingly hire specialists who understood not just the new technologies, but also the theoretical principles of online teaching and learning. In 2004, Steven J. Bell and John Shank introduced the concept of "the blended librarian," which they define "as an academic librarian who combines the traditional skill set of librarianship with the information technologist's hardware/software skills, and the instructional or educational designer's ability to apply technology appropriately in the teaching-learning process."[86] Less than two years later, Shank's analysis of library job announcements concluded "that libraries are creating positions that seek librarians who have both instructional design and instructional technology skills and knowledge."[87] By 2010, the appearance of such job titles as "instructional designer" and "educational technologist" on the mastheads of academic libraries no longer raised eyebrows, while job advertisements seeking librarians who possessed at least some skills in the areas of instructional design and/or educational technology had become commonplace.

Web Video

There is evidence dating back to the 1930s of librarians producing instructional films.[88] Although additional library instructional films would be produced over the years, they remained rare because the costs of production were high, getting finished films in front of their intended audiences was challenging, and updating a completed film was impossible. The emergence of affordable videotape cameras in the late 1970s reduced some of the costs of producing instructional videos, but the biggest breakthrough in the cost of production came with the availability of affordable, easy-to-use digital cameras and editing software. The breakthrough for distribution came with the popularity of web-based video-sharing platforms—in particular, the popularity of YouTube. An article published in *College & Research Libraries News* in June

2007 promotes the idea of librarians posting videos to YouTube (founded less than two years previously), with the author advising, "YouTube is a social software application that could radically change how we look at library instruction and training . . . if we let it."[89] There is no available data on the number of instructional videos academic libraries have uploaded to YouTube; however, finding any U.S. academic libraries *without* an instructional presence on YouTube is challenging. As popular as YouTube became, the constantly evolving nature of social media led to the emergence of other channels for posting and sharing video, including Snapchat, Bilibili, WhatsApp, X (formerly Twitter), Instagram, and TikTok. Platforms such as TikTok lent themselves to the posting of instructional library videos of less than one minute in length, a genre that has been dubbed "library snackables."[90]

Social Media

During the first decade of the twenty-first century, the growing popularity of social media inspired academic librarians to leverage its various platforms as tools for outreach and instruction. Establishing meaningful connections with students via social media, however, proved to be more challenging than simply posting the occasional library-themed meme. Librarians soon learned that generating even a modest social media following requires a continuous stream of fresh content capable of competing in a crowded marketplace of creators vying for attention. Librarians were also faced with choosing from a large, constantly expanding number of social-media platforms, each of which was competing for market share. In addition, making effective use of any social-media platform might require mastery of multiple content formats; for example, as of 2023, content could be posted to TikTok in any of seven different formats.[91] Determining which social-media platforms were worth the effort of creating and managing content was a tough call, as a trendy social-media hotspot can rapidly fall out of favor, especially with younger followers. Facebook was launched in 2004 as a social-media platform by-and-for college students, but many younger followers had abandoned "Boomerbook" by the time the platform reached its teenage years.[92] Even on social-media platforms that happen to be in favor with the young, it is all too easy for (mostly) older librarians to come off as out-of-touch, a phenomenon mocked by the long-lasting (in the context of social media) popularity of the "How Do You Do, Fellow Kids?" meme.[93] Workload was yet another factor librarians had to consider when choosing social-media platforms. Posting to a platform such as X imposes a much lighter (though still significant) workload compared to the ongoing grind of creating and maintaining an engaging blog or podcast.

The exact extent to which academic libraries invested in social media during the first quarter of the twenty-first century is difficult to quantify because precise data has yet to be collected and published. Instead, the literature contains only such hints as a 2014 survey of public and academic libraries, which finds that "70% of libraries are using social media tools, and 60% have had a social media account for three years or longer. 30% of librarians are posting at least daily."[94] Even more difficult to measure than the extent to which academic libraries have embraced social media is determining if their investments in the medium, however large or small, have produced desirable outcomes. In the penultimate chapter of *Building Communities: Social Networking for Academic Libraries*, Denise A. Garofolo writes, "there is very little information available on how to define, analyze, and measure the success of libraries in social media."[95] By all appearances, academic libraries have been, and continue to be, involved in social media without having a good handle on the outcomes. Like so many things that are relatively new, constantly changing, and hard-to-measure, more years may need to pass before the final word on academic libraries and social media can be written.

Texting

Providing reference service via text messaging (originally known as short messaging services or SMS) is similar to digital chat reference in that it involves the real-time (or near real-time) exchange of text. As cell phone use became increasingly common and communication via text was becoming the most popular form of communication among younger demographics, academic librarians began investigating texting's potential as a medium for providing reference service. One limitation of texting is that messages are short, making texting more suitable for ready-reference questions than for in-depth reference transactions.[96] A study published in 2014 reports that text (and video reference) were then beginning to emerge as tools for virtual reference, but "Current research suggests usage of these emerging reference media is limited."[97] That some unknown critical mass of libraries were offering texting as an option is suggested by the availability of commercially produced software that integrates texting into other library virtual reference services, specifically digital chat reference. However, a 2020 study of user preferences found that concerns about the ambiguity of response times and the highly personal nature of texting—coupled with safety and security concerns—combined to make library users reluctant to employ texting as a means of obtaining reference service.[98]

Videoconferencing

Popular films like *2001: A Space Odyssey*[99] and articles like "The Computer as Communication Device,"[100] both dating from 1968, had planted in the popular imagination the idea of two-way video communication years before it would become a practical reality. In 1995, an article published in *Information Today* reported on a proposal to enable law students to "to listen, talk and search online while their LEXIS-NEXIS representative offers tips and prompts via video conferencing."[101] Not much came of the proposal because, like many early attempts at providing reference via videoconferencing, the LEXIS-NEXIS experiment relied on technology that was proprietary, expensive, unreliable, and hard to use. Reference via videoconferencing would only be made practical with the advent of such low-cost, reliable, and easy-to-use web-based teleconferencing services as Adobe Connect, BlueJeans, Skype, and, most impactfully, Zoom. For one early example, in February 2007 librarians at the Ohio State University launched "a video reference kiosk pilot program" using Skype videoconferencing technology.[102] In the years leading up to 2020, a number of academic libraries experimented to varying degrees with providing reference services and instruction via videoconferencing; then, quite unexpectedly, both practices would be supercharged by a virus, though not one of the computer variety.

Covid-19 as a Driver of Change

By the early spring of 2020, campuses around the world were suspending all in-person activities in response to the Covid-19 pandemic. Almost overnight, academic librarians were forced to innovate and, often, improvise ways of serving students and faculty who could no longer access in-person services or physical collections.

In a case of fortuitous timing, the pandemic hampered access to physical collections of books and periodicals much less than it would have had the virus spread as little as a decade previously. By 2020, academic library periodical collections, as well as interlibrary-loan delivery of requested articles, had so extensively transitioned to electronic formats that the pandemic disrupted end-user access to periodicals little if at all. Access to books was a more difficult problem to solve, but the widespread availability of digital books answered most needs. By the time of the pandemic, U.S. academic libraries had added large numbers of e-books to their collections. In addition, the launches of the Internet Archive's National Emergency Library on March 24, 2020, and the HathiTrust Emergency Temporary Access Service (ETAS) on March 31, 2020 (as described in Chapter 4), provided full-text access to millions of digital books and other content regardless of copyright status. When access to physical books and other analog materials was called for, academic libraries turned to such practical solutions as postal mail and curbside pickup services.[103]

Providing reference services and library instruction during the pandemic posed a bigger problem than providing access to collections. For reference services, librarians were able to find solutions in a number of existing virtual tools, email, and digital chat. While some academic libraries had been providing reference via videoconferencing prior to 2020, the pandemic inspired far more libraries to add this service as an option. A survey of academic libraries conducted in the fall of 2022 found that over 78 percent of respondents reported providing virtual one-on-one consultations due to the Covid-19 pandemic, and that 90.9 percent (n = 298) reported using "Zoom as their chosen communications platform for providing virtual consultations."[104]

More challenging than the transition to virtual reference services was the lightning-quick transition from in-person to virtual instruction. One option available to librarians was to provide synchronous instruction using the same videoconferencing technology used to provide reference service, with Zoom being a popular choice.[105] The problem for librarians was less mastering the technology and techniques of synchronous virtual instruction and more getting their virtual instruction sessions written into course syllabi. A survey conducted at the University of Southern Mississippi in October 2020 found, "While a few faculty members indicated having used a librarian for a synchronous online instruction session, the majority indicated having used asynchronous methods such as the video and web tutorials provided." Though the above survey was limited to a single institution, it seems only natural that harried faculty and instructors caught up in the chaos and confusion of the pandemic-driven shift to online instruction would have placed making class time for a synchronous virtual instruction session led by a librarian near the bottom of their priorities.

The pandemic put pressure on academic libraries to produce asynchronous digital-learning objects in the form of virtual tours, tutorials, and videos. The sense of pandemic-induced urgency compelled academic libraries that had not previously participated in virtual learning to get into the game; at the same time, the need for quick results compelled instruction librarians to forgo the risk-avoiding, time-consuming processes of rigorous planning, development, and testing that typically preceded the deployment of any new form of instruction. For example, librarians at the University of North Carolina, Greensboro employed an existing template created by the library's Online Learning Librarian and the Information Literacy Coordinator to rapidly produce virtual tutorials of consistent quality.[106] Similarly, librarians at Rowan University devised their own "rapid distributed development model" that allowed librarians with more instructional-design experience to quickly develop learning modules on their own while less-experienced librarians worked as a group with the Instruction & Education Librarian toward the same end.[107] Taking a different approach, librarians at the University of Oregon looked outside their own organization by adapting open-source tutorials created (and magnanimously shared) by librarians at the University of Arizona.[108] For many academic librarians, moving instruction online became a matter of necessity being the mother of invention and expediency taking precedence over cautious deliberation.

For academic libraries, the magnitude of sudden disruptions brought about by the Covid-19 pandemic was unprecedented. Even so, examples of good arising out of a bad situation can be seen in the anecdotal accounts of how the trials of the pandemic expanded the professional horizons of many academic librarians. Mercer University reference librarian Gail Morton writes of how the pandemic caused her and her colleagues to learn that they could effectively use virtual tools for teaching, reference, and the creation of large numbers of tutorials. More importantly, during the pandemic, Morton and her colleagues discovered that virtual tools were allowing them to "reach members of our campus community we had been missing all along."[109] Of course, the pandemic did not provide the most favorable conditions for academic libraries and their librarians to become fully adept at the tools and techniques of virtual teaching and learning, and certainly few would disagree with the conclusion that "nobody making the transition to online teaching under these [pandemic] circumstances will truly be designing to take full advantage of the affordances and possibilities of the online format."[110] Imperfections aside, the pandemic-driven transition to virtual teaching and services forced a transition that many academic libraries would have waited years to make, if they made the transition at all. With the transition once made, academic libraries found they had crossed over a virtual threshold with no way back to a fully in-person past. After the pandemic, academic libraries would never be what they were before.

Library Facilities

In *The Evolution of the American Library Building*, David Kaser (1924–2017) puts the total number of new U.S. academic library buildings opened between 1951 and 1970 at 665, with a low of 18 new academic library buildings in 1951 and a high of 71 new academic library buildings in 1967.[111] In comparison, between 1971 and 1990, the United States opened 281 new U.S.

academic library buildings.[112] While 281 new buildings is considerably less than half of 665, the numbers look even more lopsided when factoring in the extent to which enrollments had increased over each twenty-year span. From 1951 to 1970, the United States built a new academic library building for every 8,361 students added to total higher-education enrollments; from 1971 to 1990, the nation added a new academic library building for every 19,694 additional students.[113] The years after 1990 saw a continued decline in the construction of new academic library buildings. (See Figure 6.1.) The drop after 2009 was especially steep, with little recovery over the following years. From 2010 to 2023, a total of forty-three new academic library buildings were constructed. (This time span includes the two pandemic years, 2020 and 2021, when no new academic library buildings were constructed.) Seemingly counterintuitively, as the number of new academic library buildings shrank, their average square footage tended to increase. (See Figure 6.2.) In 1990, the average square footage of the twenty-two new academic library buildings constructed that year was 53,976 square feet.[114] By 2019, the year before the pandemic set in, the average square footage of the three new academic library buildings constructed that year had grown to 190,000 square feet.

The Mixed-Use Library Building

The increase in square footage does not, however, tell the whole story. Through the 1990s and into the twenty-first century, academic library buildings were increasingly constructed as, or remodeled to be, mixed-use buildings in which substantial amounts of square footage were routinely assigned to non-library uses. Academic libraries were in part to blame for the

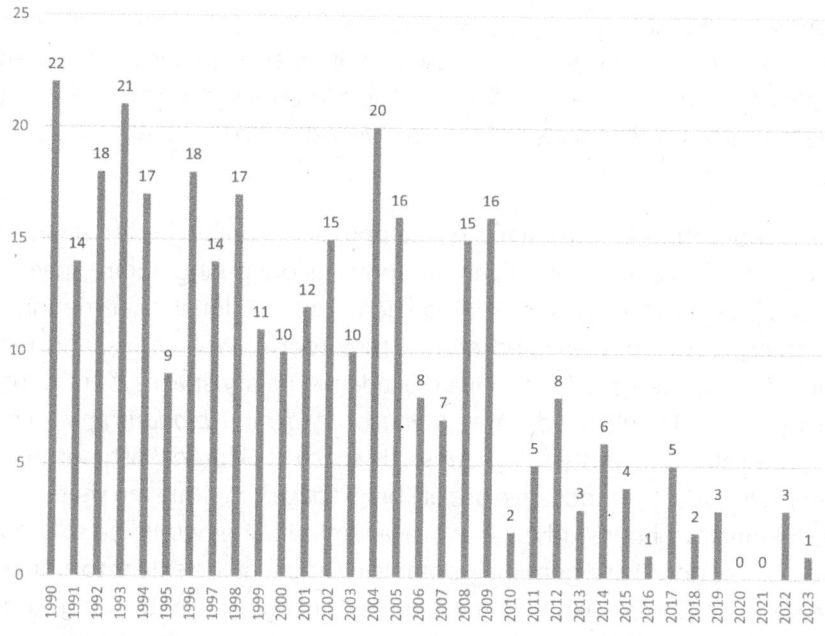

Figure 6.1 New U.S. academic library buildings 1990–2023.
Source: Library Journal annual articles on library construction.

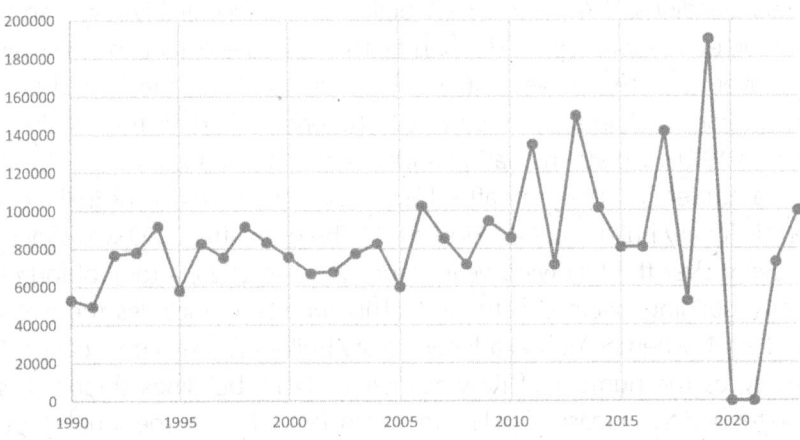

Figure 6.2 Average square footage of new academic library buildings 1990–2023.
Source: Library Journal annual articles on library construction.

appropriation of academic library space: by successfully providing their users with vast amounts of digital information accessible from any place at any time, academic libraries unintentionally lessened the need for stack space while simultaneously ceding their status as the best, if not only, place for students to do research and study. In response, campus administrators, faculty, and other special interests conveniently hypothesized dust-covered bookstacks and ghost-town library study spaces as justifications for colonizing library space. For one example, 10,000 square feet of Penn State Hershey's Harrell Library were cleared out in 2005 to make space for a medical simulation lab.[115] Similarly, in 2012, the Louisiana State University Law Library was summarily notified that it had one year to vacate 6,000 square feet to be occupied by a new Energy Law Center.[116] Concerns over these and other appropriations of academic library space are reflected in the 2009 article, "Library Space in the Digital Age: The Pressure Is On," in which the author warns librarians to be proactive lest outsiders make unilateral decisions about library space.[117]

Whether their motivation was to stave off campus land grabs, better serve users, or a combination of both, academic librarians set about reconfiguring library spaces to better meet changing user expectations, providing such non-traditional, user-friendly amenities as loaner laptops, technology-enabled group study rooms, Wi-Fi, cafes, and twenty-four-hour building access. The speed with which academic library spaces were transformed is reflected in a 1994 article published in the *Journal of Academic Librarianship* which describes the opening of a cafe and twenty-four-hour study space at George Washington University's Melvin Gelman Library as "an innovative use of library space."[118] Within ten years, the presence of cafes and twenty-four-hour study spaces in academic libraries would be so commonplace as to be unworthy of note. For a genuinely notable example of the extent to which academic library spaces were being reimagined, the Goucher College library building, known as the "Athenaeum," opened in 2011 with not only a café but also an art gallery, an information commons, a radio station, exercise equipment, a readers' loft, and "plenty of classrooms."[119]

> ### The Undergraduate Library Building
>
> The postwar era saw many U.S. research campuses not only grow into megacampuses but also become increasingly focused on graduate education and research. On such campuses, undergraduates were not well served by the model of a massive central library supplemented by multiple specialized libraries—especially on those campuses where central libraries continued to uphold the traditional prohibition against undergraduates entering the stacks, and specialized libraries might not be particularly welcoming to undergraduates. A few dozen large U.S. research campuses responded to this problem by constructing stand-alone libraries specifically designed to meet the needs of undergraduates. Commonly known as "undergraduate libraries," these purpose-built facilities are distinct from libraries that happen to be built on campuses that admit only undergraduates.
>
> While Harvard's Lamont Library, opened in 1949, is considered to be the first true undergraduate library, the boom period for new undergraduate libraries was the 1960s. An article published in 1969 reports that twelve undergraduate libraries had opened between 1960 and 1968 and that another twelve would soon be opening.[120] Changing economic and demographic circumstances brought the construction of new undergraduate libraries to a halt in the early 1970s. (The opening of Wayne State University's David Adamany Undergraduate Library in 1997 makes it the lone outlier among undergraduate libraries.) A 1996 review of the state of undergraduate libraries notes that, while a few of the original group of undergraduate libraries had ceased to exist, a core group of twenty continued serving their original purpose.[121]

The Library as Place

Motivated by the realization that digital collections had freed library buildings to consist of more than rows of bookstacks flanked by traditional wooden library tables and chairs, twenty-first century academic librarians began writing on the topic of *library as place*. Though the concept of library as place could mean different things to different people, most of the literature about the library as place centered on the idea that academic libraries provide a unique type of space, a "third place" that was neither a classroom nor a residence. In the words of Susan E. Montgomery and Jonathan Miller:

> The library as a third place provides users the space to learn from each other and build a community of learners. It demonstrates how academic libraries are advancing the mission of the academy by evolving into a place for active learning where students create their community.[122]

In the interest of converting academic libraries into user-centered third places, academic libraries took such steps as relaxing long-standing prohibitions against food and drink; remodeling buildings to include spaces for a wider variety of activities than silent reading; incorporating new styles of furniture designed both for comfort as well as group learning; and moving to off-site storage facilities little-used books and periodicals (many of which were accessible via digital surrogates) in order to make room for students. One notable example of the academic library as a third place is seen in the University of California, Berkeley's James K. Moffitt Library, a building originally designed and constructed in the late 1960s as an undergraduate library. The renovation of Moffitt Library involved relocating all the books to the Gardner Stacks—an adjacent underground facility outfitted with accessible compact shelving—and totally remodeling Moffitt's top two floors. When the work was completed in 2016, the amenities of the remodeled, re-envisioned Moffitt Library included spaces for both noisy and quiet study, a studio for practicing presentations, a wide variety of technology available for student use, plenty of comfortable furniture, movable glass walls that doubled as marker boards, and nap pods.[123]

Both because Moffitt Library is an undergraduate library on a campus with dozens of subject libraries and because its books remained on campus, its makeover did not meet with serious resistance from faculty or other defenders of tradition. This was not always the case when academic librarians sought to relocate physical collections to create third places for students. In 2016, librarians at the University of California, Santa Cruz, removed print materials, most of which were old, low-use bound journals, from the McHenry Science Library to make room for the construction of an active-learning classroom, a new information commons, and the building's first gender-neutral bathroom. Thanks mostly to social-media activism, the facts of the renovation project got spun into an apocalyptic fantasy of technology-addled librarians recklessly destroying 50,000 books worth millions of dollars.[124] The resultant wave of indignation nearly stopped the entire project from going forward.

From the Computer Lab to the Learning Commons

Of all the reconfigurations of academic library buildings in response to the changes digital technology wrought on students' discovery, access, and use of information, the most noteworthy was the evolution from the installation of the first public-access computers in academic libraries to the creation of the academic library learning commons.

In the late 1980s, even a large academic library would have provided at most a handful of stand-alone public-access computers, with those machines being devoted to running CD-ROM bibliographic databases. Throughout the 1990s, it became common for academic libraries to host increasingly large clusters of networked desktop computer workstations featuring web browsers, email applications, word-processing software, and other productivity tools. Along with workstations, libraries also installed and managed networked printers so that students could take away physical copies of their work. By the end of the decade, academic libraries had entered into something of an arms race to see who could claim bragging rights to the largest number of public-access workstations. When Wayne State's David Adamany Undergraduate Library opened in fall 1997, it featured a jaw-dropping 700 public-access desktop workstations.[125]

Seeing new opportunities to serve students, academic libraries began transitioning computer clusters (generically referred to as *computer labs*) into what came to be known as the *information commons*. Among the first mentions of an information commons in the library literature is an item in *College & Research Libraries News* announcing the August 1996 opening of the Information Commons of the University of Iowa's Hardin Library for Health Sciences.[126] While in some respects the neologism *information commons* was not much more than a five-dollar name for a computer lab that happened to be located in a library building, the higher purpose of the information commons was to encourage and enable students to make use of the entire span of library services and information resources rather than simply using the library as a convenient place to sit down at a computer. A typical example of an information commons (though, like many information commons, it did not go by that exact name) was the University of Houston Library's Electronics Publication Center (EPC) *circa* 1997. Housed in a large open space on the first floor of the university's M. D. Anderson Library, the EPC housed over 100 networked desktop workstations supported by a dozen networked printers. Among all the rows of workstations stood a service desk staffed by a combination of librarians, classified staff, and student employees. Those who approached the EPC service desk could get help with anything from a paper jam to an in-depth reference question.[127] To employ an over-used expression of the day, the EPC was "a computer lab on steroids."

By the 2000s, the information commons was evolving into the learning commons, a more sophisticated type of library space "centered on the creation of knowledge and self-directed learning."[128] In "Libraries Designed for Learning," a 2003 report published under the auspices of the Council on Library and Information Resources, Yale University Librarian Emeritus Scott Bennett writes:

> *The core activity of a learning commons would not be the manipulation and mastery of information, as in an information commons, but the collaborative learning by which students turn information into knowledge and sometimes into wisdom. A learning commons would be built around the social dimensions of learning and knowledge and would be managed by students themselves for learning purposes that vary greatly and change frequently.*[129]

"Libraries Designed for Learning" is notable in that it is among the first documents to frame the philosophical foundations of the learning commons. From a less philosophical, more practice-oriented point of view, the purpose of a learning commons can be boiled down to providing "computer and library resources as well as a range of academic services that support learners and learning."[130] The practical aspects of implementing and managing a learning commons were, early on, well documented by the North Carolina State University Library's Learning Space Toolkit. For anyone planning a learning commons, the Learning Space Toolkit offered, and continues to offer, "tools and techniques for assessing needs, understanding technology, describing spaces, planning and delivering support services, and assembling space, technology, and services to meet needs, even as they change."[131]

As "Libraries Designed for Learning" suggests, the original developers of the learning commons looked beyond the traditional model of a student working in solitude to research and write an academic *paper*. Instead, the goal of the learning commons was to articulate with higher-education pedagogies that were increasingly emphasizing communal work and the production of such alternatives to the classic academic paper as group presentations, multimedia productions, learning games, digital maps, blogs, Wikipedia entries, and other non-traditional forms of academic coursework. Though the particulars vary from one library to the next, the types of academic support services learning commons provided include not only traditional library reference services but also services that might range from basic tutoring in math and writing to expert assistance with projects involving the digital humanities, data management, or geographic information systems (GIS).

As ownership of portable computer devices became nearly universal among U.S. college students, it became less important for libraries to provide access to large numbers of desktop workstations, the bread and butter of the information commons, and more important to provide access to the types of specialized technology that students did not routinely carry around in their backpacks and pockets. To this end, learning commons might provide access to, and in-person assistance with, such specialized technologies as video-production facilities, computer-aided design software, 3D printers, and tools for data visualization. Some academic library learning commons offered even more specialized technologies. For example, in 2024, North Carolina State University's Hill Library Makerspace was supporting the study of textiles and fashion by providing students with access to high-end sewing machines and computer-guided fabric cutters while also offering expert support for using this equipment.[132]

As both "Libraries Designed for Learning" and the Learning Space Toolkit warn, a major challenge of creating and managing a learning commons is keeping up with the relentless pace of change in both technology and pedagogy. The latest, most innovative technology can become outdated before the warranty expires. And managers had to find ways to ensure their learning commons remained relevant to what students were being asked to do in the classroom in the face of "learning purposes that vary greatly and change frequently."[133] When keeping a learning commons up-to-date meant acquiring expensive new technology or undertaking costly renovations of library space, it was easy to fall behind. Campus administrators who may have been delighted to cut the ribbon at the grand opening of the library's new learning commons were typically not so delighted when later informed that the once shiny-new facility had, in just a few short years, fallen hopelessly behind the times and was in need of a complete, and costly, refresh.

The Simple Matter of Meeting Changing User Expectations

In 2005, the *Chronicle of Higher Education* published an article reporting on the state of academic libraries. In this article, University of Chicago professor Andrew Abbott expressed concerns that students were using the library "more like a student union" than a library. The faculty-endorsed solution to this state of affairs was to insist on keeping the entire library book collection on campus rather than sending any part of it to remote storage. According to Abbott, "The faculty is united in thinking that this building is supposed to be the research center of one entire wing of intellectual life at the campus, and we can't afford to let it turn into an Internet cafe."[134] Abbott and his like-minded University of Chicago faculty got what they wanted. Sort of. The University of Chicago's Joe and Rika Mansueto Library opened in October 2011. In keeping with tradition, the Mansueto Library's 180-seat Grand Reading Room was designed for quiet study and reading. Other than the modernist glass dome overhead, the Grand Reading Room looks as if it could date from 1911 rather than 2011. Which is not to argue that some hard-to-quantify amount of quiet space is no longer necessary nor valued in the twenty-first-century academic library. Indeed, the value of quiet space may have become greater than ever as the challenge of finding affordable housing compelled many students to occupy increasingly crowded and noisy living quarters.

Below the surface of the Mansueto Library's quiet space, 3.5 million books and other physical items are held in compact storage where they can be quickly retrieved via an automated system.[135] The collection remained on campus as the faculty wished, but the part of it stored underground is neither visible to, nor browsable by, all those born-digital undergraduates in need of protection from themselves. Whether you count the Mansueto Library as a triumph or a failure, it may well stand as the final example of an on-campus library building constructed to serve, first and foremost, as a book warehouse. To be fair, other libraries on the University of Chicago campus offer services and facilities well-aligned with twenty-first-century user expectations, including the Media Arts, Data & Design Center; the Crerar Library GIS Hub; and the Center for Digital Scholarship. The situation at the University of Chicago neatly frames, however, the challenge academic libraries faced in the first quarter of the twenty-first century. On the one hand, academic libraries had little choice but to adapt to rapidly changing, technology-driven user expectations. On the other, they needed to simultaneously maintain print-centric traditions dating back decades. In the end, how hard could that be?

Notes

1. Orvin Lee Shiflett, *Origins of American Academic Librarianship*, Libraries and Librarianship (Norwood: Ablex Pub. Corp., 1981), 255–6.
2. Shiflett, *Origins of American Academic Librarianship*, 143.
3. Michael Gorman, "Values for Human-to-Human Reference," *Library Trends* 50, no. 2 (2001): 172, https://www.ideals.illinois.edu/items/8350/bitstreams/28393/object.
4. James D. Hart, "Search and Research: The Librarian and the Scholar," *College and Research Libraries* 19, no. 5 (September 1958): 365.
5. Catherine Sheldrick Ross, Kirsti Nilsen, and Marie L. Radford, *Conducting the Reference Interview: A How-To-Do-It Manual for Librarians*, 3rd ed. (Chicago: ALA Neal-Schuman, 2019).
6. Thelma Freides, "Current Trends in Academic Libraries," *Library Trends* 31, no. 3 (Winter 1983): 467.
7. Barbara J. Ford, "Reference Beyond (and Without) the Reference Desk," *College & Research Libraries* 47, no. 5 (1986): 492.
8. Keith Ewing and Robert Hauptman, "Is Traditional Reference Service Obsolete?," *The Journal of Academic Librarianship* 21, no. 1 (1995): 3.
9. Jerry D. Campbell, "Clinging to Traditional Reference Services," *Reference & User Services Quarterly* 39, no. 3 (2000): 224.
10. Dennis B. Miles, "Shall We Get Rid of the Reference Desk?," *Reference & User Services Quarterly* 52, no. 4 (June 1, 2013): 320–33, https://doi.org/10.5860/rusq.52n4.320.

11 Anthea Sutton and Maria J. Grant, "Cost-Effective Ways of Delivering Enquiry Services: A Rapid Review," *Health Information and Libraries Journal* 28, no. 4 (December 2011): 253.

12 Susan M. Ryan, "Reference Transactions Analysis: The Cost-Effectiveness of Staffing a Traditional Academic Reference Desk," *The Journal of Academic Librarianship* 34, no. 5 (September 2008): 396.

13 Monty L. McAdoo, "What Do Reference Librarians Do Now?," *Evidence Based Library and Information Practice* 17, no. 3 (September 19, 2022): 63, https://doi.org/10.18438/eblip30129.

14 McAdoo, "What Do Reference Librarians Do Now?," 63.

15 American Library Association Office of Research and Statistics, "Academic Libraries in the United States: Statistical Trends," American Library Association, https://www.ala.org/tools/research/librarystats/academic/academiclibraries (accessed October 26, 2024).

16 Nancy Carey, Natalie Justh, and Jeffrey Williams, "Academic Libraries: 2000" (Washington, DC: U.S. Department of Education: National Center for Education Statistics, 2003), 23, https://nces.ed.gov/pubs2004/2004317.pdf.

17 Tai Phan, Laura Hardesty, and Jamie Hug, "Academic Libraries: 2012" (Washington, DC: U.S. Department of Education: National Center for Education Statistics, 2014), 6, https://nces.ed.gov/pubs2014/2014038.pdf.

18 Janine A. Kuntz and Jeannette E. Pierce, "The 2019 ACRL Academic Library Trends and Statistics Annual Survey: Mapping Results to the ACRL Standards for Libraries in Higher Education," *College & Research Libraries News* 82, no. 2 (February 8, 2021): 87, https://doi.org/10.5860/crln.82.2.87.

19 Homer V. Ruby, "Computerized Circulation at Illinois State Library," *Illinois Libraries* 50, no. 2 (February 1968): 159–62.

20 Association of College & Research Libraries, "The State of U.S. Academic Libraries: Findings from the ACRL 2023 Annual Survey" (Chicago: Association of College & Research Libraries, 2024), https://www.ala.org/sites/default/files/2024-10/2023%20State%20of%20Academic%20Libraries%20Report.pdf.

21 Halcyon R. Enssle, "Reserve On-Line: Bringing Reserve into the Electronic Age," *Information Technology & Libraries* 13, no. 3 (September 1994): 197.

22 Mary F. Salony, "The History of Bibliographic Instruction: Changing Trends from Books to the Electronic World," *The Reference Librarian* 24, no. 51–52 (July 20, 1995): 33.

23 United States Bureau of Education, *Public Libraries in the United States of America; Their History, Condition, and Management. Special Report, Department of the Interior, Bureau of Education. Part I* (Washington, DC: United States Government Printing Office, 1876), 240–51, https://catalog.hathitrust.org/Record/100570955.

24 Spencer Jardine, Sandra Shropshire, and Regina Koury, "Credit-Bearing Information Literacy Courses in Academic Libraries: Comparing Peers," *College & Research Libraries* 79, no. 6 (2018): 768, https://doi.org/10.5860/crl.79.6.768.

25 Richard Rubin, "Azariah Smith Root and Library Instruction at Oberlin College," *The Journal of Library History* 12, no. 3 (Summer 1977): 250–61.

26 Emma Louise Adams, "Instruction in the Use of Reference-Books and Libraries," *Library Journal* 23 (August 1898): 85.

27 Anne F. Roberts, *Library Instruction for Librarians*, Library Science Text Series (Littleton, Colorado: Libraries Unlimited, 1982), 16–17.

28. University of Illinois (Urbana-Champaign campus), *Handbook of the Library* (Urbana: University of Illinois, 1908), https://hdl.handle.net/2027/mdp.39015036812801.

29. Lucy M. Salmon, "Instruction in the Use of a College Library," in *Papers And Proceedings*, Thirty-Fifth Annual Meeting of the American Library Association (Kaaterskill: American Library Association, 1913), https://www.gutenberg.org/files/47134/47134-h/47134-h.htm.

30. Mabel Harris, "Non-professional Library Instruction in Teachers' Colleges," *Peabody Journal of Education* 12, no. 2 (1934): 86–95.

31. Frances L. Hopkins, "A Century of Bibliographic Instruction: The Historical Claim to Professional and Academic Legitimacy," *College & Research Libraries* 43, no. 3 (May 1, 1982): 194, https://doi.org/10.5860/crl_43_03_192.

32. Haskell M. Block and Sidney Mattis, "The Research Paper: A Co-Operative Approach," *College English* 13, no. 4 (January 1952): 212.

33. Mary Bolner Butterfield, "Project LOEX Means Library Orientation Exchange," *RQ* 13, no. 1 (1973): 39.

34. American Library Association, "ACRL Bibliographic Instruction Section Formed," *College & Research Libraries News* 38, no. 5 (1977): 125.

35. Paul G. Zurkowski, "The Information Service Environment Relationships and Priorities. Related Paper No. 5," National Commission on Libraries and Information Science (Washington, DC: National Program for Library and Information Services, November 1974), http://files.eric.ed.gov/fulltext/ED100391.pdf.

36. American Library Association, "Actions: ACRL Board of Directors, February 1995," *College & Research Libraries News* 56, no. 4 (1995): 240.

37. Cheryl Gunselman and Elizabeth Blakesley, "Enduring Visions of Instruction in Academic Libraries: A Review of a Spirited Early Twentieth-Century Discussion," *Portal: Libraries and the Academy* 12, no. 3 (2012): 262–71.

38. William M. Randall, *The College Library* (Chicago: American Library Association and the University of Chicago Press, 1932), 54.

39. Risë L. Smith, "Teach the Faculty to Teach Information Literacy," 8th National Conference of the Association of College and Research Libraries, Nashville, Tennessee, Association of College & Research Libraries, 1997, https://www.ala.org/acrl/publications/whitepapers/nashville/smith.

40. Corey M. Johnson, Sarah K. McCord, and Scott Walter, "Instructional Outreach Across the Curriculum: Enhancing the Liaison Role at a Research University," ed. Linda S. Katz, *The Reference Librarian* 39, no. 82 (2004): 33.

41. William Miller and Steven Bell, "A New Strategy for Enhancing Library Use: Faculty-Led Information Literacy Instruction," *Library Issues* 25, no. 5 (May 2005): 1, https://works.hcommons.org/records/36xp6-g5028.

42. Khalid Mahmood, "Do People Overestimate Their Information Literacy Skills? A Systematic Review of Empirical Evidence on the Dunning-Kruger Effect," *Communications in Information Literacy* 10, no. 2 (2016): 199, https://doi.org/10.15760/comminfolit.2016.10.2.24.

43. Linda Shirato and Joseph Badics, "Library Instruction in the 1990s: A Comparison with Trends in Two Earlier LOEX Surveys," *Research Strategies* 15, no. 4 (1997): 228–9.

44. Nadine Cohen et al., "A Survey of Information Literacy Credit Courses in US Academic Libraries: Prevalence and Characteristics," *Reference Services Review*, 2016.

45. William Badke, "A Rationale for Information Literacy as a Credit-Bearing Discipline," *Journal of Information Literacy* 2, no. 1 (July 29, 2008): 1–22, https://doi.org/10.11645/2.1.42.

46. Larry Hardesty, Nicholas P. Lovrich, and James Mannon, "Library-Use Instruction: Assessment of the Long-Term Effects," *College & Research Libraries* 43, no. 1 (January 1, 1982): 38, https://doi.org/10.5860/crl_43_01_38.

47. Tom Eadie, "Beyond Immodesty: Questioning the Benefits of BI," *Research Strategies* 10, no. 3 (Summer 1992): 108.

48. Andrea Brooks, "Information Literacy and the Flipped Classroom: Examining the Impact of a One-Shot Flipped Class on Student Learning and Perceptions," *Communications in Information Literacy* 8, no. 2 (2014): 225–35, https://doi.org/10.15760/comminfolit.2014.8.2.168.

49. ACRL Information Literacy Competency Standards for Higher Education Task Force, "Framework for Information Literacy for Higher Education," The Association of College and Research Libraries A division of the American Library Association, 2015, https://www.ala.org/acrl/sites/ala.org.acrl/files/content/issues/infolit/framework1.pdf.

50. Bibliographic Instruction Task Force of the Association of College and Research Libraries, "Guidelines for Bibliographic Instruction in Academic Libraries," *College & Research Libraries News*, April 1, 1977, https://crln.acrl.org/index.php/crlnews/article/view/22065.

51. Patricia Iannuzzi et al., "Information Literacy Competency Standards for Higher Education," Association of College & Research Libraries, January 18, 2000, https://alair.ala.org/server/api/core/bitstreams/ce62c38e-971a-4a98-a424-7c0d1fe94d34/content.

52. ACRL Information Literacy Competency Standards for Higher Education Task Force, 7.

53. Jan H. F. Meyer and Ray Land, "Threshold Concepts and Troublesome Knowledge (2): Epistemological Considerations and a Conceptual Framework for Teaching and Learning," *Higher Education* 49, no. 3 (April 2005): 373.

54. "ACRL Seeks Feedback on Third Draft of Proposed Framework for Information Literacy for Higher Education," *College & Research Libraries News*, December 2014, https://www.ala.org/news/2014/02/acrl-seeks-feedback-draft-framework-information-literacy-higher-education.

55. Irene Korber and Jodi Shepherd, "Teaching the Information Literacy Framework: Creating Choose-Your-Own-Adventure Flip-Books," *Reference Services Review* 47, no. 4 (October 2019): 461–75.

56. Glenn Koelling and Lori Townsend, "Research Clinics: An Alternative Model for Large-Scale Information Literacy Instruction," *Communications in Information Literacy* 13, no. 1 (March 2019): 77–8, https://doi.org/10.15760/comminfolit.2019.13.1.6.

57. Heather Dalal, "An Open Letter Regarding the Framework for Information Literacy for Higher Education," *ACRLog* (blog), January 7, 2015, https://acrlog.org/2015/01/07/an-open-letter-regarding-the-framework-for-information-literacy-for-higher-education/.

58. Kim Leeder Reed, "Square Peg in a Round Hole? The Framework for Information Literacy in the Community College Environment," *Journal of Library Administration* 55, no. 3 (April 3, 2015): 237.

59. Christine Bombaro, "The Framework Is Elitist," *Reference Services Review* 44, no. 4 (October 2016): 552–63.

60. "How to Spot Fake News," IFLA (International Federation of Library Associations and Institutions (IFLA), March 2017), https://repository.ifla.org/handle/20.500.14598/167.

61 Ilene F. Rockman, "Virtual Reference and Our Changing Roles," *Reference Services Review* 21, no. 2 (June 1993): 5.

62 Jay K. Lucker, "Technological Advances and the Changing Research Library: From Yesterday to Tomorrow (Paper Presented at the 4th International Seminar, Kanazawa Institute of Technology, Library Center, Kanazawa, Japan, 1985)," in *Research Libraries: Yesterday, Today, and Tomorrow*, ed. William J. Welsh, Contributions in Librarianship and Information Science; No. 77 (Westport: Greenwood Press, 1993), 251–2.

63 Margaret W. Cahalan, Natalie M. Justh, and Jeffrey W. Williams, "Academic Libraries: 1996" (Washington, DC: U.S Department of Education. National Center for Educational Statistics, October 1999), 45, https://nces.ed.gov/pubs2000/2000326.pdf.

64 Phan, Hardesty, and Hug, "Academic Libraries: 2012," 2.

65 Michael Rogers and Margaret Gordon, "UCSC Creates InfoSlug," *Library Journal*, April 1, 1993.

66 Charles W. Dean, "The Public Electronic Library: Web-Based Subject Guides," *Library Hi Tech*, 1998.

67 Sara E. Morris and Marybeth Grimes, "A Great Deal of Time and Effort: An Overview of Creating and Maintaining Internet-Based Subject Guides," *Library Software Review* 18, no. 3 (January 2, 1999): 213–16.

68 "LibGuides: Web 2.0 for Libraries," *Public Libraries* 47, no. 6 (November/December 2008): 71.

69 Jimmy Ghaphery and Erin White, "Library Use of Web-Based Research Guides," *Information Technology and Libraries* 31, no. 1 (March 1, 2008): 21–31, https://doi.org/10.6017/ital.v31i1.1830.

70 "Email Marketing and Engagement–Springshare Platform Use Case," Corporate, Springshare, https://www.springshare.com/uses/marketing-engagement.html (accessed October 15, 2024).

71 Emily Daly, "Embedding Library Resources into Learning Management Systems: A Way to Reach Duke Undergrads at Their Points of Need," *College & Research Libraries News* 71, no. 4 (April 1, 2010): 208–12, https://doi.org/10.5860/crln.71.4.8358.

72 Kelly Broughton, "Our Experiment in Online, Real Time Reference," *Computers in Libraries*, April 2001.

73 Karen G. Schneider, "The Distributed Librarian: Live, Online, Real-Time Reference," *American Libraries*, November 2000.

74 Nita Dean and Guy Lamolinara, "Library of Congress and OCLC to Collaborate on Digital Reference Project," Library of Congress, February 11, 2001, https://www.loc.gov/item/prn-01-015/library-of-congress-and-oclc-to-collaborate-on-digital/2001-02-12/.

75 "LC's Virtual Reference Project Becomes QuestionPoint," *Library Journal* 127, no. 9 (May 15, 2002): 13.

76 Marshall Breeding, "Springshare Acquires QuestionPoint from OCLC," *Smart Libraries Newsletter*, July 1, 2019, https://journals.ala.org/index.php/sln/issue/viewIssue/728/491.

77 "OCLC Annual Report 2008/2009" (Dublin: OCLC, 2009), https://www.oclc.org/content/dam/oclc/publications/AnnualReports/2009/2009.pdf.

78 "OCLC Transfers QuestionPoint 24/7 Reference Cooperative, Subscriptions to Springshare," *College & Research Libraries News*, August 2019.

79 R. David Lankes, Melissa Gross, and Charles R. McClure, "Cost, Statistics, Measures, and Standards for Digital Reference Services: A Preliminary View," *Library Trends* 51, no. 3 (Winter 2003): 407.

80 Survey conducted by the author.

81. Pixey Anne Mosley and Daniel Xiao, "Touring the Campus Library from the World Wide Web," *Reference Services Review* 24, no. 4 (1996): 7–14.

82. Susan Mikkelsen and Sara Davidson, "Inside the iPod, Outside the Classroom," *Reference Services Review* 39, no. 1 (February 15, 2011): 67.

83. Lori Mestre, *Designing Effective Library Tutorials: A Guide for Accommodating Multiple Learning Styles*, 1st ed., Chandos Information Professional Series (San Diego: Elsevier Science, 2012).

84. Hannah Gascho Rempel and Maribeth Slebodnik, *Creating Online Tutorials: A Practical Guide for Librarians*, 1st ed., vol. 17, Practical Guides for Librarians (Lanham: Rowman & Littlefield Publishers, 2015).

85. Graham Sherriff, "Guide on the Side and LibWizard Tutorials Side-By-Side: How Do the Two Platforms for Split-Screen Online Tutorials Compare?," *Journal of Web Librarianship* 11, no. 2 (April 3, 2017): 124–42.

86. Steven J. Bell and John Shank, "The Blended Librarian: A Blueprint for Redefining the Teaching and Learning Role of Academic Librarians," *College & Research Libraries News* 65, no. 7 (July 1, 2004): 374, https://doi.org/10.5860/crln.65.7.7297.

87. John D. Shank, "The Blended Librarian: A Job Announcement Analysis of the Newly Emerging Position of Instructional Design Librarian," *College & Research Libraries* 67, no. 6 (November 1, 2006): 523, https://doi.org/10.5860/crl.67.6.514.

88. Necia Parker-Gibson, "Reference and Media-Instruction by Any Means Necessary," *The Reference Librarian* 31, no. 65 (July 7, 1999): 61.

89. Paula L. Webb, "YouTube and Libraries: It Could Be a Beautiful Relationship," *College & Research Libraries News*, June 1, 2007, http://crln.acrl.org/index.php/crlnews/article/view/7815.

90. Robert Tomaszewski, "Library Snackables: A Study of One-Minute Library Videos," *The Journal of Academic Librarianship* 49, no. 2 (March 2023): 1–10.

91. Lewey Tanner, "'How Do You Do, Fellow Kids?': Staying Relevant with College Students on Your Academic Library's Social Media," *Public Services Quarterly* 19, no. 3 (July 3, 2023): 236.

92. Helen Lewis, "What Happened When Facebook Became Boomerbook," *The Atlantic* (blog), October 5, 2021, https://www.theatlantic.com/ideas/archive/2021/10/facebook-midlife-crisis-boomerbook/620307/.

93. "How Do You Do, Fellow Kids?," Know Your Meme, https://knowyourmeme.com/memes/how-do-you-do-fellow-kids (accessed October 24, 2024).

94. Taylor & Francis Group, "Use of Social Media by the Library Current Practices and Future Opportunities," October 2014, 2, https://doi.org/10.6084/m9.figshare.1221673.v1.

95. Denise A. Garofalo, *Building Communities: Social Networking for Academic Libraries*, 1st ed., Chandos Publishing Social Media Series (Oxford: Chandos Publishing, 2013)., 161.

96. J. B. Hill, Cherie Madarash Hill, and Dayne Sherman, "Text Messaging in an Academic Library: Integrating SMS into Digital Reference," *The Reference Librarian* 47, no. 1 (July 12, 2007): 25.

97. Anthony S. Chow and Rebecca A. Croxton, "A Usability Evaluation of Academic Virtual Reference Services," *College & Research Libraries* 75, no. 3 (May 1, 2014): 309–61, https://doi.org/10.5860/crl13-408.

98. Tara Mawhinney, "User Preferences Related to Virtual Reference Services in an Academic Library," *The Journal of Academic Librarianship* 46, no. 1 (January 2020): 1–8.

99 *2001: A Space Odyssey*, directed by Stanley Kubrick (Metro-Goldwyn-Mayer, 1968).

100 J. C. R. Licklider and Robert W. Taylor, "The Computer as Communication Device," *Science & Technology*, April 1968, https://moodlearchive.epfl.ch/2021-2022/pluginfile.php/2704820/mod_resource/content/3/LickliderApr68.pdf.

101 "Two-Way Video Conferencing Puts Law Students in Touch With LEXIS-NEXIS," *Information Today*, February 1995.

102 Char Booth, "Developing Skype-Based Reference Services," *Internet Reference Services Quarterly* 13, no. 2–3 (June 30, 2008): 151.

103 Julie A. Murphy and Joshua Newport, "Reflecting on Pandemics and Technology in Libraries," *Serials Review* 47, no. 1 (January 2, 2021): 39–40.

104 Coleen Meyers-Martin, "It's All about the Chat and COVID-19: Virtual One-on-One Research Consultations Surveyed," *The Journal of Academic Librarianship* 50, no. 4 (July 2024): 6.

105 Kathia Ibacache, Amanda Rybin Koob, and Eric Vance, "Emergency Remote Library Instruction and Tech Tools: A Matter of Equity During a Pandemic," *Information Technology and Libraries* 40, no. 2 (June 15, 2021): 6, https://doi.org/10.6017/ital.v40i2.12751.

106 Rachel Olsen and Samantha Harlow, "Creating Library Tutorials to Provide Flexibility and Customized Learning in Asynchronous Settings," *Public Services Quarterly* 18, no. 1 (January 2, 2022): 24.

107 Ashley Lierman, Bret McCandless, and Michelle Kowalsky, "Learning from Academic Libraries' Pivot to Online Instruction during the COVID-19 Pandemic," *Journal of Library & Information Services in Distance Learning* 16, no. 2 (April 3, 2022): 140–1.

108 Yvonne Mery, Rayne Vieger, and Annie Zeidman-Karpinski, "Reuse and Remix: Creating and Adapting Open Educational Tutorials for Information Literacy," *Portal: Libraries and the Academy* 22, no. 3 (July 2022): 559–69.

109 Gail Morton et al., "COVID's Lasting Impact on Georgia Libraries," *Georgia Library Quarterly* 60, no. 2 (May 1, 2023): 12, https://doi.org/10.62915/2157-0396.2607.

110 Charles Hodges et al., "The Difference Between Emergency Remote Teaching and Online Learning," *EDUCAUSE Review*, March 27, 2020, https://er.educause.edu/articles/2020/3/the-difference-between-emergency-remote-teaching-and-online-learning.

111 David Kaser, *The Evolution of the American Academic Library Building* (Lanham: Scarecrow Press, 1997), 119.

112 Kaser, *The Evolution of the American Academic Library Building*, 156.

113 Thomas D. Snyder, "120 Years of American Education: A Statistical Portrait" (Washington, DC: National Center for Education Statistics, 1993), 7, https://nces.ed.gov/pubs93/93442.pdf.

114 Bette-Lee Fox et al., "Service to the People," *Library Journal*, December 1, 1990.

115 Cynthia K. Robinson, "Library Space in the Digital Age: The Pressure Is On," *The Bottom Line* 22, no. 1 (May 19, 2009): 6.

116 Natalie Palermo, "Loss of Space and Relocation of Library Collections," *Codex* 4, no. 4 (January 2016): 23.

117 Robinson, "Library Space in the Digital Age," 5–8.

118 Deborah C. Masters and Jessica Arneson, "Cafe Gelman: An Innovative Use of Library Space," *Journal of Academic Librarianship* 19, no. 6 (January 1994): 388.

119 Louise Schaper, "Crafted for a New Worldview. (Cover Story)," *Library Journal* 137, no. 12 (July 1, 2012): 22–3.

120 Warren B. Kuhn, "Undergraduate Libraries in a University," *Library Trends* 18, no. 2 (October 1969): 188.

121 Mark Watson, Jody Bales Foote, and Roland Person, "Twenty Years of Undergraduate Libraries: Whence and Whither?," *College & Undergraduate Libraries* 3, no. 2 (1996): 11–15, https://opensiuc.lib.siu.edu/cgi/viewcontent.cgi?article=1043&context=morris_articles.

122 Susan E. Montgomery and Jonathan Miller, "The Third Place: The Library as Collaborative and Community Space in a Time of Fiscal Restraint," *College & Undergraduate Libraries* 18, no. 2–3 (April 2011): 235, https://scholarship.rollins.edu/as_facpub/32.

123 Gretchen Kell, "Reimagined and Revitalized Moffitt Library Opens Wednesday," *Berkeley News*, November 1, 2016, https://news.berkeley.edu/2016/11/01/reimagined-and-revitalized-moffitt-library-opens-wednesday/.

124 Richard Montgomery, "Montgomery: On UCSC Outrageous Mass Destruction of Books," *San Jose Mercury News*, December 27, 2016.

125 Sheryl Moore, "Libraries to Labs: Managing Public Access Computer Labs in an Academic Library Environment," *The Reference Librarian* 35, no. 74 (June 2001): 208, https://doi.org/10.1300/J120v35n74_13.

126 "Univ. of Iowa Opens Info Commons...," *College & Research Libraries News* 57, no. 9 (October 1996): 567, https://crln.acrl.org/index.php/crlnews/article/view/18989/21892.

127 The author's second job as a professional librarian was as the manager of the University of Houston's Electronic Publications Center, a post he held from October 1996 to November 1997.

128 Elizabeth K. Heitsch and Robert P. Holley, "The Information and Learning Commons: Some Reflections," *New Review of Academic Librarianship* 17, no. 1 (March 25, 2011): 65.

129 Scott Bennett, "Libraries Designed for Learning" (Washington, DC: Council on Library and Information Resources, 2003), 38, https://www.clir.org/wp-content/uploads/sites/6/pub122web.pdf.

130 Barbara Blummer and Jeffrey M. Kenton, "Learning Commons in Academic Libraries: Discussing Themes in the Literature from 2001 to the Present," *New Review of Academic Librarianship* 23, no. 4 (October 2, 2017): 329.

131 North Carolina State University Library, "About," Learning Space Toolkit, https://learningspacetoolkit.org/about/index.html (accessed October 7, 2024).

132 "Textiles," North Carolina State University Libraries, https://www.lib.ncsu.edu//do/textiles (accessed October 9, 2024).

133 Bennett, "Libraries Designed for Learning," 38.

134 Scott Carlson, "Thoughtful Design Keeps New Libraries Relevant," *The Chronicle of Higher Education*, September 30, 2005, sec. News.

135 "Mansueto Library Dedication Set for Oct. 11 | University of Chicago News," October 6, 2011, https://news.uchicago.edu/story/mansueto-library-dedication-set-oct-11.

7 The Future of the U.S. Academic Library

I began my career as a professional academic librarian in 1990. I know that if I had been asked at that time to predict what academic libraries would be like in thirty-five years, my guesses would have been closer to, "Trying to find space for all those print journals," than, "Negotiating transformative agreements with scholarly publishers." It will be 2025 before this book is published, and, of course, it is impossible to know with complete certainty what will transpire for academic libraries, or the world at large, over the coming decades. With the perils of predicting the future in plain sight, the remainder of this chapter will outline a few broad future scenarios.

The Future of U.S. Higher Education

As the first quarter of the twenty-first century draws to a close, there are some ominous signs for the future of U.S. higher education. The rising cost of obtaining a college education coupled with an ongoing student-loan debt crisis has caused many reasonable people to question the return on investment of a college education. The specter of artificial intelligence (AI) possibly gobbling up jobs once performed by well-educated human beings only adds to fears that a college degree may no longer hold the value it once did. It is not completely far-fetched to ask if there is a future for someone with a graduate library degree if AI gets to the point where it can answer any reference question and manage a library collection without the need for human input. The fact that similar questions are being asked about the future of those holding degrees in law, medicine, engineering, education, and other traditionally secure professions is of little comfort to librarians.

Counterintuitively, at the same time that the value of a college education is being questioned, getting into a competitive, highly selective college or university has become a more coveted status symbol than ever before, a reality made evident by the "Varsity Blues" college-admissions scandal of 2019.[1] At least some of the blame for the marketing of an elite college education as yet another luxury consumer good can be laid at the door of the various systems of college rankings. In the years since the *U.S. News & World Report*'s influential college rankings first debuted in 1983, the annual announcement of which institutions have moved up or down in the estimation of the for-profit *U.S. News & World Report* has grown to become an annual pop-culture event rivaling the announcement of the March Madness college basketball tournament brackets or the Oscar nominees for Best Picture. As the power of college rankings to attract both students and donor contributions has grown, some higher-education institutions have made improving their standing in the rankings a formal organizational goal.[2] Whether the intentional pursuit of higher rankings has resulted in overall improvements to the quality of education and research remains a question of some debate.

The rising costs of obtaining a college education have gone hand in hand with the rising costs of providing a college education. Over the course of several decades, higher education has been burdened with new costs, ranging from spending on the acquisition and maintenance of digital technology to the escalating expenses of complying with increased state and federal regulatory mandates. At the same time that expenses were growing, many public institutions lost income as state legislatures reduced spending on higher education. Regardless of the reasons, the high cost of running a campus resulted in over 500 U.S. private, nonprofit, four-year institutions closing from 2014 to 2024.[3] While the closed institutions were all private and mostly small, there is no guarantee against the future closure of larger public institutions should legislative bodies choose to reduce or eliminate funding for higher education. It is no secret that U.S. higher education has become a target of populist politicians who portray colleges and universities as the source of both elitist agendas and inconvenient scientific findings. More than one populist politician has leveled threats to defund higher education. Obviously, the future of academic libraries is inextricably tied to the future of the institutions they serve. If the United States were to experience a downsizing of higher education for any reason—political, economic, demographic, or technological—academic libraries would suffer as a result.

The Future of Scholarly Communication

The future of the academic library is closely tied to both the economics and reputation of scholarly communication. On the economic side, the cost of scholarly literature, especially journal literature, remains high.[4] Any expectations that the open access movement would lower the total costs of academic library collections remain unfulfilled as of 2025. In the words of the authors of *Library Journal*'s 2023 article on the cost of scholarly journals:

> *And as more publishers successfully transition their revenue streams from annual or multiyear subscriptions to transformative OA agreements, some librarians wonder if academia will remain locked in a "different lipstick, same pig" model that does nothing to fundamentally change the way scholarly communications is dominated by a few large publishers.*[5]

Although it seems unlikely, if a few large scholarly publishers were to so dominate the marketplace that the acquisition of scholarly information became more a case of campus purchasing officers paying a handful of annual information-services bills than librarians purposefully building a collection, the academic library's role as the intermediary between scholars and scholarly information would be greatly diminished, if not rendered entirely redundant.

As much as the future of academic libraries is tied to the economics of scholarly communication, it is equally tied to the reputation of scholarly communications. As anyone who has been paying attention for the last few decades knows, a number of valid criticisms have been leveled against the scholarly communications enterprise, including charges of profiteering by publishers, manipulation of impact factors, plagiarism, the use of bad data, flawed peer-review processes, lack of replication studies, and ethical questions surrounding scholars' use of AI. While it falls to scholars and the scholarly publishing industry to respond to valid criticisms about the things they can control, scholarly communication's reputation has also been tarnished by forces beyond the control of publishers and the academy. The proliferation of predatory journals has served to undermine the authority of scholarly publications by flooding the market with questionable scholarship that is difficult to distinguish from the genuine article. At the same time, the spread of disinformation and the rise of anti-intellectual populism have served to discredit scholars and their publications in the eyes of an uncomfortably large segment of the public. This situation is not helped by the fact that special interests have done everything they can to discredit scholarship that they find inconvenient, most notably the discrediting of the strong scientific consensus that climate change is real and a result of human activity.[6] The possibility of post-truth populism further diminishing the influence of scientists and other scholars in public decision-making is not merely a threat to scholarship, the academy, and academic libraries, but to the world at large.

Diversity and the Future of the Academic Library

As early as the 1960s, librarians were addressing the need to diversify the profession "concomitant with the Civil Rights Act."[7] However, it was not until 1990 that the Association of College & Research Libraries Board of Directors created the Racial and Ethnic Diversity Committee (renamed the Equity, Diversity and Inclusion Committee in 2019) as a formal mechanism for addressing both workplace diversity and "the promotion of library and information services for diverse library users."[8] A review of the library literature, especially the literature of the twenty-first century, shows that librarians have put considerable thought and effort into diversifying the profession, though without a lot to show for it. As of 2022, the demographics of librarians employed in all types of libraries (academic, public, school, etc.) break down as shown in Figure 7.1.

The reasons put forward to explain the lack of diversity among academic librarians have ranged from ingrained institutional racism to the low earnings potential of a library career. While nobody can know for certain the extent to which the profession of librarianship will diversify in the future, forecasts have the racial makeup of the profession hovering around 75 percent white in the year 2033.[9]

The other aspect of diversity which academic librarians are likely to continue addressing in the coming years concerns the makeup of library collections. Historically, U.S. academic library collections have followed the lead of the scholarly communications enterprise by focusing on the works of mostly white, mostly male, mostly Western-oriented creators. Librarian-curated archival collections have demonstrated a similar bias. Wide-ranging solutions to diversifying academic library collections include forming collection-diversity committees, seeking out publishers who focus on creators from underrepresented groups, incorporating into collections content other than the traditional printed book, and "creating special collections

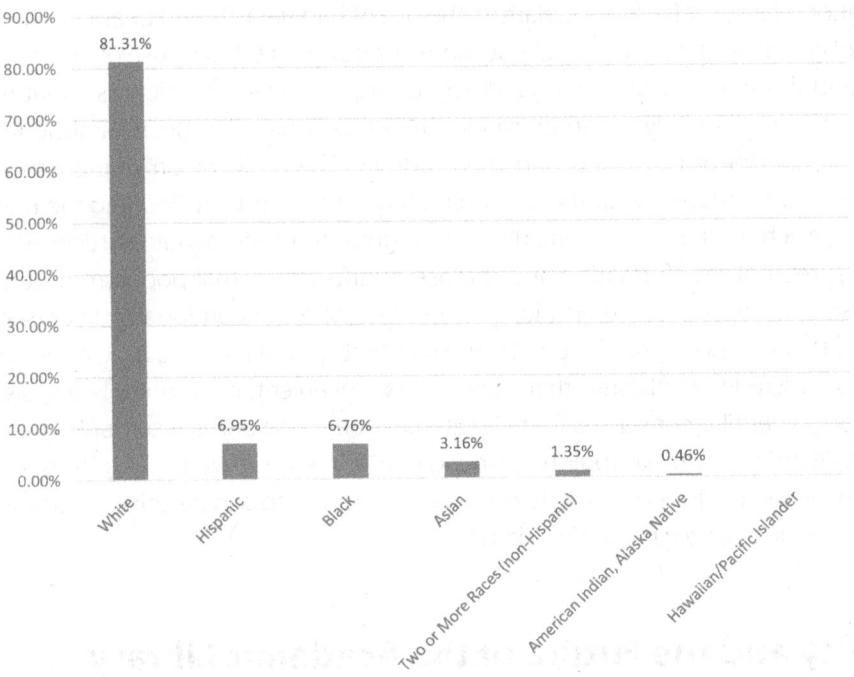

Figure 7.1 Percentage of employed librarians by race-ethnicity in 2022.
Source: Curtis Kendrick and Ioana Hulbert, "By Any Measure: The Racial Demographics of Librarians," Ithaka S+R, April 18, 2023, 7, https://doi.org/10.18665/sr.318716.

from traditionally underrepresented communities."[10] Because academic libraries have a considerable degree of control over the archival materials they choose to incorporate into their collections, the diversification of such collections is one goal which academic libraries are likely to achieve in coming years.

Will Artificial Intelligence Disrupt Everything?

When it comes to the future of academic libraries, and academia as a whole, the elephant in the room is AI. Although everyone seems to agree that the spread of AI will bring some level of disruption, nobody can say for sure what the exact nature and extent of that disruption will be. As noted in previous chapters, there are several AI-replaces-humans scenarios that might disrupt, or are already disrupting, such aspects of academic libraries as reference services, instruction, cataloging, and collections. From the perspective of scholarly authors comes the concern that scholarly publications can be mined and exploited by AI without the consent of the creator.[11] Similarly, any library-curated digital collections that are made freely available online are at risk of being mined and exploited by AI technologies. Although there is no shortage of chilling, often apocalyptic, AI prophecies, AI is like every other technology in that it has the potential to be used for purposes both ethical and unethical. For one example, just as

AI can be used to generate fake scholarly publications, it can also be used to detect and expose such publications.[12]

Although it is repetitious to again point it out, the obvious truth is that anyone who attempts to predict the future of the academic library, with or without AI clouding the glass, runs the risk of joining the ranks of the "Gentleman of Quality," who, in 1971, ridiculed the idea of libraries using computer technology.[13] I would very much like to confidently predict that the academic library will still be going strong at the conclusion of the twenty-first century, but such an outcome is more sincere hope than certainty. If the academic library survives to see New Year's Day 2100, it may differ as much from the academic library of today as the academic library of today differs from the eighteenth-century colonial college library. It must be left to future historians to write the definitive history of academic libraries during the remaining three-quarters of the twenty-first century. I wish both those future historians and future academic librarians good luck.

Notes

1. Melissa Korn, Jennifer Levitz, and Erin Ailworth, "Federal Prosecutors Charge Dozens in College Admissions Cheating Scheme," *Wall Street Journal (Online)*, March 13, 2019.
2. Elizabeth F. Farrell and Martin Van Der Werf, "Playing the Rankings Game," *Chronicle of Higher Education* 53, no. 38 (May 25, 2007): 5.
3. Milla Surjadi, "A New Problem with Four-Year Degrees: The Surge in College Closures," *Wall Street Journal (Online)*, August 19, 2024, sec. US.
4. Bo-Christer Björk, "Why Is Access to the Scholarly Journal Literature So Expensive?," *Portal: Libraries and the Academy* 21, no. 2 (2021): 177–92.
5. Stephen Bosch et al., "Periodicals Price Survey 2023: Going for Gold, Deep in the Red," *Library Journal* 148, no. 4 (April 2023): 32.
6. Peter J. Jacques, Riley E. Dunlap, and Mark Freeman, "The Organisation of Denial: Conservative Think Tanks and Environmental Scepticism," *Environmental Politics* 17, no. 3 (June 2008): 349–85.
7. Ann Allen Shockley, "Negro Librarians in Predominantly Negro Colleges," *College & Research Libraries* 28, no. 6 (November 1, 1967): 423–6, https://doi.org/10.5860/crl_28_06_423.
8. "ACRL Equity, Diversity and Inclusion Committee," Association of College and Research Libraries, https://www.ala.org/acrl/aboutacrl/directoryofleadership/committees/acr-raed (accessed November 16, 2024).
9. Kendrick and Hulbert, "By Any Measure," 10.
10. Alice M. Cruz, "Intentional Integration of Diversity Ideals in Academic Libraries: A Literature Review," *The Journal of Academic Librarianship* 45, no. 3 (May 2019): 223.
11. Christa Dutton, "Two Major Academic Publishers Signed Deals with AI Companies. Some Professors Are Outraged," *The Chronicle of Higher Education*, July 29, 2024, sec. News.

12. Bashar Haruna Gulumbe, "Obvious Artificial Intelligence-generated Anomalies in Published Journal Articles: A Call for Enhanced Editorial Diligence," *Learned Publishing* 37, no. 4 (October 2024): e1626, https://doi.org/10.1002/leap.1626.

13. Ellsworth Mason, "The Great Gas Bubble Prick't; Or, Computers Revealed-by a Gentleman of Quality," *College & Research Libraries* 32, no. 3 (May 1971): 183–96, https://search.ebscohost.com/login.aspx?direct=true&db=lxh&AN=ISTA0700521&site=ehost-live.

Index

AACR. *See Anglo-American Cataloging Rules*
Abbott, Andrew   184
Academia.com   52, 72
Academic Complete   18
The Academic Library in the American University   1
The Academic Library in the United States: Historical Perspectives   1
Academic Press   44, 46–7
accepted author manuscript   67
access versus ownership   8–9
acquisitions   11–16, 94–7, 194
ACRL. *See* Association of College & Research Libraries
ACRL Framework. *See Framework for Information Literacy for Higher Education*
ACRL Standards. *See Information Literacy Competency Standards for Higher Education*
Adam Matthew Digital   12, 142
Adams, Emma Louise   163
Adobe Connect   176
AI. *See* artificial intelligence
A.L.A. Catalog Rules, Author and Title Entries   98
ALA. *See* American Library Association
Alabama, University of at Birmingham   49
Albion College   12
Alexander Street Press   12
Alibris   95
altmetrics   51
ALTO   17
AM. *See* Adam Matthew Digital
Amazon
    Kindle   16
    Kindle Direct Publishing   28
    (online retailer)   95
American Association of Publishers   64
American Chemical Society   64
American Council of Learned Societies   18
American Libraries
    annual article, library automation   107
    annual article, periodical prices   41
American Library Association   10, 40–1, 89, 164
    Office of Research and Statistics   161
American Memory   136

American National Standards Committee on Library and Information Sciences and Related Publishing Practices   40
Ameritech Foundation   136
Amiran, Eyal   58
Anderson, Rick   15–16
Anglo-American Cataloging Rules   91, 98–9
    Second Edition   *99, 102*
ANSI Z39.20–1983   40
APC. *See* article publication charge
Apple
    (corporation)   58
    iPad   16
    Music   14
APPM. *See Archives, Personal Papers, and Manuscripts*
approval plan   11–12
Aram, Henriette   98
archival bond   133
Archive-It   141
archives   125–9, 131–52
    access to   145–6
    preservation   146–8
    storage costs   148–9
Archives, Personal Papers, and Manuscripts   134
ArchivesSpace   136
The Archivist's Toolkit   135–6
Archon   135–6
Arendt, Hannah   101
Arizona, University of   93, 174, 178
ARL. *See* Association of Research Libraries
article publication charge   61–2, 68–72, 75–6
Articulate 360   174
artificial intelligence   101, 112–13, 170, 182, 193, 196–7
ArtStor   142
arXiv   58–9, 67
ASERL. *See* Association of Southeastern Research Libraries
Association of American Publishers   21
Association of College & Research Libraries   161–2, 165–6
    Equity, Diversity and Inclusion Committee   195
    Racial and Ethnic Diversity Committee   195

Association of Library Collections and Technical Services   40
Association of Research Libraries   11, 47, 50, 59, 64, 66, 76, 92, 163
Association of Southeastern Research Libraries   9
Astrobiology and Humanism: Conversations on Science, Philosophy and Theology   7
Atkins, Stephen E.   1
Atkinson, Richard C.   11
Atkinson, Ross   96
Atwood, Margaret   10
Audit and Certification of Trustworthy Digital Repositories: Recommended Practice   147
Authors Guild   21
automated retrieval systems   8, 185

Beall, Jeffrey   71–2, 107
Beall's List   71–2
Bell & Howell Information & Learning   44
Bell, Steven   166, 174
Bennett, Scott   183
Bepress   110
Bergstrom, Theodore C.   48–9
Berlin Conference   61, 73
Berlin Declaration on Open Access to Knowledge in the Sciences and Humanities   60
Berners-Lee, Tim   2, 101, 104–5
Bethesda Statement on Open Access Publishing   60
BIBFRAME. *See* Bibliographic Framework Initiative
bibliographic databases   40, 65, 96, 105, 138, 182
Bibliographic Framework Initiative   103–4, 112–13
bibliographic instruction. *See also* library instruction   164–5
bibliographic software   40
bibliographic utilities   92, 106, 130, 132, 149
big data   149–50
The Big Deal   43, 46–52
Big Ten Academic Alliance   21
Bigelow, Ian   104
BioMed Central   46, 61–2, 69
BioOne   44, 46
bit rot   146
Björk, Bo-Christer   49, 61, 69
black open access   73
Blackwell's   43
blanket order   11–12
blended librarian   174
BlueJeans (videoconferencing software)   176
Bombaro, Christine   169–70
Books
    physical format   5–11
    shelf ready   93
BookSource   18
born-digital materials   140–3

Boston Public Library   8
Bowling Green State University   172
boycotts   65–6, 75
Boydston, Jeanne M. K.   93
Breeding, Marshall   104, 107, 110–12
Brigham Young University   125–6
British Library   103
Brodart Company   14
bronze open access   72
Brown, Bob   17
Brown, Patrick O.   62
Brown University   129, 136
BRS   46
Budapest Open Access Initiative   60
Building the Service-Based Library Web Site: A Step-by-Step Guide to Design and Options   105
bulk order   12
Busa, Roberto   17, 150
Bush, Vannevar   17
ByWater Solutions   111

Cabell   72
California Digital Library   51, 75
California State University
    Chico   169
    Monterey Bay   24
    Northridge   8, 12
California, University of
    Berkeley   135, 182, 190
    Davis   70
    Los Angeles   141
    Merced   2, 24
    Press   77
    Riverside   106
    San Diego   10
    Santa Barbara   131
    Santa Cruz   171, 182
    System   21, 49, 65, 148, 173
Cambridge University Press   75, 77
Campbell, Jerry D.   160
Campus-Wide Information System   171–2
Canadian Research Knowledge Network (CKRN)   49
card catalog   90–2, 109
Carlyle, Thomas   5
Carnegie Mellon University   20
CASE Act (2020)   20
cataloging
    as a profession   89–93, 112–14
    shared   92–3, 107
    standards   98–104
Catalogue of Printed Books in the British Museum   98
CatchWord   44
CD-ROM   1, 18, 39, 47, 109, 136, 150
Center for Research Libraries   9
CFDP. *See* Collaborative Federal Documents Program

Chandler, Robin L. 137
Chapman, Stephan 141
ChatGPT 2
Chicago, University of 10, 136, 151
    Joe and Rika Mansueto Library 184–5
circulation (of books and other items) 11, 159, 162
citation indexes, digital 46–7
classified staff 92
CLIR. *See* Council on Library and Information Resources
CLOCKSS 13
CNI. *See* Coalition for Networked Information
Coalition for Networked Information 59, 67
cOAlition S 74
Cohen, Dan 137
Cohn, Joanne 58
Coleman, Mary Sue 21
Collaborative Federal Documents Program 9
collection development 94–7
college rankings 193
Columbia University 18
Committee on Institutional Cooperation. *See* Big Ten Academic Alliance
computer labs 182
computer-output microform 109
Connecticut, University of 40
consortia, library 44–5
controlled digital lending 22–3
cooperative collection-building 8–9
copyright 20–3, 26, 40, 52, 57, 60, 67, 72–3, 138–9, 145, 177
CORC. *See* OCLC Cooperative Online Resource Catalog
Core: Leadership, Technologies, Futures 114
Cornell University 44, 136, 141
Council on Library and Information Resources 142, 167, 183
COUNTER 50
Counting Online Usage of Networked Electronic Resources. *See* COUNTER
Covid-19 Pandemic 2, 22–3, 161, 170, 177–8
Creative Commons 60, 67, 144
critical thinking 164, 168
Crossref 45
Crowley Digitization Services 141
Current Science Group 61
Cutter, Charles A. 98
CWIS. *See* Campus-Wide Information System
cybrarian 105

DAMS. *See* digital assets management system
Dana, John Cotton 165
dark web 73
Data Carpentry 149
data librarian 149

data management plans 149–50
data visualization 150
David Rumsey Map Collection 142
DDA. *See* demand-driven acquisition
de Havilland, Dame Olivia 102
Deep Dyve 45
Deka, Dipen 101
Dekker 46
demand-driven acquisition 14–15
Dewey Decimal Classification 91
Dewey, Melvil 92
DeZelar-Tiedman, Christine 96
DIALOG 46
diamond open access 72
Diener, Ron 90
digital assets management system 147
digital books. *See* electronic books
Digital Commonwealth 137
digital humanities 17, 132, 150–1, 184
Digital Millennium Copyright Act (1998) 26
Digital Preservation Network 148
Digital Public Library of America 137, 194
Digital Rights Management (DRM) 25–6
digitization 10, 19–23, 110, 130–2, 136–46, 149
Dillon, Martin 113
Directory of Electronic Journals, Newsletters and Academic Discussion Lists 37–8, 41–2
Directory of Open Access Journals 63, 68, 72
Directory of Scholarly Electronic Journals and Academic Discussion Lists 37
disinformation 168, 195
diversity
    library collections 195–6
    library staff 195–6
D-Lib Magazine 136
DMP Tool 149–50
DOAJ. *See* Directory of Open Access Journals
document type definition 135, 150–1
Dot Com Super Bowl 104–5, 107
Dow Jones News Retrieval 47
DPLA. *See* Digital Public Library of America
DPN. *See* Digital Preservation Network
Drexel University 8
DSpace 46
DTD. *See* Document Type Definition
Dublin Core 99–100
Duguid, Paul 131–2
Duke University 136
dumb terminals 108
Dunning-Kruger Effect 166
Dynabook 17

EAC-CPF. *See* Encoded Archival Context—Corporate bodies, Persons, and Families
EAD. *See* Encoded Archival Description

Eadie, Tom   167
EAST. *See* Eastern Academic Scholars Trust
EAST: Eastern Academic Scholars Trust   9
Eberhard, Martin   16
E-biomed   61, 63
e-books. *See* electronic books
Ebrary   18
EBSCO   18, 41–4, 104
EBSCO Discovery Service   110–11
Eden, Brad   113
educational technology   174
Eisen, Michael   62
e-journal. *See* electronic journals
Elbakyan, Alexandra   73
electronic books   3, 5, 14–28, 177
    numbers of   24
    textbooks   28
    usability   27–8
electronic journals   2, 5, 37–52
    advantages of   39–40
    archiving   45
    cost   39–52, 194
    growth of   38–9
    navigating   44–5
    perpetual access   13
electronic records management systems   109
electronic theses and dissertations   78
Elsevier   44, 49–50, 58, 64–5, 75, 110
email   38, 40, 58, 105, 114, 130, 140, 143, 162
email reference service   171, 177
E-Metrics   50
Enciclopedia Mecánica   17
Encoded Archival Context—Corporate bodies, Persons, and Families   135
Encoded Archival Description   135–6
    EAD Working Group   135
Endeavor (library system vendor)   110
.epub standard   26
Espresso Book Machine   28
ESRI (GIS company)   29, 150
Evans, Meredith R.   125
Evergreen ILS   111
Evidence Based Library and Information Practice   50
The Evolution of the American Library Building   178
Ex Libris   23, 109–10, 147
Extensible Markup Language   60, 123, 135
Eysenbach, Gunther   71

Facebook   175
Fair Access to Science and Technology Research Act   64
Fair Copyright in Research Works Act   64
fair use   22, 26, 138
fake news   170

Farmington Plan   9
FASTR. *See* Fair Access to Science and Technology Research Act
FDLP. *See* Federal Depository Library Program
Federal Depository Library Program   9
Federal Research Public Access Act   64
FEDORA (digital assets management system)   146
figshare+   148
file transfer protocol   37–8, 57–8, 105
The Finch Report   73
FindAID   135
finding aids   132, 134–6
firm order   11
First Sale Doctrine   26
Fiske, (Admiral) Bradley A.   17
Fiske Reading Machine   17
Flickr (photo sharing website)   144
flipped classroom   168, 170
Florida Polytechnic University   24
Florida State University   49
Florida, University of   137
FOLIO (open source library system)   111
Follet Higher Education Access   27
fonds   133. *See also respect des fonds*
Ford, Barbara J.   160
FRAD. *See* Functional Requirements for Authority Data
Framework for Information Literacy for Higher Education   168–70
Frazier, Kenneth   47–8
FRBR. *See* Functional Requirements for Bibliographic Records
Freides, Thelma   160
FRESS (File Retrieval and Editing System)   17
FRPAA. *See* Federal Research Public Access Act
FRSAD. *See* Functional Requirements for Subject Authority Data
FTP. *See* file transfer protocol
Functional Requirements for Authority Data   102
Functional Requirements for Bibliographic Records   100, 102–3
Functional Requirements for Subject Authority Data   102

Gale (publisher)   142
Garabedian, Michael   128
General International Standard Archival Description   134
geographic information systems   29, 150
George Washington University   180
Get It Now   45
gifts   12
Ginsparg, Paul   58
GIS. *See* geographic information systems
gold open access   65, 68–71

Google
    Books Project   21–2, 76, 131, 140
    corporate acquisitions   110
    Scholar   65, 110, 168
    search engine   105–6, 109–10, 143, 166, 168
Gopher (internet protocol)   2, 105, 130, 135, 171–2
Gorman, Michael   10, 93, 99, 160
Goucher College   180–1
government documents   22, 90–1
gray literature   140–1
gray open access   72
green open access   67
Greene, Mark   143
Gregor, Dorothy M.   97
Grolier Academic Encyclopedia   18
Guide on the Side   174
"Guidelines for Bibliographic Instruction in Academic Libraries"   168

Hamlin, Arthur T.   1
Handbook of the Library   163, 187
The Handmaid's Tale   10
Harnad, Stevan   58, 66–7, 77
Harris, Mabel   164
Harris, Roma   93
Hart, James D.   160
Hart, Michael S.   17–18
Harvard University   12, 49, 136–7, 159, 163, 181
    Task Force on University Libraries   8–9
Harvey, Miles   127
HathiTrust Digital Library   7, 21–3, 76, 104, 131
    Emergency Temporary Access Service   22–3, 177
    Research Center   22, 151
High Altitude Rocket Research   6–7
Highwire Press   44
Hilton, James L.   147
Hirtle, Peter B.   131, 136
Holt, Glen   93
Hopkins, Frances L.   164
Houghton, Bernadette   145
Houston, University of   2, 183
Howath, Lynne C.   102
HTML. *See* Hypertext Markup Language
HUMANIST (listserv)   57
hybrid journal   68
Hypertext Markup Language   105, 135

ICOLC. *See* International Coalition of Library Consortia
ICPR. *See* Inter-university Consortium for Political Research
ICPSR. *See* Inter-university Consortium for Social and Political Research
Idaho, University of   126

IFLA. *See* International Federation of Library Associations and Institutions
ILL. *See* interlibrary loan
Illinois, University of   128, 163–4
ILS. *See* integrated library systems
Index Thomisticus   17, 150
Indian Institute of Science   20
InfoGlobe   47
INFOMINE   105–6
information commons   182–3
information literacy   165–6
Information Literacy Competency Standards for Higher Education   168
information organization   113
InfoSlug   171
Ingenta   44
IngramSpark   28
Institute for Scientific Information   41–2
institutional repositories   67–8, 110, 113, 147–8
instructional design   174
instructional video   174–175
integrated library systems   103, 107–9, 111–12
intellectual property   25
Interlibrary Loan   8, 26–7, 51–2, 130, 162–3, 177
International Coalition of Library Consortia   50
International Council on Archives   134
International Federation of Library Associations and Institutions   99–100, 104, 116–17, 170
Internet Archive   19, 20, 22–3, 141, 177
    National Emergency Library   23, 177
    Open Library: Digital Lending Library project   23
    Wayback Machine   141
Inter-university Consortium for Political Research   149
Inter-university Consortium for Social and Political Research   149
Intner, Sheila   103
Iowa State University   15
Iowa, University of   183
iPad. *See* Apple iPad
ISAD-G. *See* General International Standard Archival Description
ISBD(M)   99
ISI. *See* Institute for Scientific Information
The Island of Lost Maps: A True Story of Cartographic Crime   127
ISO 16363   147
ISO Standard 14721:2003   146
ITHAKA   13
iTunes   14, 29

Jewett, Charles Coffin   98
Johns Hopkins University   18, 24
Johnson, Spencer   11
Joint Library Facility, Bryan, Texas   10

Joint Steering Committee for Revision of AACR   102
journal impact factor   50
Journal of Cataloging and Classification   89
Journal of Internet Cataloging   106
Journal of Library Metadata   107
journal usage, measurement of   50–2
Joyce, James   139
JSTOR   13, 44
Jul, Erik   113
Jurassic Park   18

Kahle, Brewster   19, 141
Kalita, Deepjyoti   101
Karger   46
Kaser, David   178
Kay, Alan   17
Kenney, Anne   141
Kentucky Digital Library   137
King, Stephen   26
Kluwer   44, 46
Knovel   18
Knowledge Unlatched   75, 77
Koha   111
Kuali OLE   112
Kurth, William H.   40

Lafayette College   49
Lampert, Cory   138
Land, Ray   169
Landis, William E.   151
LaserDiscs   136
learning commons   183–4
Learning Space Toolkit   183–4
leases   13–14
Lessig, Lawrence   60
Leysen, Joan M.   93
LibAnswers   173
LibGuides   172
LibLime   111
"Libraries Designed for Learning"   183–4
library as place   181–2
Library at Alexandria   20
library automation   107–12
   hosting   112
   migration of records   111
   open source systems   111
   RFP process   111
library buildings   178–85
   mixed use   179–80
   number constructed   178–9
   space within   8–9
   undergraduate   181–2
library instruction   162–78
   assessment   167
   for-credit courses   164, 166–7

   post-1990   167–70
   prior to 1990   162–6
   virtual   170, 173–5, 177–8
Library Journal
   annual article, library automation   107
   annual article, periodical prices   40–6, 49–50, 58
Library Materials Price Index Committee   40
Library of Congress   8, 90, 92, 98, 103, 106, 134–6, 142, 173
   Cataloging in Publication   92
   Classification   91
   Collaborative Digital Reference Service   173
   National Digital Library Program   136
   Subject Headings   91–2
library pathfinders. *See* research guides
Library Publishing Directory   66
Library Reference Model   104
Library Resources and Technical Services   40, 89
library services platform   112
Library Systems and Services   173
library tours, virtual   173–4
library tutorials, virtual   173–4
LibWizard   174
licensing agreements   26
link resolvers   40, 45
linked data   101–4
Linking Science and Industry   20
ListServ   37–8, 57, 130
LOCKS. *See* Lot of Copies Keep Stuff Safe
LOEX   165
Logsdon, Richard H.   89
Lot of Copies Keep Stuff Safe   6, 148
Louisiana State University   180
Lowery, Charles B.   1
LRM. *See* Library Reference Model
LSP. *See* library services platform
Lucker, Jay K.   11
Lulu Xpress   28
Lyman, Peter   141
Lynch, Clifford A.   67

MAchine Readable Cataloging. *See* MARC
Mackie-Mason, Jeffrey   68
magazines   46–7
Makerspace   184
The Making of America   44, 131
Malin, Gwynneth   136
Mamma Haidara Library (Timbuktu)   146
Mandel, Carol   97
Mapbox   29
maps   29, 94, 140, 142, 150
MARC   1, 92, 96, 98–101, 103–4, 106, 109, 111, 113, 134–5, 149
MARC AMC. *See* USMARC Archival and Manuscripts Control

MARC 21   100, 104
Massachusetts Institute of Technology   75, 77
Matthews, Joseph R.   107
Max Planck Institute   49
Max Planck Society   65
McCallon, Mark L.   1
McCallum, John C.   148
McCord, Alan   147
McDonald, Terrance J.   138
McMurtry, Larry   95
McNaughton Book Service   14
media, non-print formats   27–9, 90, 125, 131, 133, 148
megajournal   61–2
Meissner, Dennis   143
Mellon Foundation   77, 88, 106, 112
Memex   17
Mendeley   72
Mercer University   178
Metadata   101–3, 106–7
   Archival   143–7
Metcalf, Henry Clayton   20
Meyer, Jan H.   169
Michaelson, Robert C.   48
Michigan, University of   18, 44, 77, 131, 137–8, 163, 166
microfilm   46
Microsoft   18
Miles, Harvey   127
Miller, Jonathan   181
Miller, Steven Jack   145
Miller, William   166
Million Book Project   20
MOBIUS Consortium   111
Montgomery, Susan E.   181
More Product, Less Process   143–4
Morton, Gail   178
Mosaic (web browser)   37
MPLP. *See* More Product, Less Process
Muddit, Alison   76
Müller, Katja   138

National Archives (United States)   137
National Center for Educational Statistics   161–2, 171
National Endowment for the Humanities   77, 149
National Institutes of Health (U.S.)   61, 63–4, 149
National Library of Australia   111
National Library of Medicine Classification System   91
National Science Foundation   149
National Union Catalog   130, 132
National Union Catalog of Manuscript Collections   132
Nature Publishing Group   46, 59, 65

NCES. *See* National Center for Educational Statistics
Neal-Schuman Publishing   105
Netflix   29
NetLibrary   18, 27
Netscape   37
Nevada, University of, at Reno   137
New England Depository Library   7
New Horizons in Adult Education (*NHAE*)   37, 58
New Mexico, University of   169
New York Public Library   8, 137
New York Times   47
New York University   18
Newell, Homer E., Jr.   6–7
Newsbank   47
newspapers   46–7
NEXIS   46
NLS (oN-Line System)   17
non-print media   28–9, 140, 164
North Carolina State University   183–4
North Carolina, University of
   Chapel Hill   136, 138
   Greensboro   178
North Dakota State University   136
North Texas, University of   140
Northeast Document Conservation Center   141
Northern Iowa, University of   27
NUC. *See* National Union Catalog
NUCMC. *See* National Union Catalog of Manuscript Collections
NuvoMedia   16

OA2020. *See* Open Access 2020
OAI-PMH. *See* Open Archives Initiative Protocol for Metadata Harvesting
OAIS. *See* Space Data and Information Transfer Systems: Open Archival Information System Reference Model
OAIster   66
Oberlin College   163
OCLC   1, 66, 92, 99, 106–7, 130, 132, 134–5, 147, 173
   Cooperative Online Resource Catalog   107
   FirstSearch   130
   Intercat   106
   TECH-PRO   93
   Worldcat   7, 106
OCR. *See* optical character recognition
The Ohio State University   133, 136, 143–4, 176
OhioLink   45
Oklahoma, University of   49
One L: The Turbulent True Story of a First Year at Harvard Law School   22–3
one-shot instruction   167–8
online indexes   1
online public access catalog   1, 15, 40, 91, 97, 105–6, 108, 110, 130

OPAC. *See* online public access catalog
open access publishing   46, 57–88
    discovery tools   65
    funders   73–4
    growth   61–3
    resistance to   63–5
    scholarly monographs   76–8
Open Access 2020   73–4
Open Access Week   61
Open Archives Initiative Protocol for Metadata Harvesting   60, 66, 146
Open Content Alliance   19
open educational resources   78
open source library systems. *See* library automation; open source systems
OpenURL   45, 51, 109
optical character recognition   19, 139
Orbis Cascade Alliance   137
Oregon, University of   49
Organic Letters   46
original order (archives)   133
Origins of American Academic Librarianship   1
orphan works   20
outsourcing   12, 93, 141–2
overlay journals   72
Ovid   44
Owens, Trevor   146
Oxford Reference Online   18
Oxford University   18

Page, Larry   21
Panizzi, Anthony   98
PAPR. *See* Print Archives Preservation Registry
paraprofessionals. *See* classified staff
Paris Principles   98, 101
Partnership for Research Integrity in Science and Medicine   64
patron driven acquisition   14–15
Pay It Forward: Investigating a Sustainable Model of Open Access Article Processing Charges for Large North American Research Institutions   70
pay-per-view access   45, 52
PDA. *See* patron driven acquisition
peer review   58
Pennsylvania State University   180
Pennsylvania, University of   18
periodical indexes   109, 164–5
Peters, Thomas A.   96
Phillips & Hunt   12
physical collections, size   5–7
PINES (open source library system)   111
Pitti, Daniel   135
Plan S   74
platinum open access. *See* diamond open access
Plenum   46

PLOS. *See* Public Library of Science
PLOS Biology   62
PLOS One   63
Plum Analytics   100
Portico   13
PostModern Culture   58
Poynder, Richard   49, 79
predatory publishing   71–2, 168, 195
Preventing Real Online Threats to Economic Creativity and Theft of Intellectual Property Act   64
price indexes, journals   40–1
Princeton University   7, 91
Princeton University Press   18
Print Archives Preservation Registry   9
print disabilities, persons with   22
print on demand   28, 78
PRISM. *See* Partnership for Research Integrity in Science and Medicine
privacy   138–40, 145
Proffitt, Merrilee   106
Project Gutenberg   17–18, 76
Project Muse   44
Project Xanadu   17
Projekt DEAL   75
ProQuest   44
ProQuest Direct   47
provenance (archives)   133–4
Psycoloquy   58
PubChem   64
Public Knowledge Project   60
Public Library of Science   61–2
publish-and-read agreement   75
PubMed Central   61–3, 65, 67

Questia   19
QuestionPoint   173

Randall, William M.   165
RBM: A Journal of Rare Books, Manuscripts, and Cultural Heritage   127
RDA. *See* Resource Description and Access
RDA Steering Committee   103
RDA Toolkit, 103
RDF. *See* Resource Description Framework
read-and-publish agreement   50, 75
ReadCube   45
The Readies   17
records management   126
Red de Revistas Científicas de América Latina y El Caribe, España y Portugal   60, 72
Redalyc. *See* Red de Revistas Científicas de América Latina y El Caribe, España y Portugal
RedLightGreen   106
Reed, Kim Leeder   169

reference services
   cost   161, 164, 173
   digital chat, 172–173
   effectiveness   160–1
   email   171
   interview   160
   librarians   159–60
   statistics   161
   virtual   170–7
research guides   96, 171–2
Research Libraries Group   106, 147
Research Works Act   64
ResearchGate   52, 72
reserve collections   163
Resource Description and Access   102, 106
Resource Description Framework   102
Resources and Technical Services Division   89, 114
respect des fonds   133
Riding the Bullet   26
RLG. *See* Research Libraries Group
RLIN   130, 132, 134
ROARMAP   73
Robinson, Otis   5
Rocket eBook   16
Root, Azariah Smith   163
Rosenthal, David S.H.   148
Rowan University   178
RoweCom/Faxon   12, 43, 46
Royal Society of Chemistry   75
Ruiz Robles, Angela   17
Rules for a Printed Dictionary Catalogue: Public Libraries in the United States of America, Their History, Condition, and Management, Part II   98
Rules for Descriptive Cataloging in the Library of Congress   98
Rutgers University   18
Ruth, Janice E.   132

Salmon, Lucy Maynard   165
Santa Fe Convention   60
scanning   19, 139–40
scholarly communication   43, 52, 57, 170, 194–5
Scholarly Publishing and Academic Resources Coalition   49, 58–9, 62, 76–8, 95, 170, 184–5, 195
SciELO   59, 72
Science Direct   49
Scientific Reports   63
SCI-Hub   52, 73
SCOAP³   75
Semantic Web   101–4, 112
Serial Slants   89
Serials Solutions   110
SFX   45, 109
SGLM. *See* Standard Generalized Markup Language

Shank, John   174
shared print   8–9
Shea, John   159
Sherpa   72
Shiflett, Orvin Lee   1
Shoah Foundation Institute   12
silver-nitrate film   140
Skype   176
slip plan   12
Smith, Risë L.   165–6
Smithsonian Report on the Construction of Catalogues of Libraries, and Their Publication by Means of Separate, Stereotyped Titles, with Rules and Examples   98
social media   72–3, 175–6
Society of American Archivists   133–6
SoftBook   16
Solomon, David J.   69
Sonny Bono Copyright Term Extension Act (1998)   20
Southern Illinois University   49
Space Data and Information Transfer Systems: Open Archival Information System Reference Model   146–7
Spalding, C. Summer   99
SPARC. *See* Scholarly Publishing and Academic Resources Coalition
Sparling, Abigail   104
special collections   125–9, 151
Spindler, Robert P.   126
Springer   44, 50, 62, 65
Springer Link   49
Springer Nature   63, 75
Springshare   172–4
Standard Generalized Markup Language   135
Stanford University   143
Stop Online Piracy Act   64
storage costs, library   8
storage facilities, library   7–9
streaming digital content   14
Students for Free Culture   61
Suber, Peter   57, 60, 79
subject bibliographers   95–6
subscription agencies   12–13
subscriptions   12–13, 65–6
Superintendent of Documents Classification   91
Swets Information Services   12–13, 43
Syracuse University   10
systems librarians   90

Taylor & Francis   49
TEI. *See* Text Encoding Initiative
Tennant, Roy   141
Tennessee, University of, Knoxville   105
Tetrahedron Letters   46

Texas A&M University   173
Texas, University of, at Austin   10, 130, 136
Text Encoding Initiative   150–1
texting   175–6
Thompson, William Oxley   133, 136, 142–3
Threshold Concept Theory   169
TikTok   175
Tillet, Barbara   100
Times of London   47
Tolkien, J.R.R.   28
Toronto Globe and Mail   46
TRAC Standard   147
Traister, Daniel   127–8
transformative agreement   74–6
Trueswell, Richard   10
trusted digital repository   13, 147–8
Tucker, John Mark   1
Tuckman, Barbara   28
Turow, Scott   22
24/7 Reference   173
Twitter. *See* X

UCLA Online Campaign Literature Archive   141
Uniform Resource Identifier   102
UNIMARC   99
The University Library in the United States: Its Origins and Development   1
University of California Press   77
Unsworth, John   58
URI. *See* Uniform Resources Identifier
U.S. District Court, Southern District of New York   23
U.S. News & World Report   193
Usenet   57, 105, 130
Using the World Wide Web and Creating Home Pages: A How-to-Do-It Manual   105
USMARC Archival and Manuscripts Control   134

The Valley of the Shadow   151
Varmus, Harold   61–2
Varsity Blues (college admissions scandal)   193

version of record   67
videoconferencing   176
Virginia, University of   91, 151
Virtual Reference Desk (LSSI)   173
Voyager (company)   18
Vu-TEXT   47

W3C. *See* World Wide Web Consortium
Wall Street Journal   47
Washington Post   47
Washington, University of   137
Waters, William H.   15
Watson, Thomas E.   138
Wayne State University   181–2
Web. *See* World Wide Web
web directories   105–6
Web of Science   66
web search engines   105–6
websites, archiving of   141
Weihs, Jean   102
Welch, Helen M.   40
WEST: Western Regional Storage Trust   9
Westbrook, Bradley D.   137
Whatley, Kara M.   96
Wiley   44, 46, 50, 64, 75
Willinsky, John   60
Wilson, Thomas D.   64
Winkler, Paul W.   99
World Wide Web   1–2, 18, 37, 100, 104–5, 141
World Wide Web Consortium   102
Wright State University   93
Wu, Michell M.   23

X (social media platform)   175
XML. *See* Extensible Markup Language

YouTube   174–5

Z39.50 (computer protocol)   108
Zhejiang University   20
Zoom (videoconferencing)   176–7

About the Author

Donald A. Barclay worked as an academic librarian from 1990 until his retirement in 2022, holding positions at New Mexico State University, the University of Houston, the Texas Medical Center, and the University of California, Merced. Barclay began working at the University of California, Merced in 2002, before ground was broken on what would become the first (and thus far only) new U.S. research university of the twenty-first century. The unique opportunity of creating an academic research library from the ground up at a time when digital technology was expanding into every aspect of human life allowed him to both closely observe and actively participate in the biggest technological change to hit libraries since the advent of printing from movable type.

Over the course of his career, Barclay has authored numerous articles and books on topics ranging from the literature of the American West to children's literature to library and information science. His book *Fake News, Propaganda, and Plain Old Lies: How to Find Trustworthy Information in the Digital Age* was published in June 2018 and spent two months as an Amazon #1 New Release. His follow-up book, *Disinformation: The Nature of Facts and Lies in the Post-Truth Era*, was published in 2022.

Barclay earned his bachelor's degree from Boise State University and holds master's degrees in both English and Library and Information Science from the University of California, Berkeley. Prior to working as a librarian, he spent four years teaching college writing and, before that, ten seasons working as a wildland firefighter, mostly as a member of a U.S. Forest Service Hotshot Crew. He lives in Merced, California, with his wife Caroline Dawson, a professor of mathematics.